IMAGES
of America

THE BOLIVAR PENINSULA

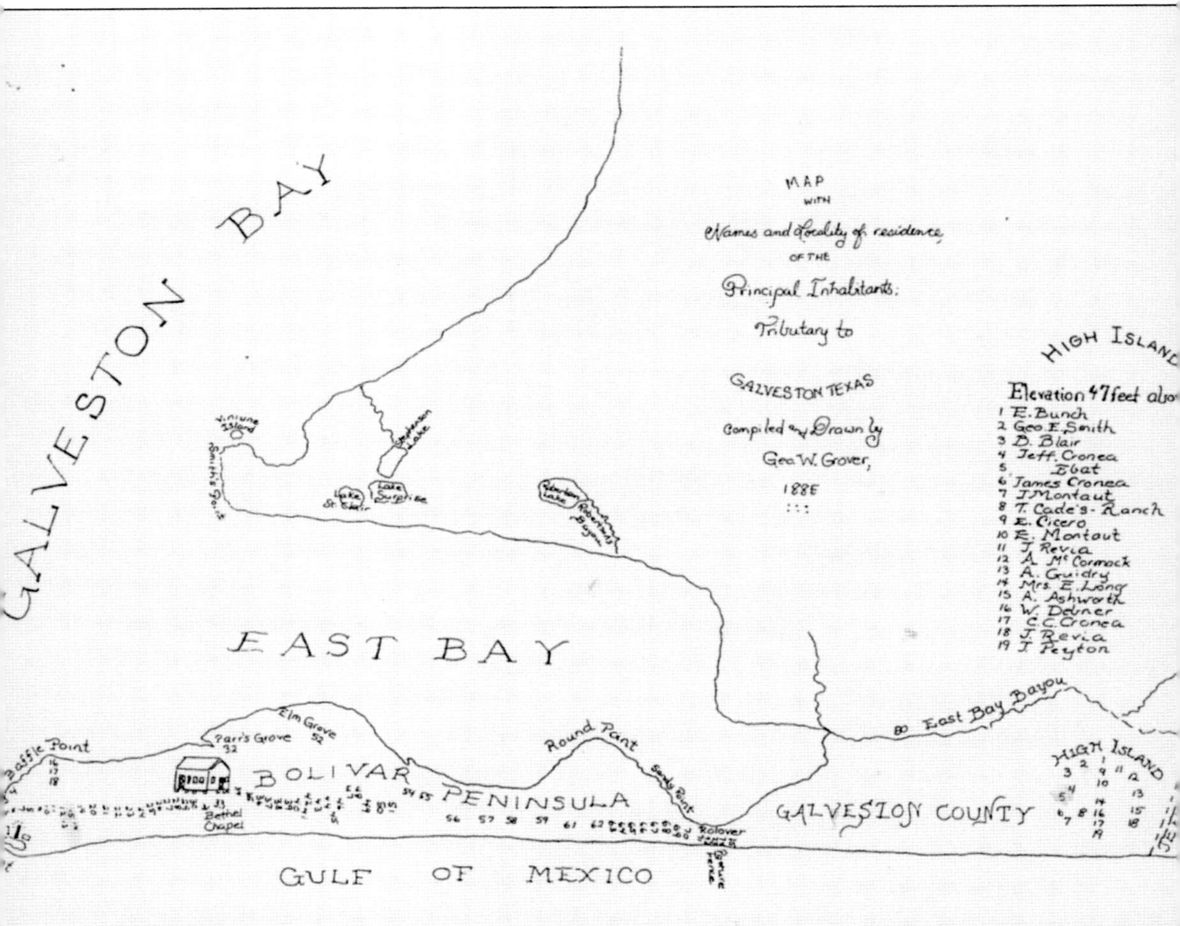

This map was compiled and drawn by George W. Gover in 1885. It depicts the names and localities of the principal inhabitants on the Bolivar Peninsula. This portion of the map makes note of all inhabitants of the peninsula at that time and lists the names of the 19 families living in High Island. (Courtesy of Clare Atkinson Wonders.)

On the Cover: Ferry service has been a part of the life for Bolivar Peninsula residents since the mid-19th century, when passengers paid individual boat owners to take them across between Galveston, Texas, and the peninsula. This ferry is shown carrying automobiles and walk-on passengers around 1950. (Courtesy of the Texas Department of Transportation.)

IMAGES
of America

THE BOLIVAR PENINSULA

Dr. Melanie Wallace

ARCADIA
PUBLISHING

ISBN 978-1-4671-3386-9

Published by Arcadia Publishing
Charleston, South Carolina

Printed in the United States of America

Library of Congress Control Number: 2015933195

For all general information, please contact Arcadia Publishing:
Telephone 843-853-2070
Fax 843-853-0044
E-mail sales@arcadiapublishing.com
For customer service and orders:
Toll-Free 1-888-313-2665

Visit us on the Internet at www.arcadiapublishing.com

To my mother, who taught me the importance of family history

Contents

Acknowledgments 6

Introduction 7

1. Landmarks: The Lighthouse, Rollover Pass, Fort Travis, Audubon Lands, and Cemeteries 9
2. Folks: Founders, Heroes, and Characters 27
3. Making a Living: Farming, Ranching, Bounty of the Sea, and a Little Oil 37
4. From Pasture to Seashore: Cowboy Boots and Bathing Suits 57
5. Transportation: By Land and By Sea 77
6. Teaching and Preaching: Schools and Churches 93
7. Going Down to Take the Breeze: Life at the Breakers 105
8. This and That: Too Good to Miss 115
9. Jane Long: Mother of Texas 121

About the Organization 127

ACKNOWLEDGMENTS

Many of my happiest days were spent on the Texas Gulf coast. I can vividly recall the feeling of waking up as a small child in an rented cabin on the beach without air-conditioning, sunburned and gritty from the sand, rocking with the memory of the waves I had been playing in all of the previous day. Those memories include cookouts with grandparents and aunts and uncles and endless games of cards with my cousins. I even remember watching the first moon landing on a nine-inch black-and-white television while staying in one of those cabins. I am convinced that there is saltwater in my veins.

Little did I know that my childhood dreams would come true when I moved to the Bolivar Peninsula decades later, as an empty-nester. The magic was still there—only deeper and more fascinating. In addition to sun, sand, and surf, the peninsula offered a wealth of history and welcoming, loving people who were more than willing to tell their stories.

Shortly after beginning the process of writing this book, I was invited to attend the Bolivar Reunion, a gathering of the families of early settlers. This allowed me to make contact with the families of the founding fathers and mothers of the peninsula. I was then invited into the homes of those wonderful people who shared their stories, insights, and photographs. I was given books and information and cake and coffee, and I made friendships that I believe will last well beyond the completion of this book.

The stories of bravery, entrepreneurship, and fun were intriguing. The real takeaway for me was the golden thread of character—love of family, country, and God—that ran through every story. The Bolivar Peninsula is a place built by good people.

Special thanks go to my friend and first reader, Linda Elissalde. She has always been my biggest supporter, and her friendship has made my life on the peninsula such fun.

Introduction

Ellen Rienstra states in her introduction to Melanie Wiggins's definitive tales of the peninsula, *They Made Their Own Law*, "Bolivar Peninsula is a world unto itself." It is truly a place like no other.

Bolivar Peninsula is named for South American hero Simón Bolívar, the leader of the fight to free South and Central America from Spanish rule. Liberator of Venezuela, Colombia, Ecuador, Peru, and Panama, Bolívar was the founder and first president of Bolivia.

The peninsula, as locals call it, is a quirky community made up of the towns of Port Bolivar, Crystal Beach, Caplen, Gilchrist, and High Island. It is a 27-mile-long barrier formation in the Gulf of Mexico and a short ferry ride from Galveston, Texas.

Access to the peninsula can be gained in two ways. One is through Chambers County, on Highway 124, then on to Highway 87 (the Jane Long Memorial Highway). The other is by ferry from Galveston. The public ferries are operated by the Texas Department of Transportation and have been run free of charge since 1934. Summer months and spring break are peak times for travel on the ferries and may require a significant wait in some instances.

The Gulf Intracoastal Waterway extends the length of the peninsula on the north side, with the Gulf of Mexico to the south. The crystal sand beaches are open and driving on them is permitted. Before Highway 87 was built, the beach was the highway. There were no roads on the peninsula until 1930.

A well-loved tourist destination famous for fishing, birding, shelling, and sea-bathing, the peninsula boasts a long and fascinating past. Even before written history, native peoples are known to have traversed the upper Gulf coast, as evidenced by the archaeological digs at Caplen Mound. Natives buried their dead at Caplen Mound, a small natural hill made larger by shell refuse. The mound, known locally as the Indian Cemetery, was desecrated over the years by people in search of artifacts.

Few artifacts were left when a team of University of Texas archaeologists conducted excavations in 1932. Analysis of the 66 human remains found in the mound showed that the people were well-fed, robust, and tall, with no evidence of malnutrition; they adapted well to the coastal environment and lived relatively long lives.

Explorer Cabeza de Vaca came to the area in 1528 and likely visited the peninsula; some evidence points to his landing at High Island and beginning his explorations from that point. Legend has it that the gentleman pirate Jean Lafitte and his crew of pirates sometimes held parties in a grove of oak trees on the peninsula. Many believe that Lafitte left some buried treasure on the peninsula, but none has been discovered to date. When he retired from life on the high seas, Lafitte's cabin boy Charles Cronea made his home at High Island. His homestead stood there for over a century. Cronea is buried at the High Island Cemetery with a historical marker.

Gen. James Long and his wife, Jane Long, the "Mother of Texas," were among the most famous residents of the peninsula. In 1821, Jane gave birth to one of the first Anglo children born in

Texas. James Long left the peninsula aboard the ship the *Three Sisters* in the autumn of 1821, leaving Jane, her young daughter Ann, servant girl Kian, and faithful dog Galveston at Fort Las Casas. The remaining 20 soldiers left the peninsula one by one. Eventually, Jane and the young girls were alone at the fort. Her food was running out, and she had only an old rusty cannon for defense. She is reported to have fired the cannon each morning. Then, lacking a proper flag, Jane raised her red flannel petticoat up the flagpole. The natives assumed the fort was still inhabited. Jane's full story is told in chapter 9.

According to the 1850 census, 15 families lived along the 27-mile stretch of land between High island and Bolivar Point. The earliest settlers included Martin Dunman of High Island, S.D. Parr, John G. Simpton, J.H. Fredenberg, William Reeves, William Allen, Solomon Bryan, Joseph Atkins, William Dorsett, William Holbrook, Thomas Bostick, and J.B. Benjamin. Other well known early settlers include A.J. Johnson, C.W. Kahla, John Crainer, Frank Crainer, Willie Patton, John Strathan, James A. Crenshaw, R.C. Bouse, Vincent Linder, Jacob Hampshire, R.C. Knuckles, Fred Schneider, R.H. Slaughter, Oscar Flake, R.M. Roberson, George Simpton, W.H. Daily, Samuel H. Hughes, and Reuben Barrow.

The Bolivar Lighthouse was built in 1852, during the heyday of lighthouse construction on the Gulf and Atlantic coasts. It was dismantled during the Civil War by Confederate troops, who used the tower's iron to make cannonballs. The lighthouse was rebuilt in 1872 and served as a beacon to travelers until the 1930s, when more sophisticated navigational devices were employed. Bolivar residents used it as a refuge during the 1900 and 1915 hurricanes. It is now privately owned and still serves as a symbol of the peninsula to residents and visitors alike.

Bolivar Peninsula boasts a long history of farming and ranching. From the late 1800s through the early 1900s, the peninsula was known as the "Breadbasket of Galveston" and the "Watermelon Capital of Texas." By 1885, the peninsula was also well known as a successful place to raise livestock. Cowboys still run cattle on the salt-grass pastures.

The Houston Audubon Society is currently one of the largest landowners on the Bolivar Peninsula. The peninsula has world-renowned bird sanctuaries and is considered a paradise to bird-watchers around the world. The Bolivar Christmas Count celebrated its 50th anniversary in 2011. The famous count includes the woods of High Island, Rollover Pass, and the entire coast of the Bolivar Peninsula. The first count, on December 23, 1962, yielded a total of 97 species. Since that first count, expected species run from 170 to 180. With 197 species identified in 1995, Bolivar tied for fifth count in the nation.

The Sea View Hotel, built in High Island in 1896 by Capt. C.T. Cade, was the first to provide deluxe accommodations for visitors. The hotel was famous for luxurious parties, provision of transportation down to the beach, and treatments of healthy mineral-spring waters. That was the beginning of tourism on the Bolivar Peninsula.

Many day visitors ride across on the ferry or motor down the highway from Beaumont and Texas locales farther east. A plethora of Easter egg–colored beach houses, high in the air on stilts, provide rental properties for visitors wanting to stay a week or a summer. A majority of homeowners on the peninsula were once visitors who fell in love with the laid-back lifestyle and came back to stay.

One

LANDMARKS

THE LIGHTHOUSE, ROLLOVER PASS, FORT TRAVIS, AUDUBON LANDS, AND CEMETERIES

The Bolivar Peninsula lies at latitude 29.4 north and longitude 94.6 west. For people crossing the bay by ferry from Galveston, Texas, on one of the busiest waterways in the world, the Bolivar Lighthouse quickly comes into clear view, standing watch over the singing seagulls and dancing dolphins. It is a magical trip.

After an approximately 17-minute free ride (courtesy of the Texas Department of Transportation), the ferry docks, and the real adventure begins. A few minutes' drive down Highway 87 brings visitors to Fort Travis Seashore Park. Fort Travis was built in 1836 to protect the Galveston Harbor entrance. Currently the home of the annual Jane Long Festival, the remains of the four batteries (Ernst, Davis, Kimball, and No. 236) still remain, and some can be toured during the festival.

One will observe acres and acres of bird sanctuary land owned by the Houston Audubon Society along the peninsula. Bolivar Flats is a Globally Important Bird Area (the highest designation) and an international site in the Western Hemisphere Shorebird Reserve Network. Boy Scout Woods and Smith Oaks Nature Sanctuaries are world-class birding areas located in High Island.

About 20 miles on down the highway, one will cross Rollover Pass, the narrowest part of the peninsula. Rollover is famous for world-class fishing and infamous for its history of smugglers "rolling over" barrels of contraband from the earliest days of Spanish rule through Prohibition.

Visitors can turn left onto Highway 124 at the end of Highway 87 and head into High Island. As the name suggests, it is the highest point on the peninsula at 38 feet, and it sits atop a large salt dome. High Island is the highest elevation of any point on the Gulf coast from Mobile, Alabama, to the Yucatan Peninsula. With its substantial wooded areas, High Island is a natural refuge for migrating birds making their way across the Gulf of Mexico and was once famous for its mineral waters.

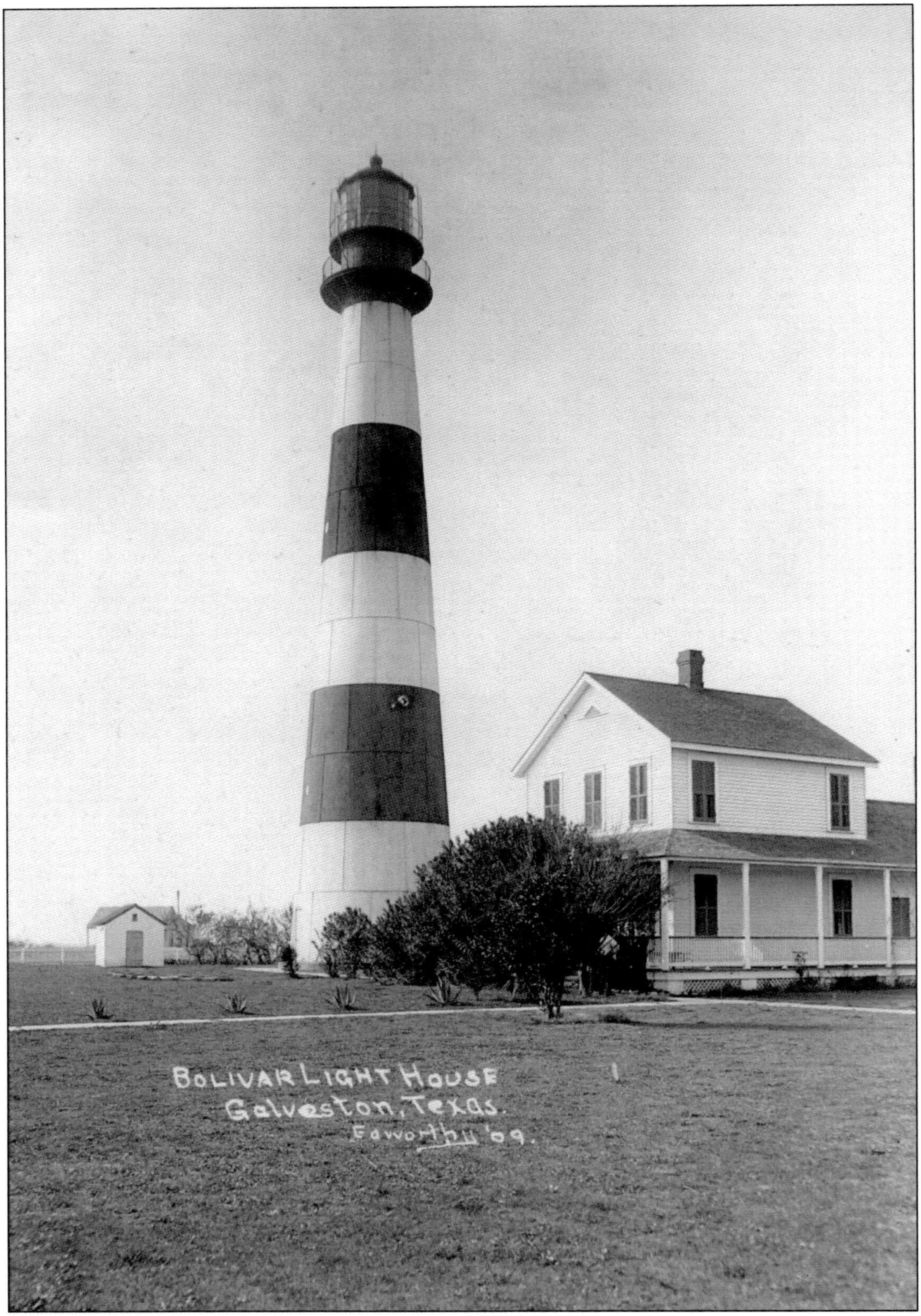

The Bolivar Lighthouse was built by the federal government in 1852 and later dismantled by Confederate soldiers during the Civil War. It was rebuilt in 1872 and served as the beacon that guided thousands of mariners into port until 1933. (Courtesy of Galveston County Museum.)

The lighthouse withstood three of the worst storms hitting the peninsula—the 1900 and 1915 storms and Hurricane Ike in 2008. During the 1900 and 1915 storms, the lighthouse harbored a number of peninsula residents, saving them from certain death. According to an inspector's report after the 1900 storm, over 6,000 lives were lost on Galveston Island. (Courtesy of Dwain Cox.)

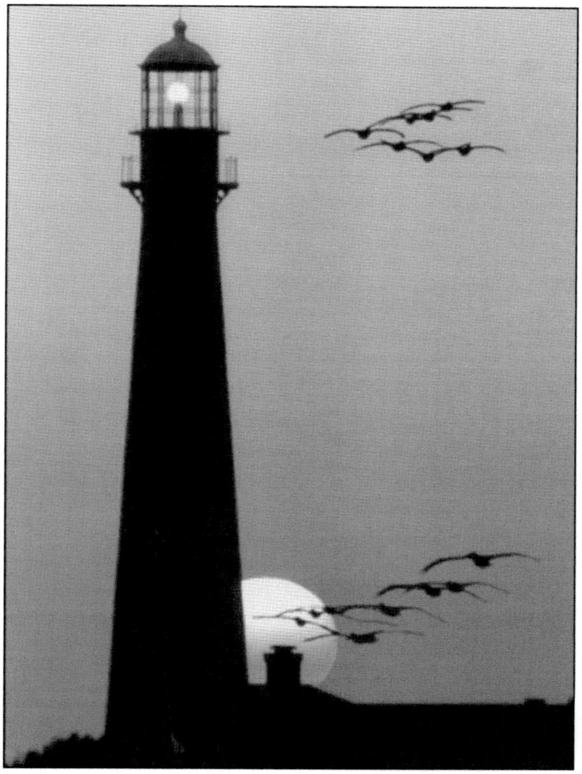

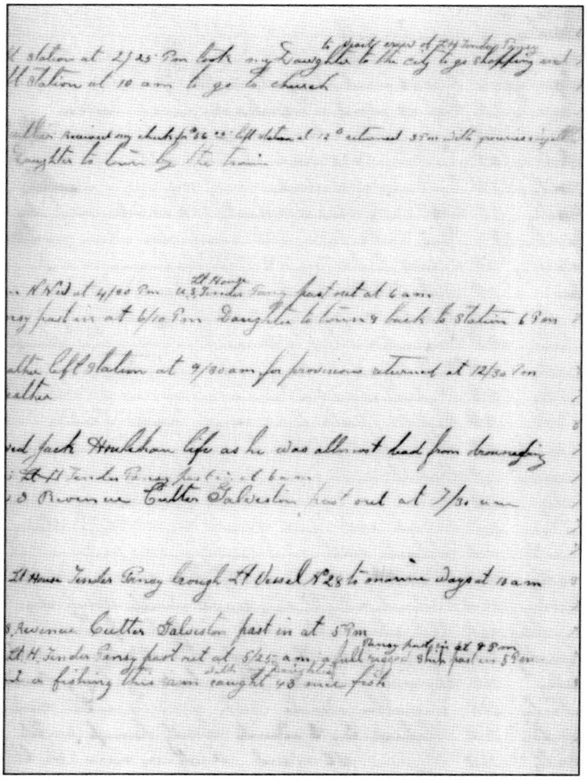

station at 2/25 Pm took my Daughter to the City to go shopping and
Station at 10 am to go to church

Daughter to town by the train

Daughter to town & back to Station 6 Pm

left Station at 9/30 am for provisions returned at 12/30 Pm

Jack Houleham life as he was almost dead from drowning
Revenue Cutter Galveston past out at 7/30 am

Lt House Tender Pansy brought Lt Vessel No 28 to marine ways at 11 am

Revenue Cutter Galveston past in at 5 Pm

caught 43 nice fish

Life in the Bolivar Lighthouse was lonely and somewhat monotonous. Mrs. H.C. Claiborne, wife of the first lighthouse keeper, said, "Life at the lighthouse is very lonely and friendless. There is very little visiting because travel is nonexistent from the point to Galveston. We pass most of our time by reading books." Entries in the lighthouse keeper's journal suggest a busy and repetitive schedule for the keeper and his family. On November 1, 1902, the keeper's wife wrote, "Scrubbing and washing floors and steps to lighthouse." "Working all day cleaning brass and plate glass," was her entry in July 1903. A very cold winter in February 1903 yielded this entry: "Lots of frozen fish in sight." The keeper's wife wrote in May 1903, "Saved Jack Houleham's life as he was almost dead from drowning." (Courtesy of the Rosenberg Library, Galveston, Texas.)

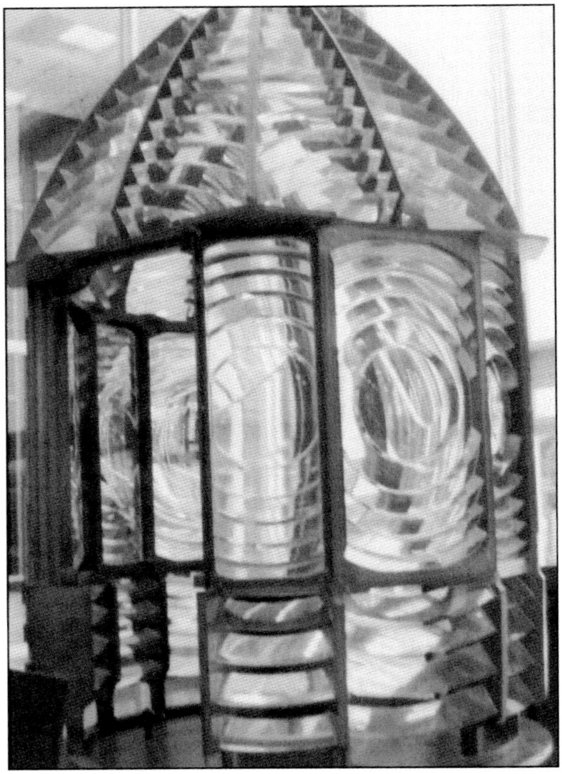

The Bolivar Lighthouse was officially retired on May 29, 1933, after 61 years of service. The lamps and reflector lenses have been reassembled and are a key artifact in the *On the Water* exhibit displayed at the Smithsonian in Washington, DC. The Fresnel lens, named for French scientist and inventor Augustin Fresnel, could be seen for miles. (Photograph by the author.)

In 1968, the made-for-television movie *My Sweet Charlie*, starring Patty Duke and Al Freeman Jr., was filmed at the lighthouse. Duke won an Emmy Award for her work in the groundbreaking movie. In the opening scene, she is seen walking up the road to the lighthouse. (Photograph by the author.)

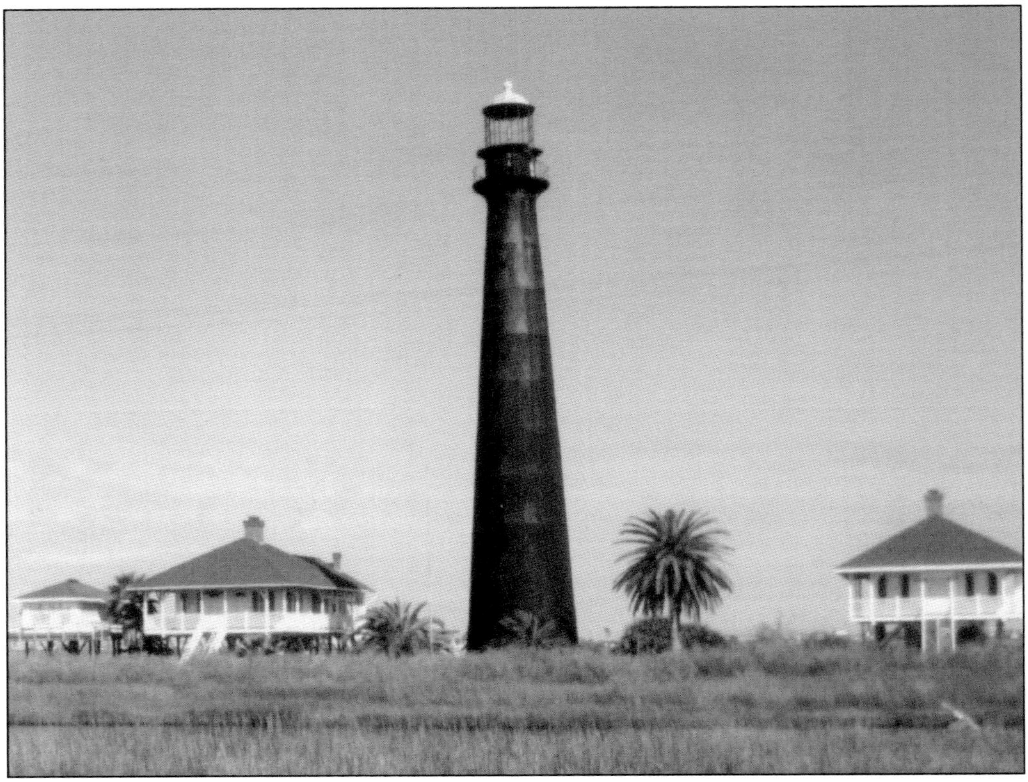

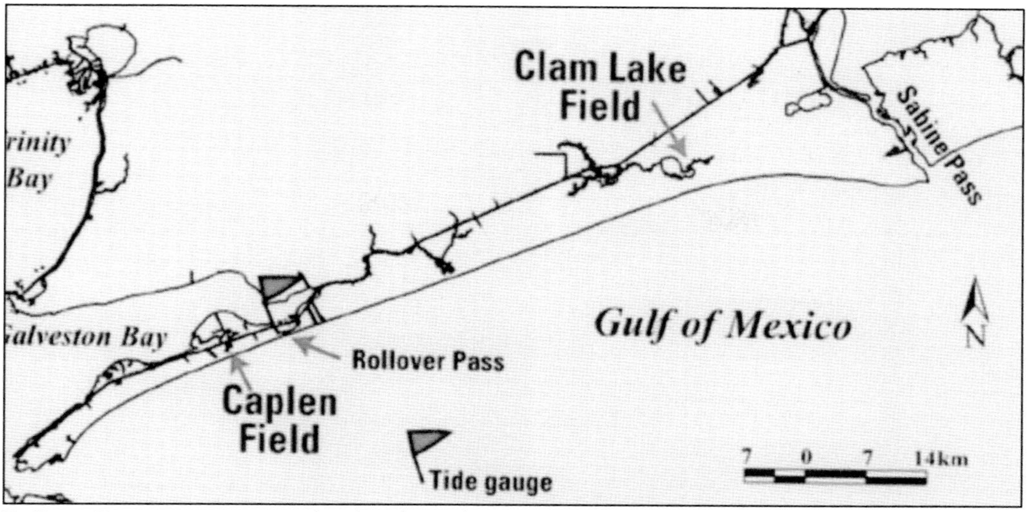

Rollover Pass is an important landmark on the Bolivar Peninsula. Smugglers used the narrow strip of land between the Gulf and Galveston Bay long before there was a man-made channel. They rolled their ill-gotten gain (usually packed in barrels) over from a ship on the Gulf to a waiting boat on the bay side, where it would be carried for distribution. The practice continued during Prohibition, with barrels of liquor being rolled over the pass to waiting boats on the other side. (Courtesy of Galveston County Parks and Cultural Services.)

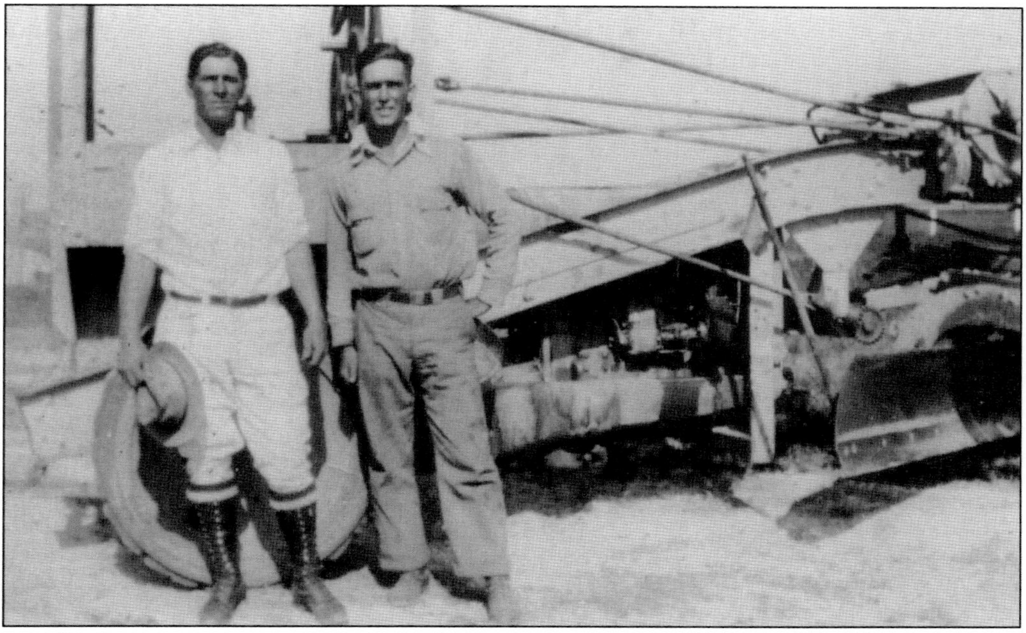

In 1955, the pass was mechanically dredged to create a new opening between the gulf and Galveston Bay. This was intended to improve ingress and egress of fish and shellfish. It was believed that this would produce better fishing. Fishermen agree that this was successful. The pass is excellent for recreational fishing, and it is a very popular location for shore-based anglers. Every weekend finds dozens of fishermen lined up on both sides of the pass. The fishing continues by lantern light at night. Croaker, flounder, redfish, sand trout, speckled trout, drum, sheepshead, saltwater catfish, and Spanish mackerel are caught from the side at Rollover Pass. (Courtesy of Robert and Jerri Bouse.)

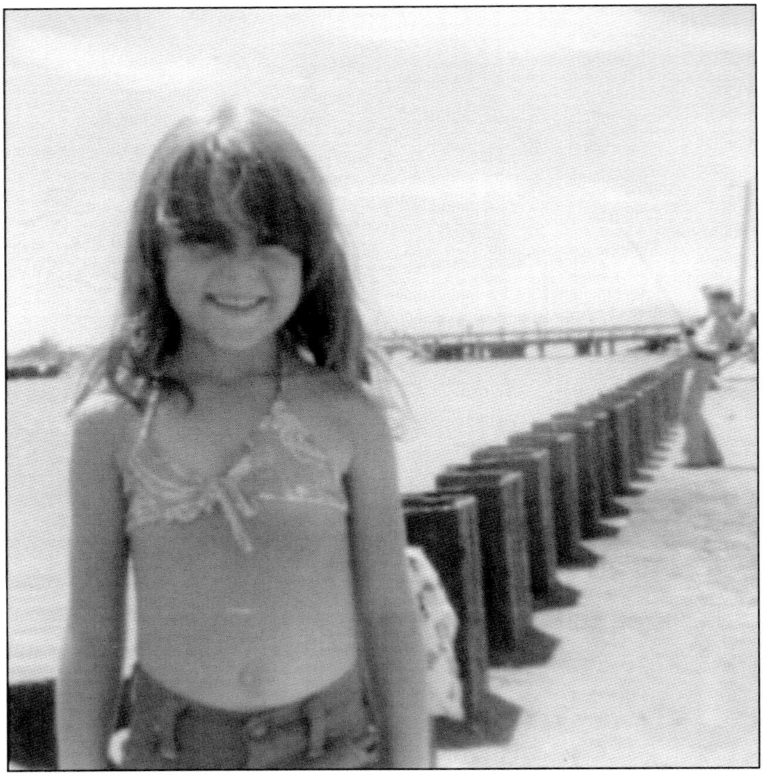

Rae Sullivan, pictured here at Rollover Pass in 1976, reports a childhood filled with happy days on the peninsula, fishing and crabbing with her grandmother. They would set out long lines between two poles that had crab lines hanging from them, then float a large washtub and fill it with crabs. Her uncle shrimped with a homemade net dragged behind his small boat. He also dug oysters. After a weekend of fishing, they gathered to make a huge pot of gumbo. (Courtesy of Rae Sullivan.)

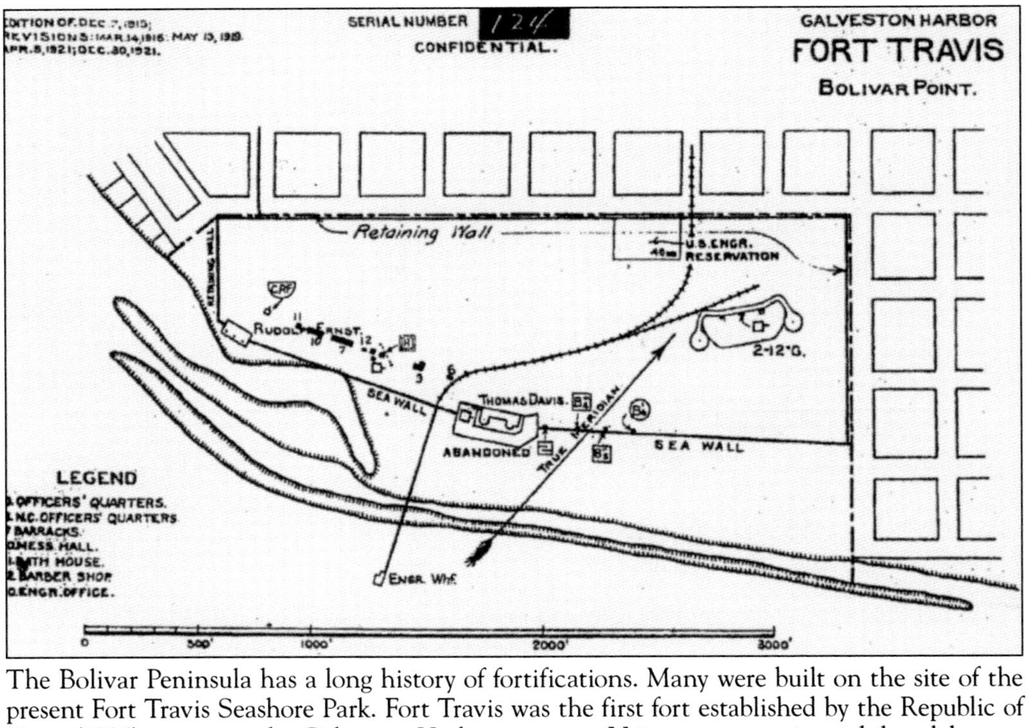

The Bolivar Peninsula has a long history of fortifications. Many were built on the site of the present Fort Travis Seashore Park. Fort Travis was the first fort established by the Republic of Texas (1836) to protect the Galveston Harbor entrance. Using army recruits and slave labor, an octagonal earth and timber fortification was built. (Courtesy of Ralph Stenzel.)

Fort Travis was named in honor of William B. Travis, a famous defender of the Alamo. The fort received a Texas Historical Marker in 1993. In the background is Battery No. 236. (Courtesy of Galveston County Parks and Cultural Services.)

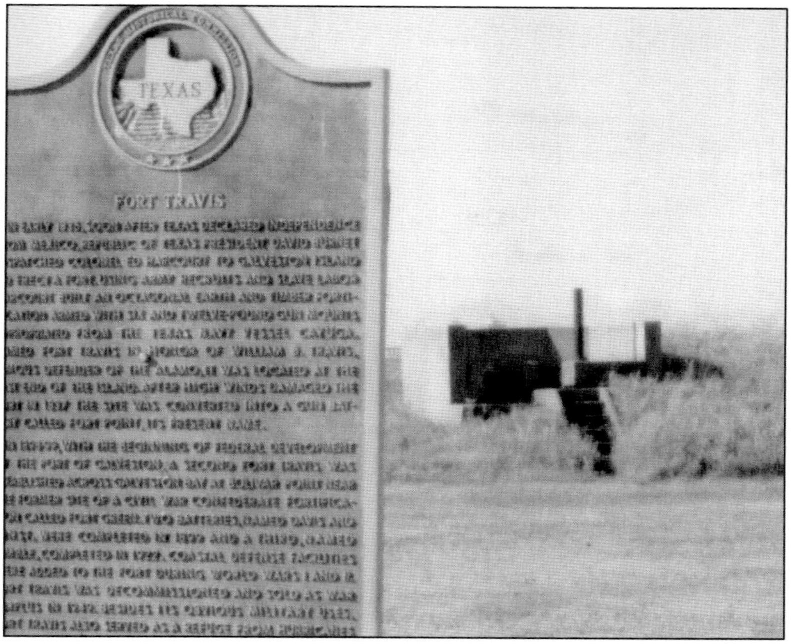

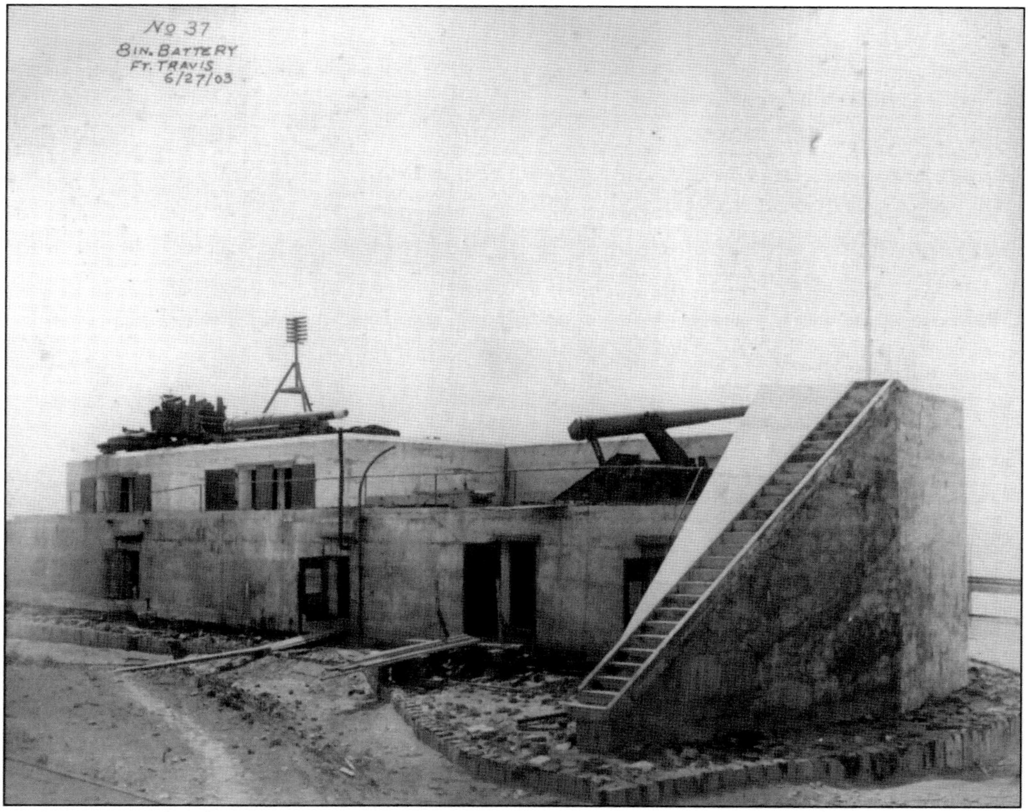

Built in 1898, this battery was named for Lt. Thomas Davis of the US Mounted Rifles. Battery Davis is currently in a state of deterioration, and visitors are no longer admitted. (Courtesy of Ralph Stenzel.)

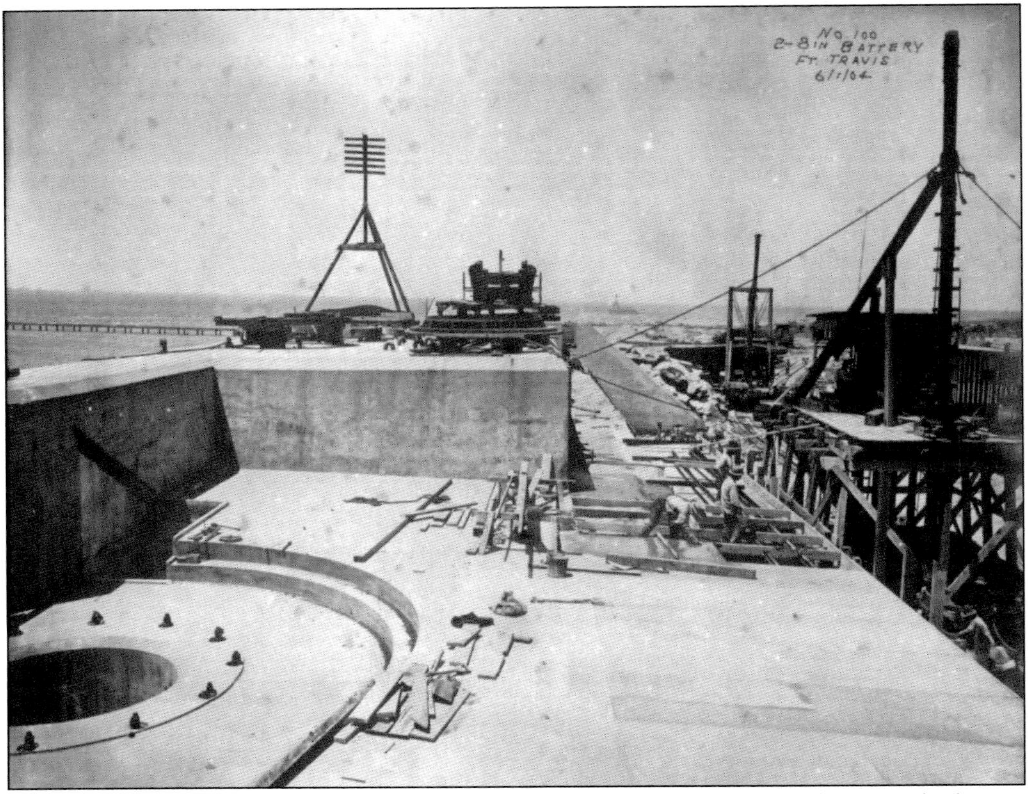

Battery Davis is pictured here in 1904. The battery contained two eight-inch guns, which were the most advanced of their day. (Courtesy of Ralph Stenzel.)

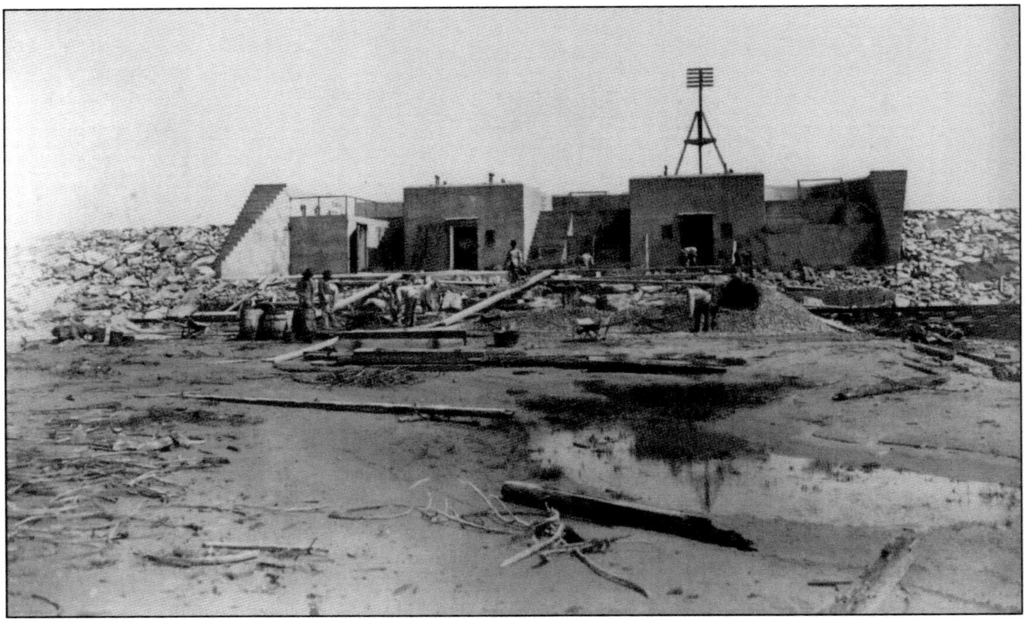
Battery Ernst was built in 1898 and named after 2nd Lt. Rudolph Ernst, US Sixth Infantry. It contained three small-caliber pedestal guns and ammunition magazines below. Battery Ernst is pictured here in April 1904. (Courtesy of Ralph Stenzel.)

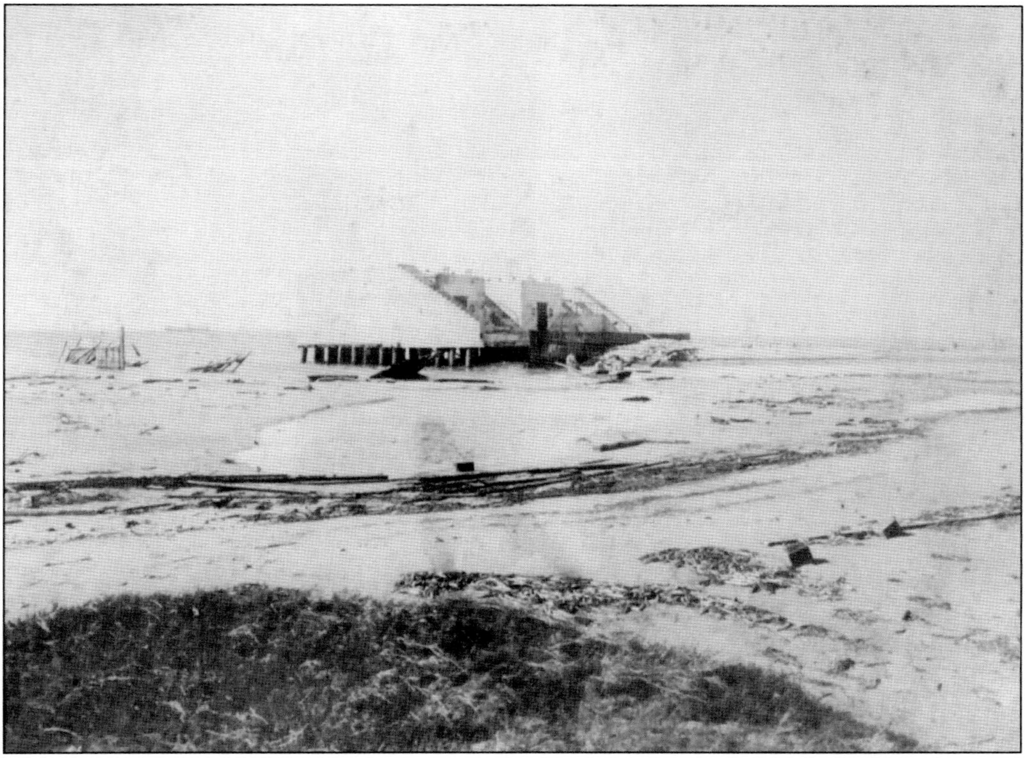

After the 1900 hurricane, a 17-foot seawall was constructed on the gulf side of the fort. Fort Travis was occupied by soldiers in both world wars and served as an internment camp for several German prisoners of war during World War II. The fort was purchased in 1973 by the Galveston County Commissioners for use as a public park. This photograph shows Battery Ernst after the 1900 storm, when it was severely damaged. (Courtesy of Ralph Stenzel.)

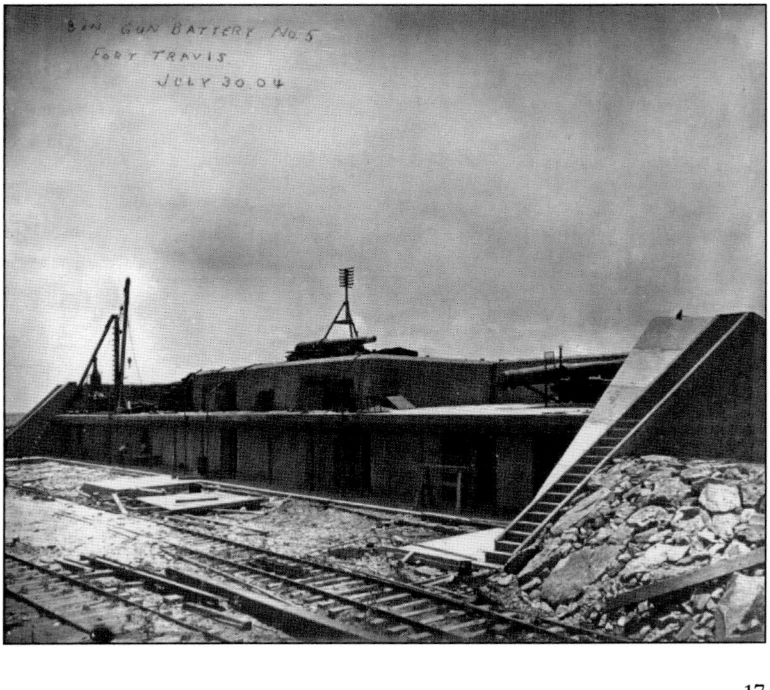

Recovery from the 1900 storm was slow. During the ensuing five years, the Army Corps of Engineers spent about $1 million to rebuild Fort Travis. Battery Davis is pictured here on July 30, 1904. (Courtesy of Ralph Stenzel.)

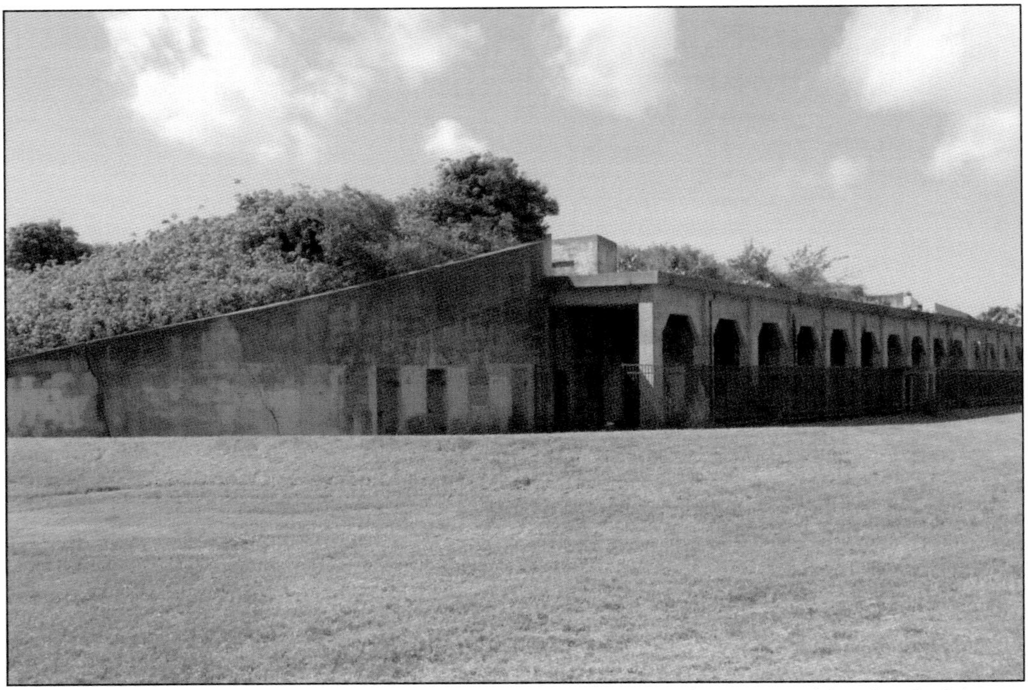

Battery Kimble was completed in 1922. It was named after Maj. Edwin R. Kimble, who died during World War I. Battery Kimble contained 12-inch guns with a range of 17 miles. Battery Kimble is pictured as it stands today. (Courtesy of Galveston County Parks and Cultural Services.)

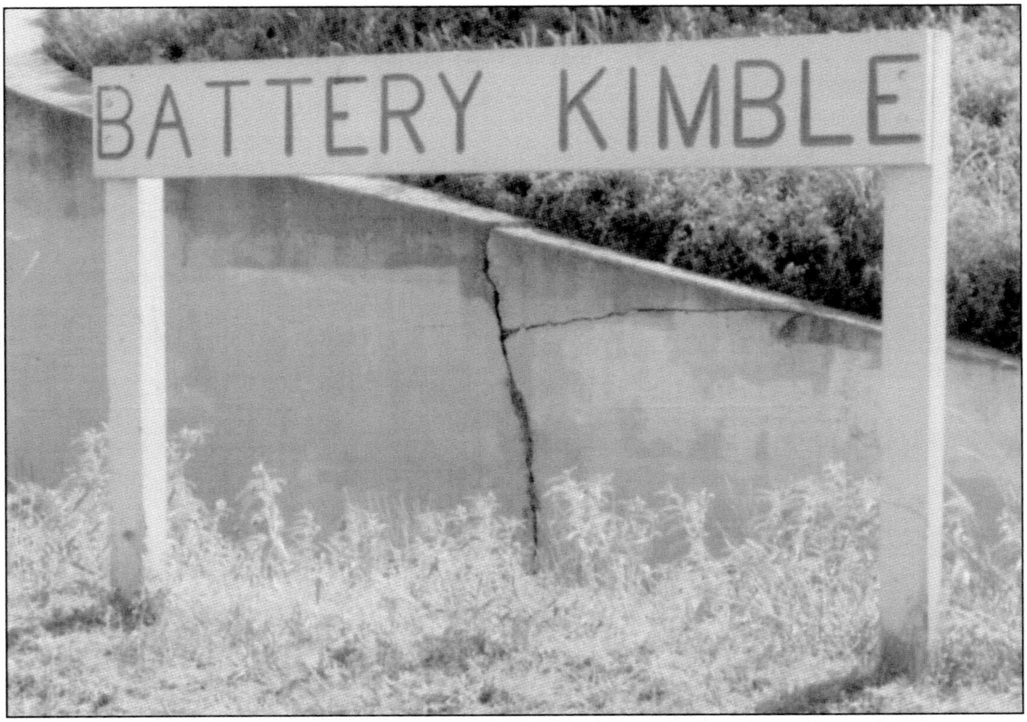

Visitors are allowed to tour the interior of Battery Kimble during the Jane Long Festival. (Photograph by the author.)

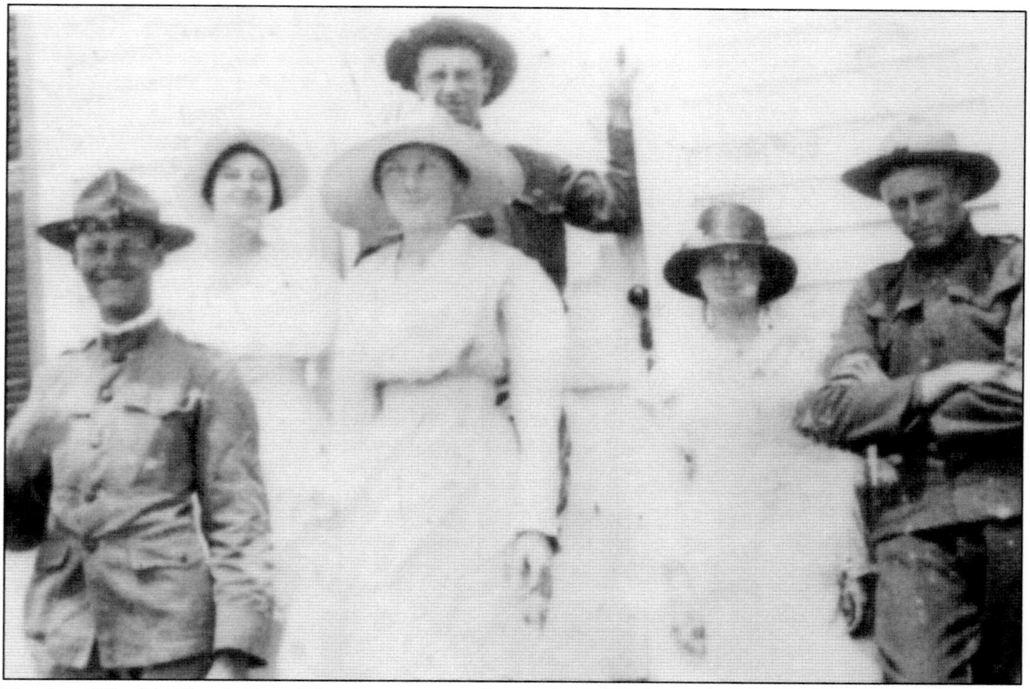

During World War I, Fort Travis garrisoned troops defending the Port of Galveston and its approaches. There were 2,500 troops stationed at the fort during World War II. The fort was enlarged, and several sizes of guns were installed. Fort Travis was sold in 1949 to private interests. It was acquired through a Moody Foundation Grant in 1976 and is currently operated by the Galveston County Parks and Cultural Services Department. (Courtesy of the Simpton family.)

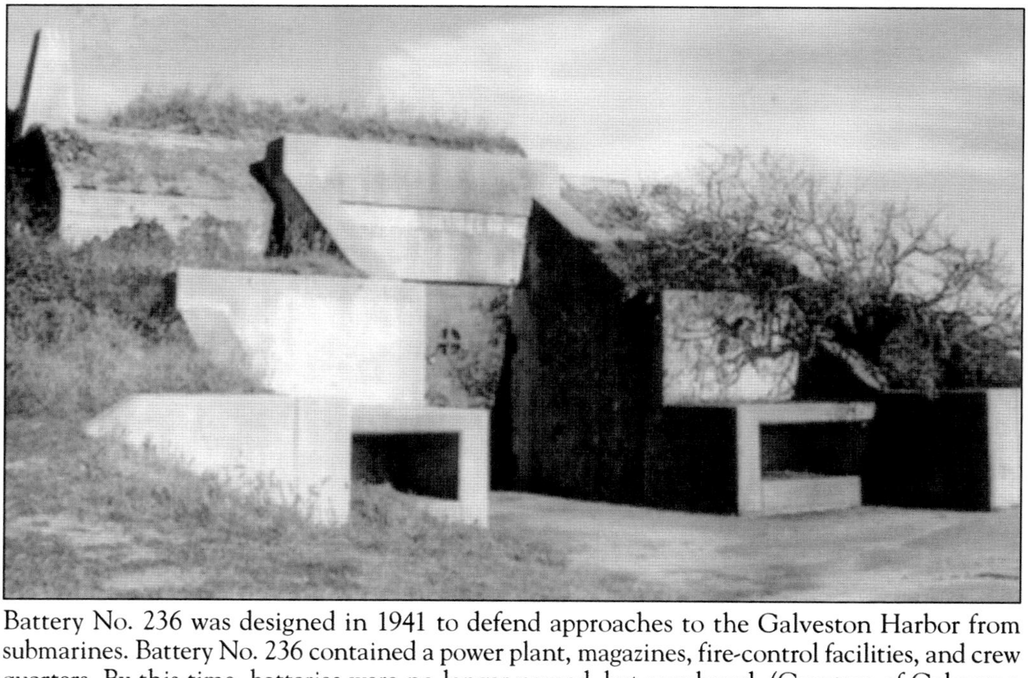

Battery No. 236 was designed in 1941 to defend approaches to the Galveston Harbor from submarines. Battery No. 236 contained a power plant, magazines, fire-control facilities, and crew quarters. By this time, batteries were no longer named, but numbered. (Courtesy of Galveston County Parks and Cultural Services.)

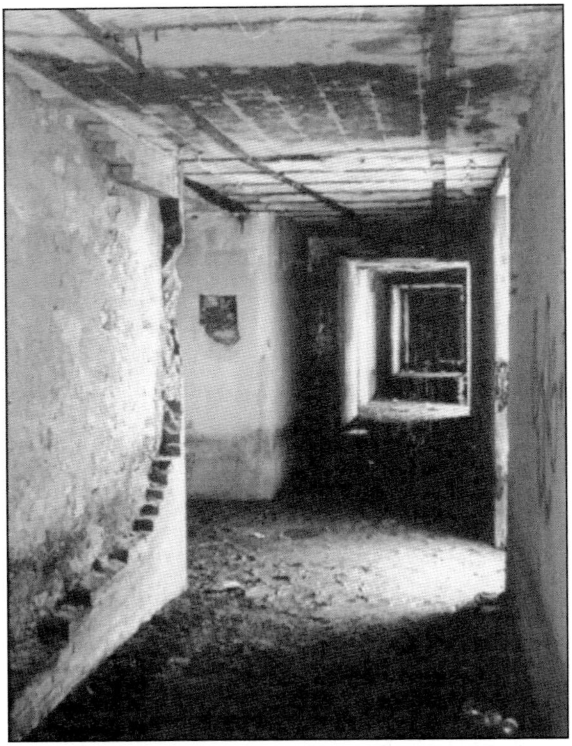

In 1961, many local residents rode out Hurricane Carla at the fort. So did their cattle and other animals. This photograph shows the interior of one of the bunkers at Fort Travis. Throughout the history of the fortifications, many residents and their livestock have weathered hurricanes in the bunkers at the fort. (Courtesy of Galveston County Parks and Cultural Services.)

The Houston Audubon Society is one of the largest landowners on the peninsula. Pictured here are John Moore (left) and Scott Watson, heading out for a day of world-class birding. (Courtesy of John Moore.)

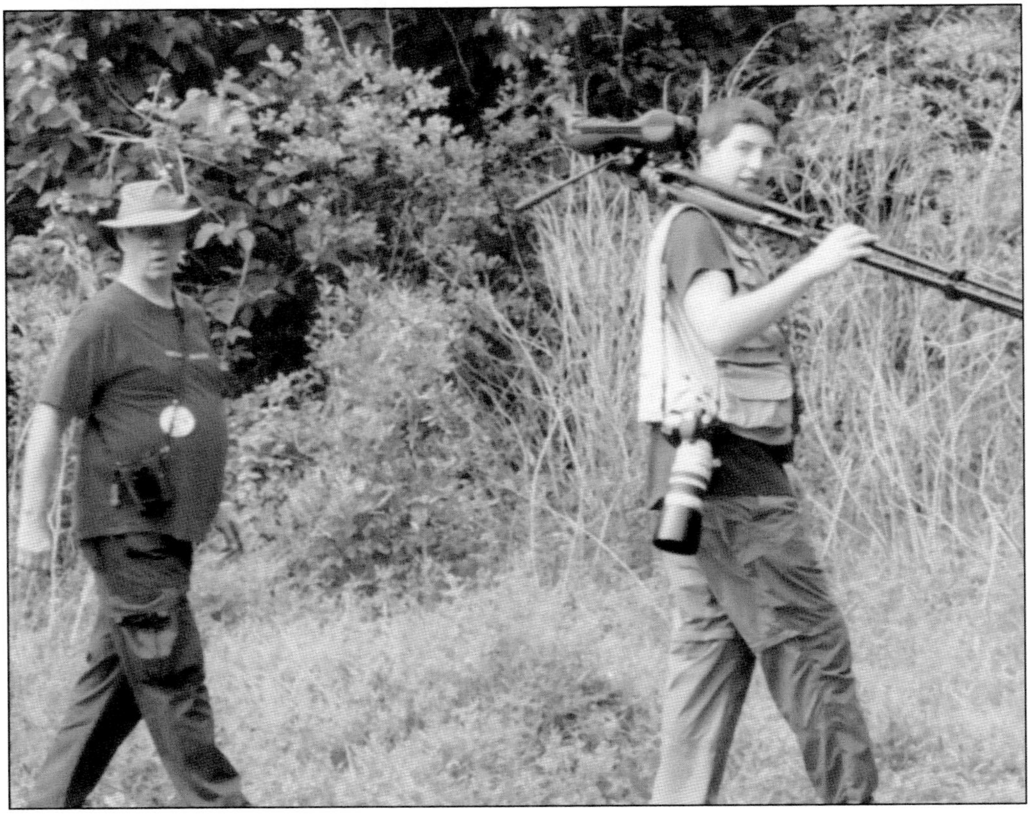

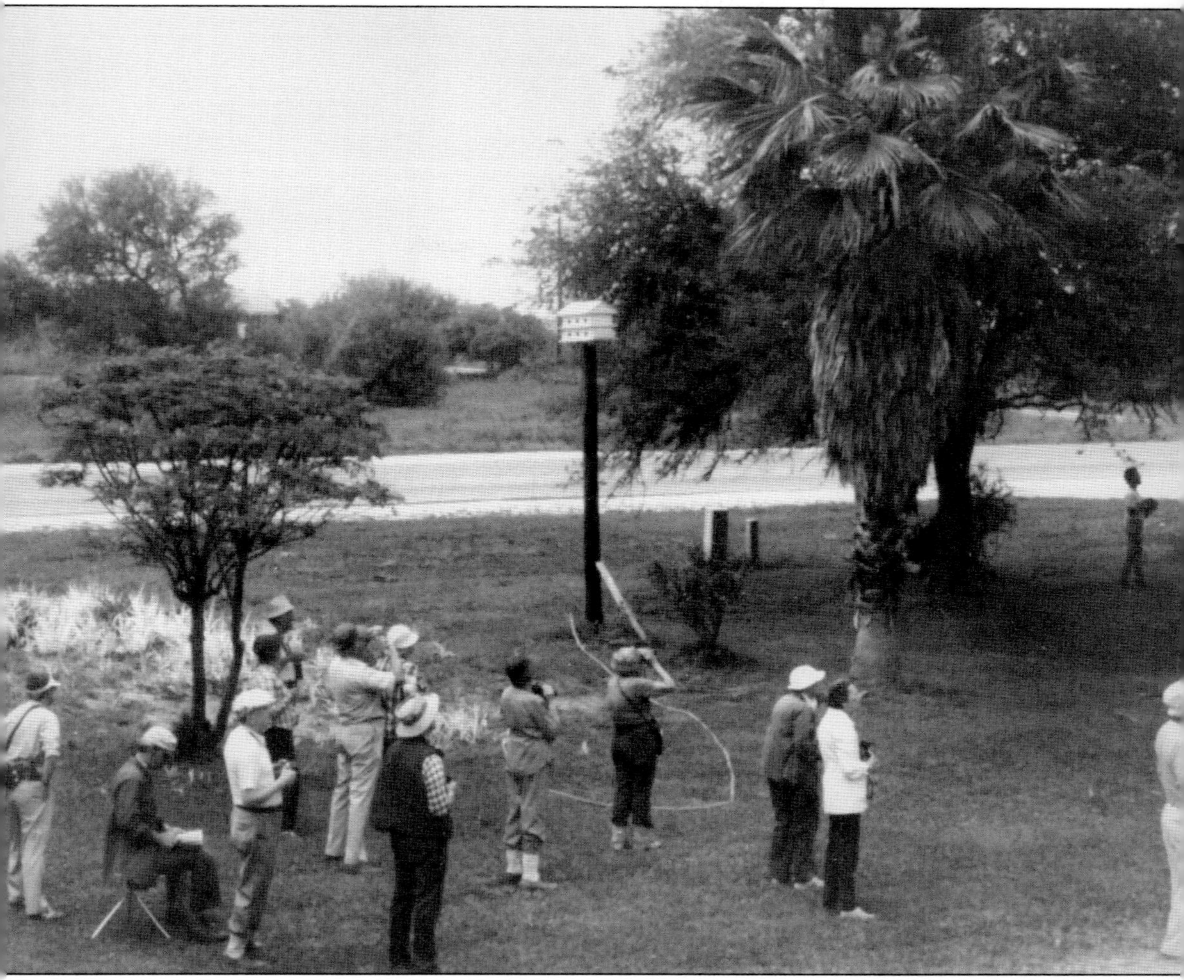

Birding is an important pastime on the Bolivar Peninsula. International birders come to admire the vast expanses of woods and marshland that provide sanctuary to migrating birds. Bolivar Flats is a Globally Important Bird Area, the highest designation, and an international site in the Western Hemisphere Shorebird Reserve Network. These birders are pictured at the Johnson Ranch in 1987. (Courtesy of Margo Johnson.)

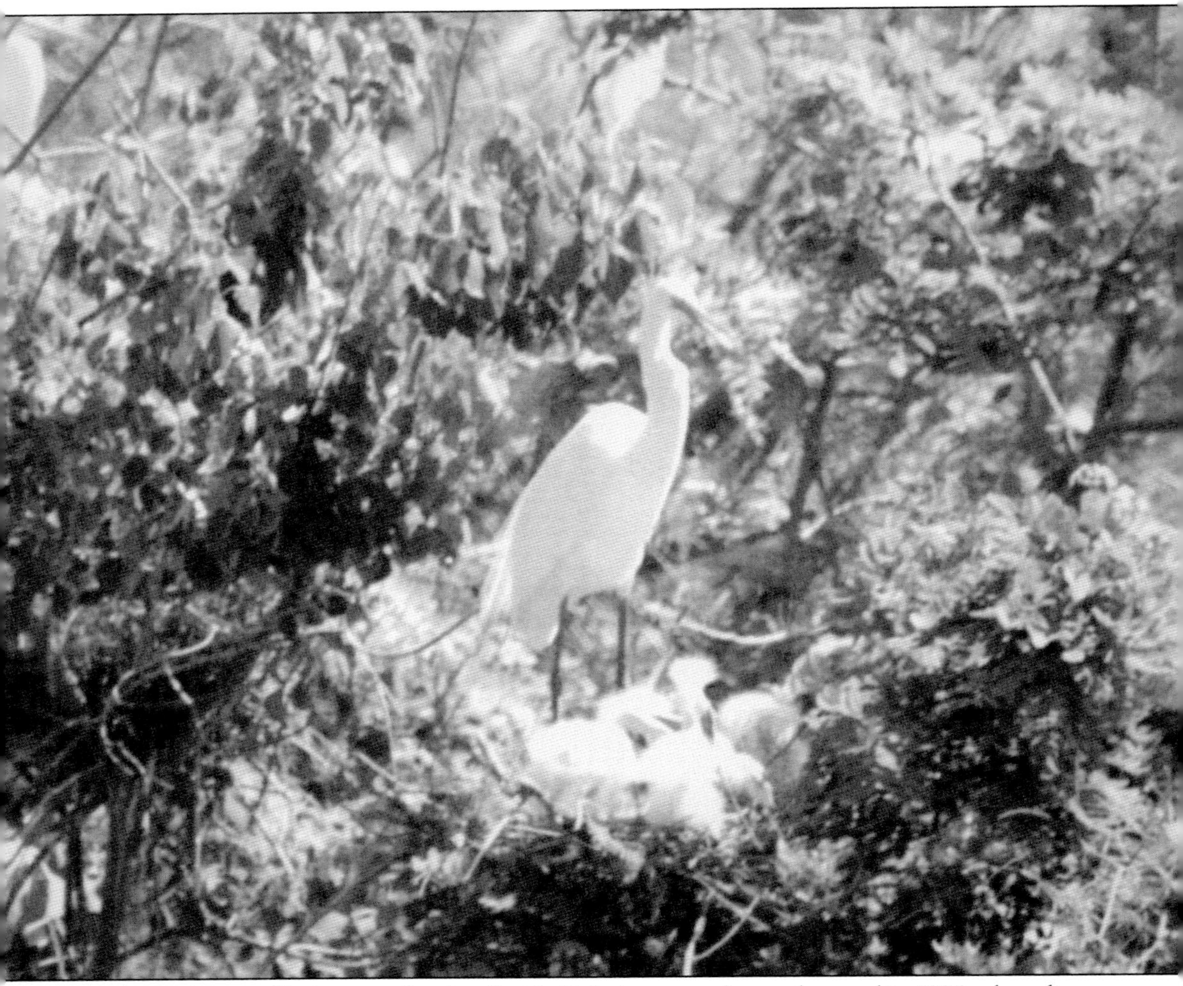

The rookery at Claybottom Pond in Smith Oaks is a part of a pond started in 1936, when dirt was needed for the railway bridge over the new intracoastal waterway. It also held the water supply for the High Island Community and provided water for the sulfur plant located to the east of the pond. Visitors to the rookery in High Island's Smith Oaks get a close look at egrets, herons, cormorants, and spoonbills nesting on the predator-free island from the platform on the northeast side of the pond. (Courtesy of John Moore.)

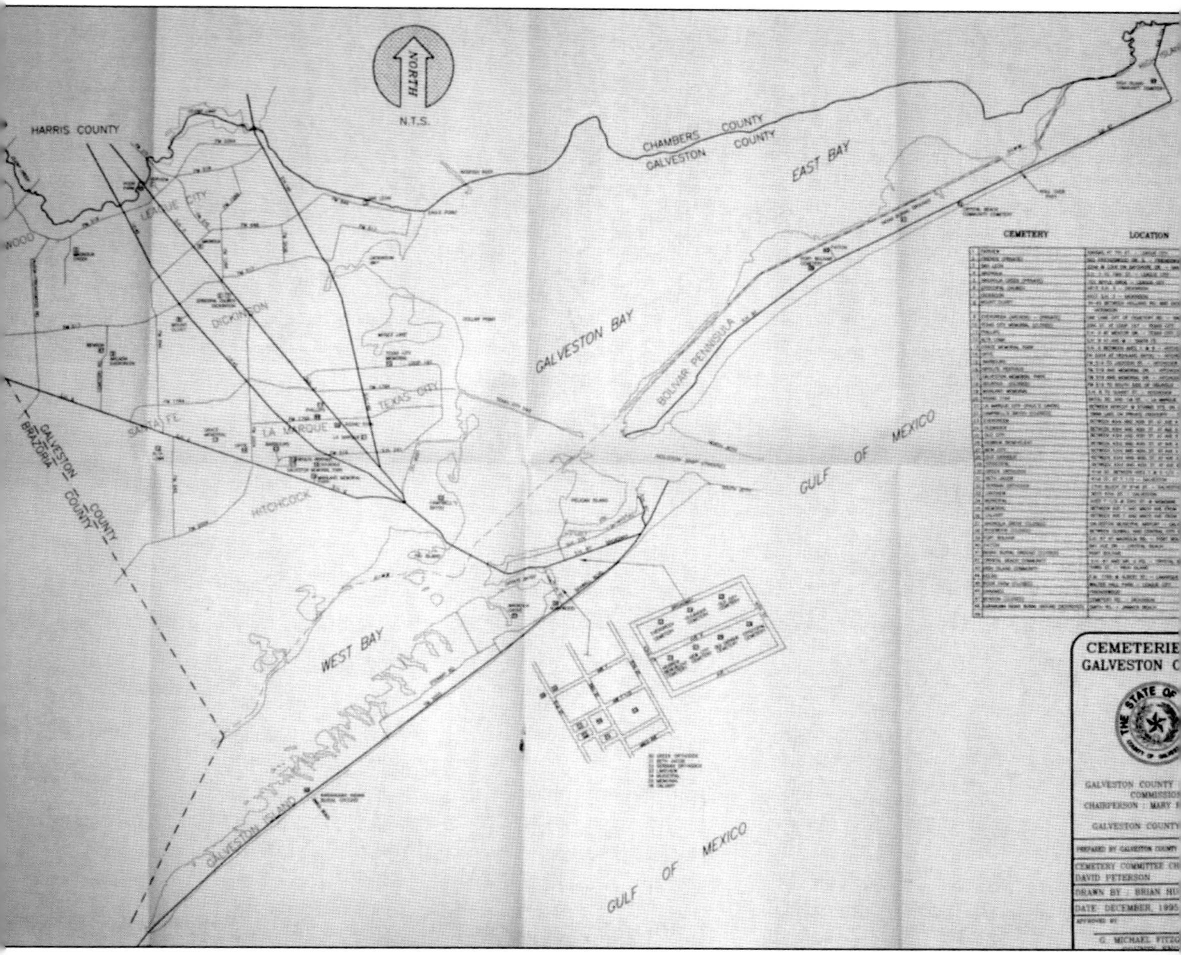

The area surrounding the cemetery at Caplen Mound (depicted on this map) was home to native peoples who hunted, gathered, and fished for centuries around the bays and inlets of the upper Texas coast. Caplen Mound, known for decades as the Indian Cemetery, is a small circular knoll a natural hill built up over the years as the native people buried their dead within the piles of shell. Excavation of the site began in 1932 with a team of University of Texas archaeologists. Remains of approximately 70 people were discovered. Only a modest number of pottery shards were found. (Courtesy of Margo Johnson.)

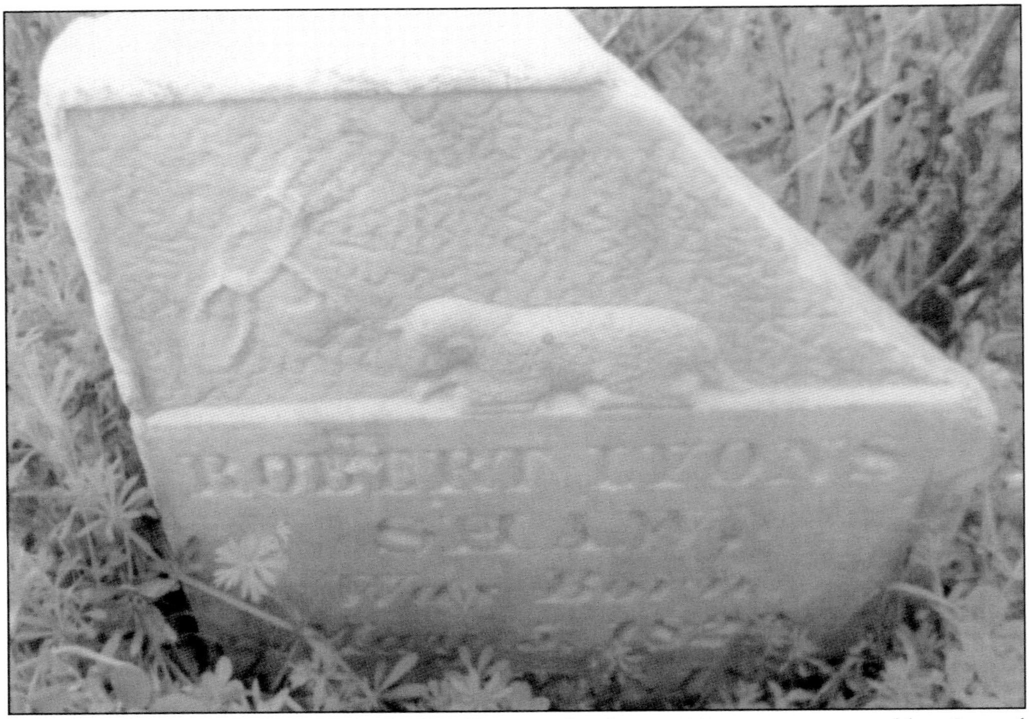

Patton Cemetery is a pioneer cemetery legally set aside when a 100-acre tract was sold to Samuel H. Robertson in 1880. When the area was first surveyed in 1954, there were six gravestones discovered. Currently, only three headstones are intact. The others were lost during the devastation of Hurricane Ike. This is the headstone of Robert Lyons Shaw, who is buried at the cemetery. He was the heir of Jonas Shaw, who surveyed a portion of the Bolivar Peninsula in the early 1830s, when Mexico still had ownership. In the 1840 Texas census, Jonas is shown to have 420 acres of land under survey, based on a grant. The land was patented to him by the State of Texas in 1846. (Photograph by the author.)

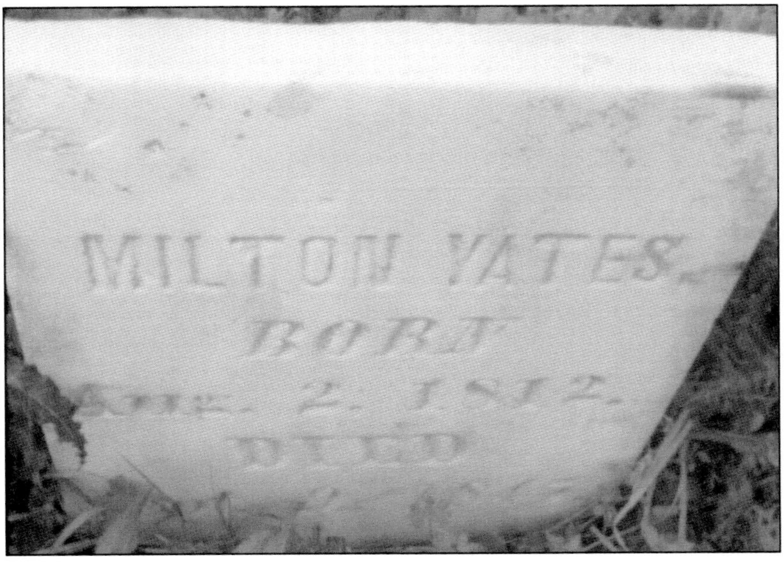

Milton Yates moved to the Bolivar Peninsula in the 1830s. He is buried in Patton Cemetery, and his headstone is pictured here. Yates was a justice of the peace and performed the first marriage ceremony on the peninsula. He fought in the Battle of San Jacinto. (Photograph by the author.)

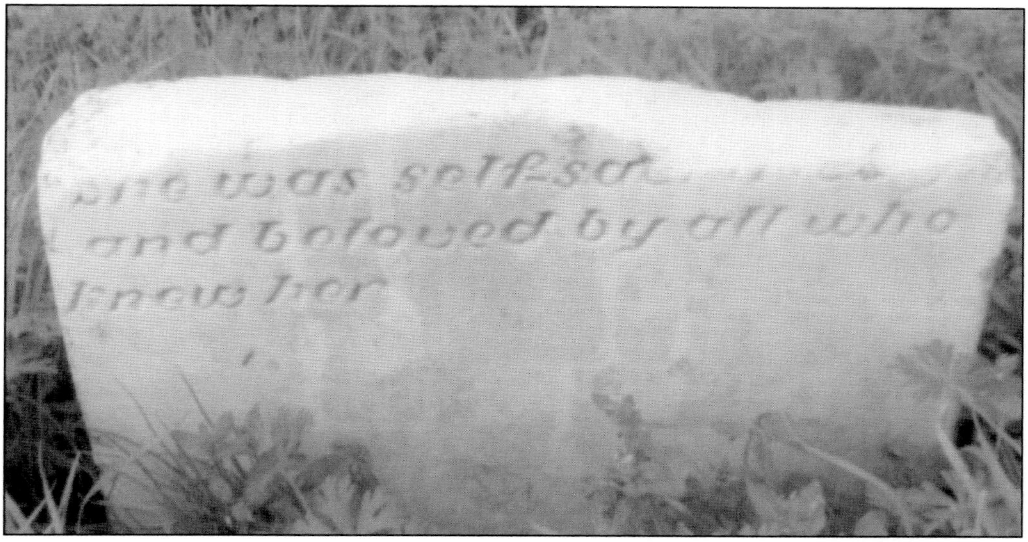

This stone, located in the Patton Cemetery, contains only the following inscription: "She was self-sacrificing and beloved by all who knew her." The identifying information is missing. It was most likely lost during one of the several hurricanes hitting the Bolivar Peninsula in the many decades since it was placed. It is believed that this stone belongs to either Johannah Abrahamson or Lizzie Griscom. (Photograph by the author.)

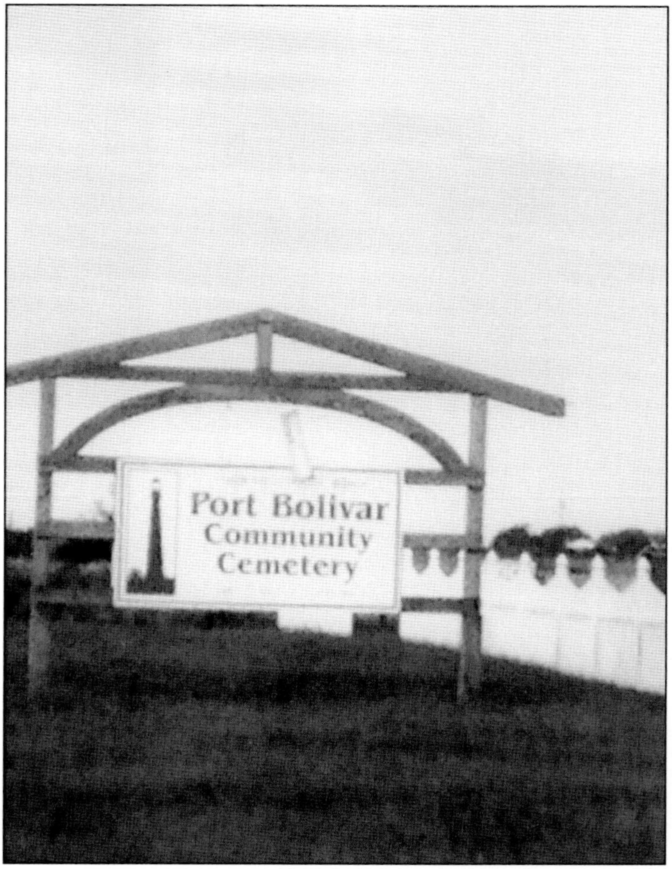

The Bolivar Community Cemetery was officially established between 1889 and 1890. However, the oldest registered grave is that of Marceline Johnson, dated January 8, 1815. Johnson was among the earliest settlers on the peninsula. There are now approximately 500 graves, with several still unmarked. Land for the cemetery was donated by the Jeffers family and later by the Johnson family. For many years, local men dug the graves. After Hurricane Ike, every headstone was turned over, and trash and timbers covered the cemetery. Local residents worked tirelessly to restore the headstones, remove the trash, and construct a new fence. In the spirit of the Bolivar Peninsula, people just driving by stopped to help. (Courtesy of Jane Ewing.)

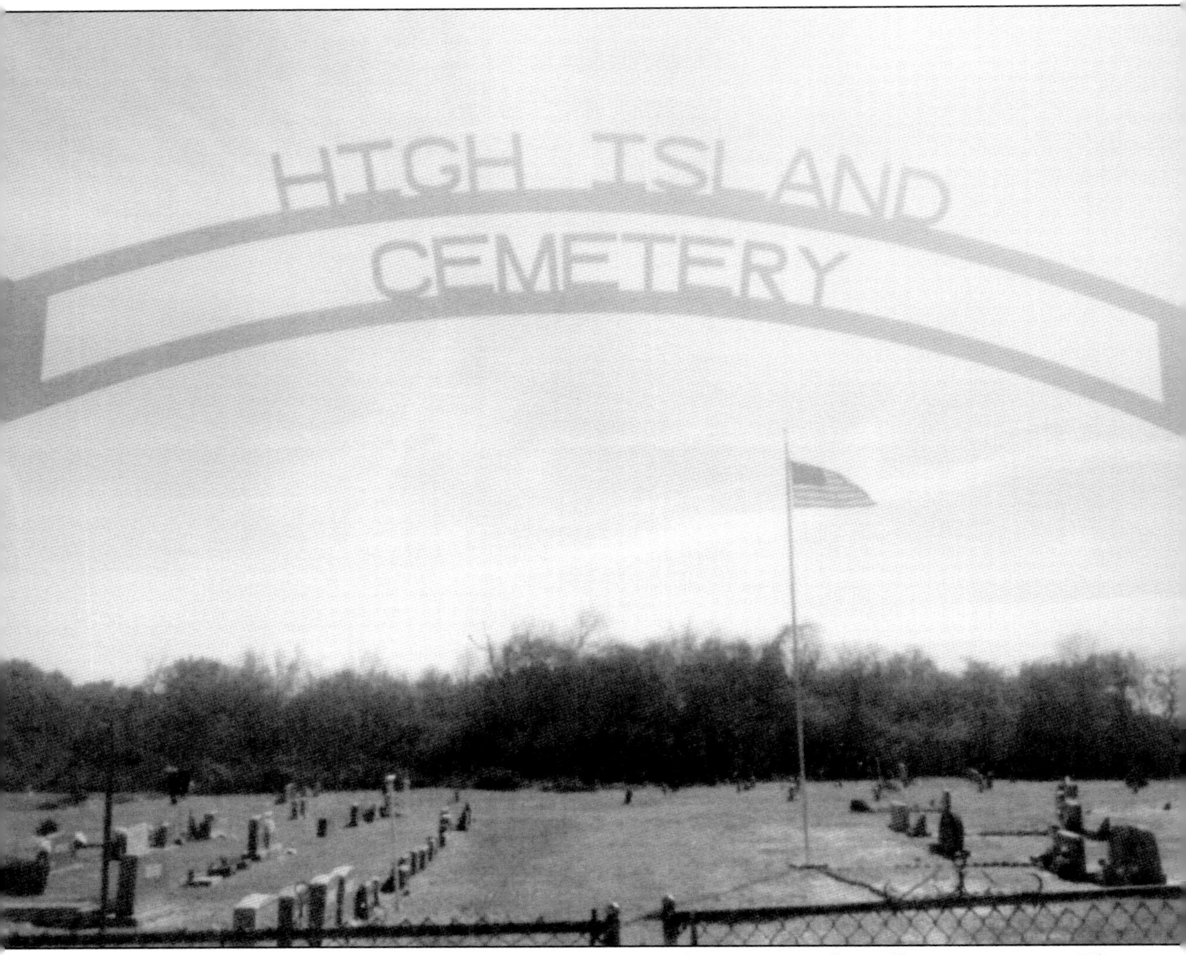

The High Island Cemetery has served the High Island community for well over 100 years. The earliest grave belongs to Minnie Sullivan, 1886. The most well-known person interred at High Island Cemetery is Charles Cronea, former cabin boy for pirate Jean Lafitte. (Photograph by the author.)

Two

FOLKS

FOUNDERS, HEROES, AND CHARACTERS

The history of any town is really just the story of the interesting people who made it their home. Nowhere is this more true than on the Bolivar Peninsula. From the lives of early native peoples, evidenced by the burial ground at Caplen, through stories of pirates and filibusterers, to the early settlement by farmers and cattle ranchers, the Bolivar Peninsula is full of rich, exciting stories.

The peninsula became notorious between 1816 and 1822 as a base of filibustering activities against Spain. For about 15 years after the era of filibustering, the peninsula reverted to a land of wildlife, devoid of civilization.

On August 5, 1838, the first permanent settler, Samuel D. Parr, claimed a league of land beginning at Bolivar Point. The town that is now Port Bolivar was also known as Ismail, Parrsville, and Gabion. A handful of farmers settled at Bolivar during the 1840s. By 1850, there were 15 families (half of whom were English immigrants) living along the 27-mile stretch between High Island and Bolivar Point.

The earliest settlers included Martin Dunman of High Island, S.D. Parr, John G. Simpton, J.H. Fredenberg, William Reeves, William Allen, Solomon Bryan, Joseph Atkins, William Dorsett, William Holbrook, Thomas Bostick, and J.B. Benjamin. Other well known early settlers include A.J. Johnson, C.W. Kahla, John Crainer, Frank Crainer, Willie Patton, John Strathan, James A. Crenshaw, Vincent Linder, Jacob Hampshire, R.C. Knuckles, Fred Schneider, R.H. Slaughter, Oscar Flake, R.M. Roberson, George Simpton, W.H. Daily, Samuel H. Hughes, and Reuben Barrow. By 1885, about 80 families were living on the peninsula. Many of their stories are told in this book.

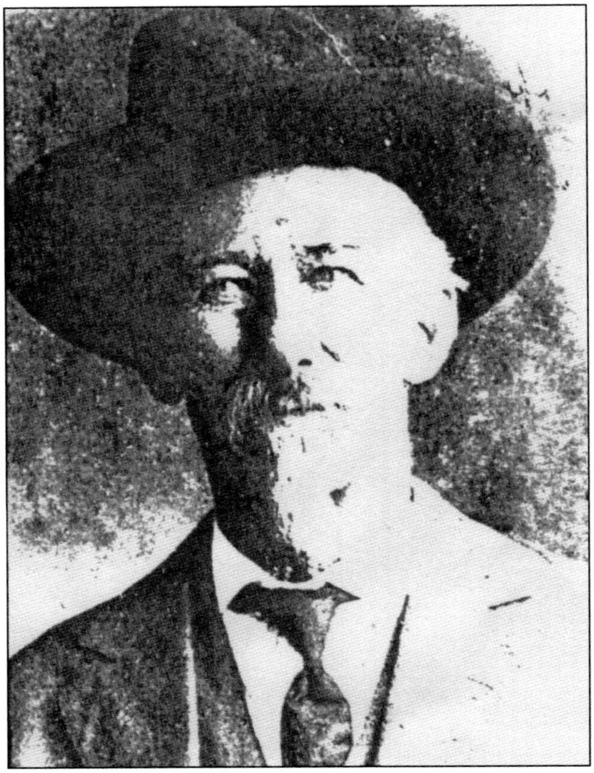

Pictured here is James Anderson Crenshaw. The Crenshaw family settled in Bolivar in January 1872. (Courtesy of Clare Atkinson Wonders.)

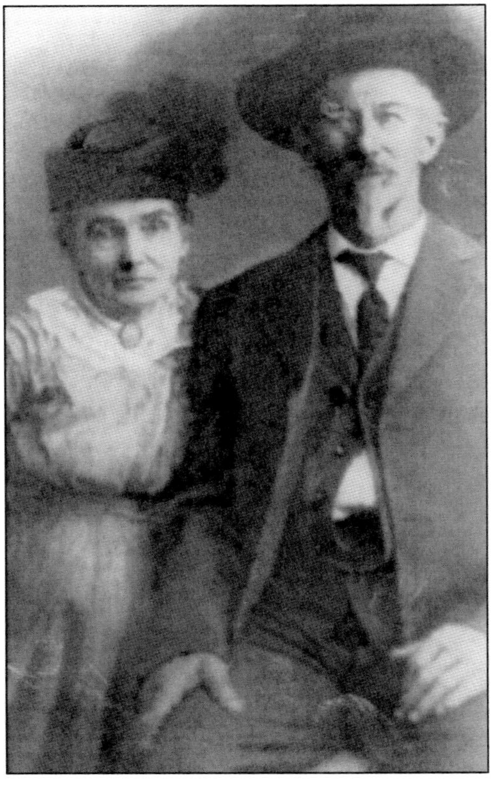

James Anderson Crenshaw and Henrietta Barker Elliott Crenshaw bought their first piece of property, a 250-acre tract, on August 20, 1872. The family owned a produce farm on Bolivar and boated produce to Galveston. (Courtesy of Clare Atkinson Wonders.)

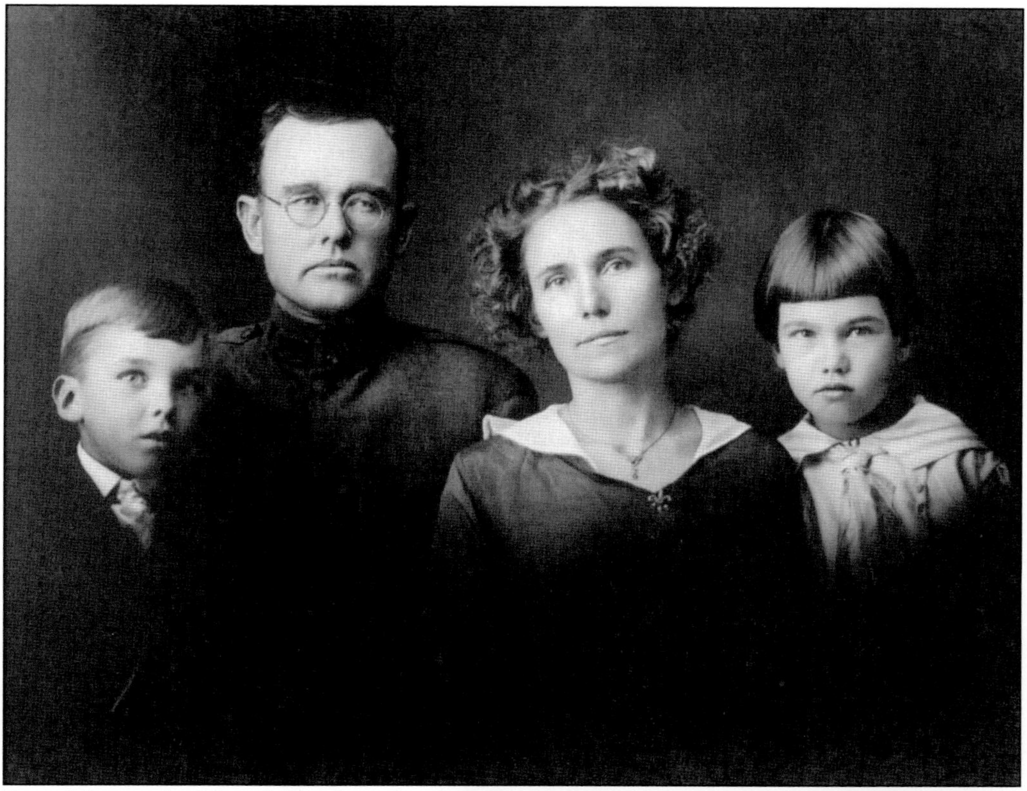

From left to right, Newell Wrigley Atkinson II, Dr. Newell Wrigley Atkinson Sr., Helen Crenshaw Atkinson, and Mary Helen Atkinson are pictured here. One of Dr. Atkinson's professors told him that he would one day meet and marry a lovely Bolivar girl named Helen Crenshaw. This prediction came true. Dr. Atkinson courted Crenshaw for 10 years, and they married on June 26, 1907. The Crenshaw school, which opened in 2004, is named for this family. (Courtesy of Clare Atkinson Wonders.)

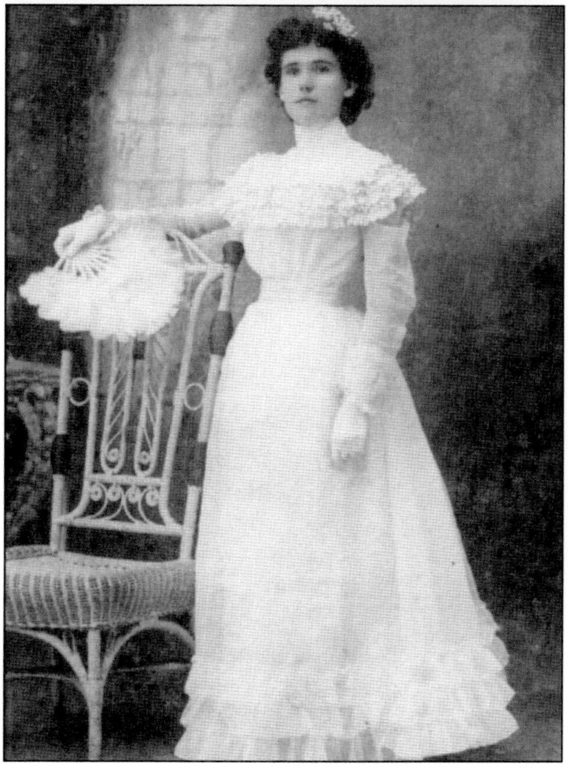

Mary Macklin Crenshaw was the eldest daughter of James A. Crenshaw. She was born on January 24, 1871, in Kentucky. She later married A.L. Snoody. (Courtesy of Clare Atkinson Wonders.)

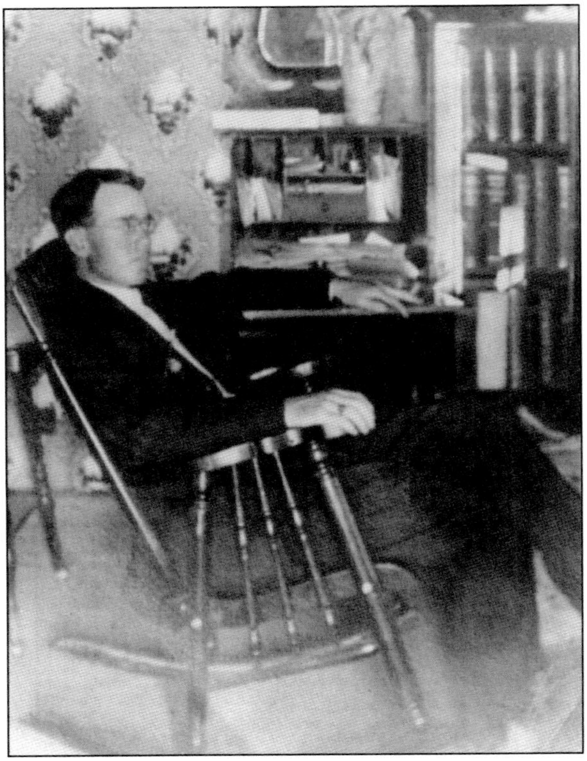

Dr. Newell Atkinson graduated from medical school at the University of Texas Medical Branch (UTMB) in 1898. Dr. Atkinson, who came from a modest background, rowed a small boat to the Bolivar Peninsula to get produce to sell in Galveston. This work funded his medical school tuition. (Courtesy of Clare Atkinson Wonders.)

The first doctor's office on the Bolivar Peninsula was opened in 1899 and run by Dr. Newell Atkinson. (Courtesy of Clare Atkinson Wonders.)

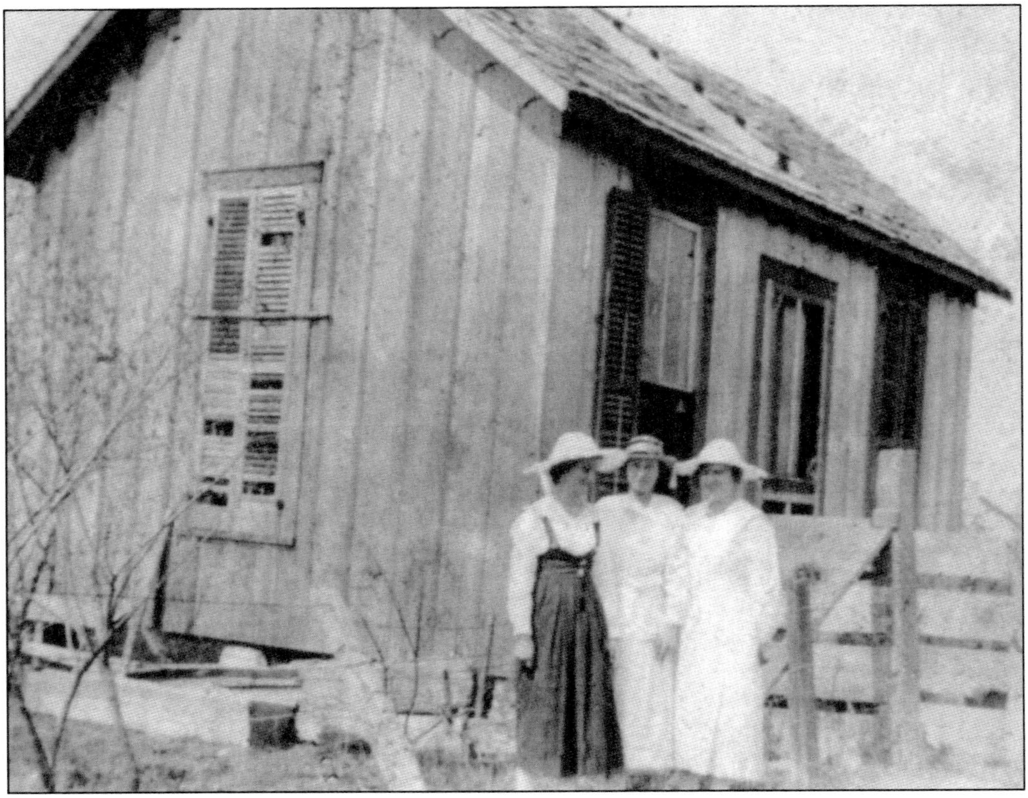

Raymond Clarence Bouse, Jr., age 15, is pictured here in 1917. Notice that Bouse is wearing lace-up cowboy boots. In the early 1900s, lace-up boots were common on the American frontier. (Courtesy of Robert and Jerri Bouse.)

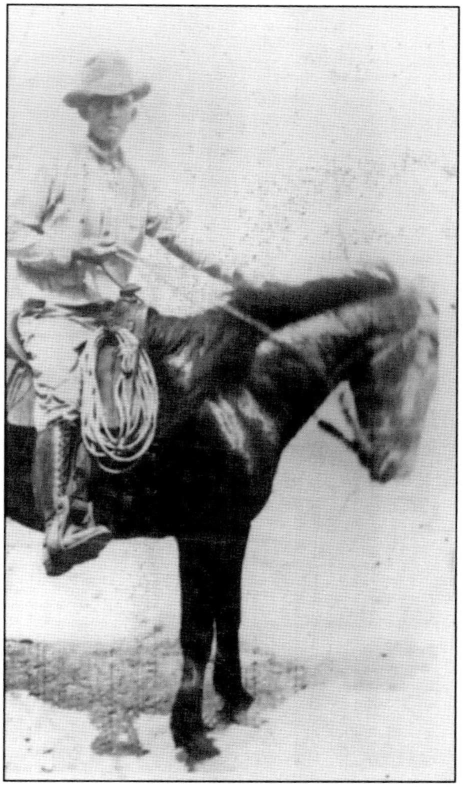

The Bouse family ran the general store, service station, and post office in Port Bolivar for many years. The Bouse Store had the only telephone on the peninsula during the 1930s. The post office was located inside the store. In the early days of the store, there was no refrigeration. Bouse would slaughter a calf and hang the meat from a tree. Community members would come on that day to purchase their meat. (Courtesy of the Bouse family.)

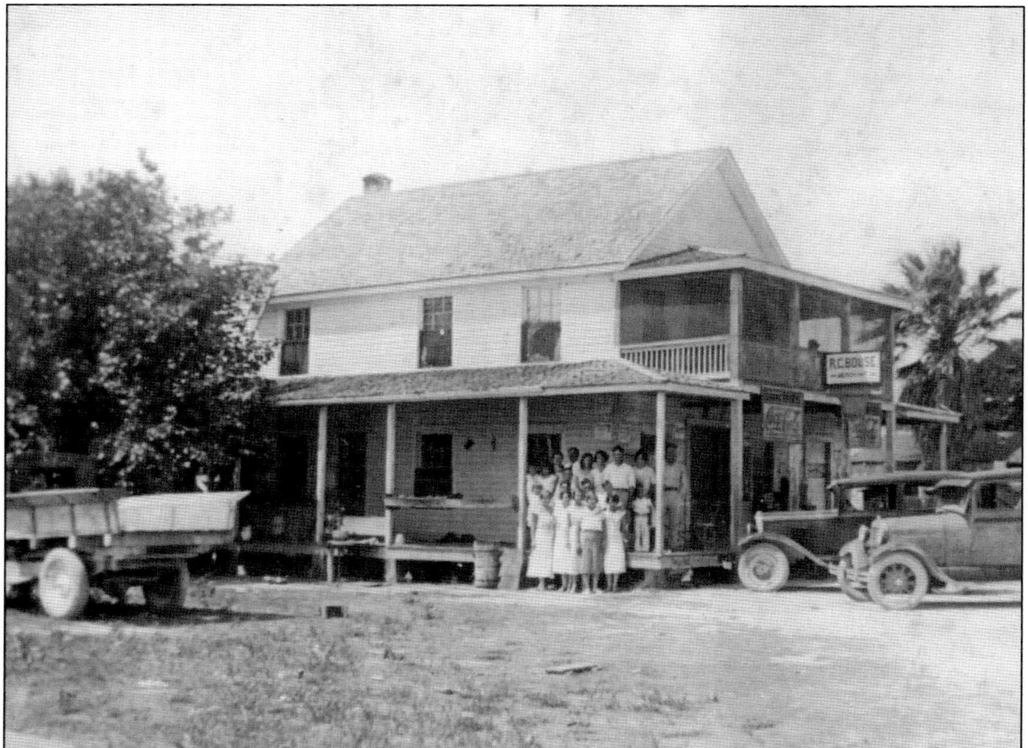

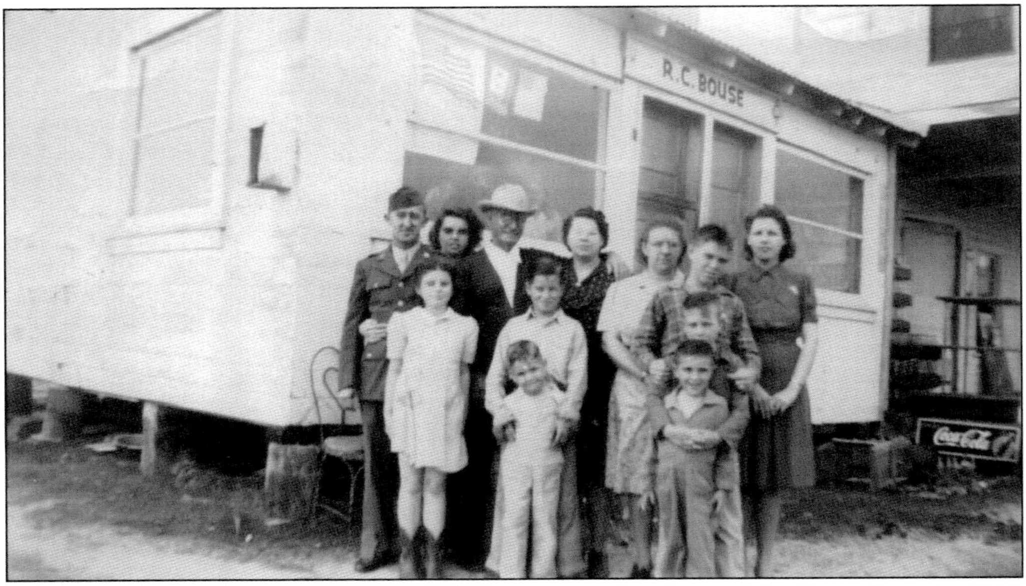

Members of the Bouse and Simpton families are pictured in front of the Bouse Store in 1944. (Courtesy of the Simpton family.)

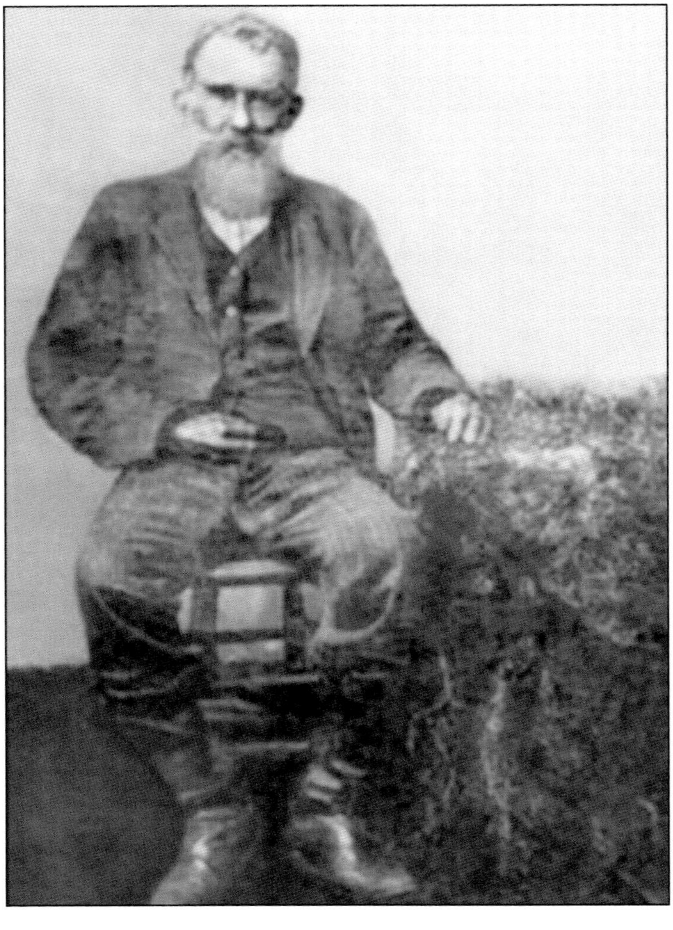

Charles Cronea was not only a cabin boy on one of Lafitte's ships but also fought in the Texas Revolution. He was present at the capture of Santa Anna. Cronea's house, recently destroyed by Hurricane Ike, stood at High Island for over a century. It was built on the 1,200 acres granted to him as a reward for his participation in gaining the independence of Texas. He is buried at the High Island Cemetery, and there is a Texas State Historical Marker on his grave. (Courtesy of Revis Bell.)

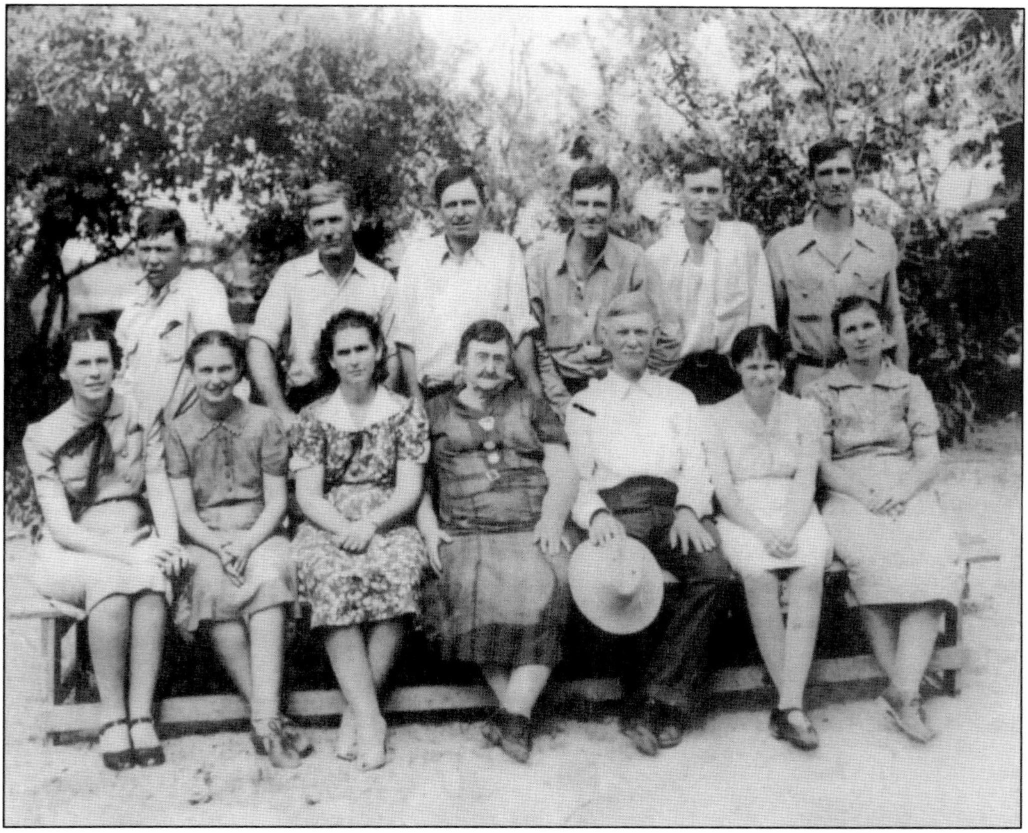

The Kahla family is one of the oldest on Bolivar, having been on the peninsula since the mid-19th century. This photograph was taken on August 15, 1940, on the occasion of John and Martha Kahla's 50th anniversary. Pictured are, from left to right, (first row) Ethel Shaw, Emily Guidry, Augusta Strimple, Martha, John, Effie Kreuzen, and Frances Smith; (second row) Bill Kahla, John Kahla Jr., Brad Kahla, Cornell Kahla, Monroe Kahla, and Victor Kahla. (Courtesy of Klela Bentley and Jane Ewing.)

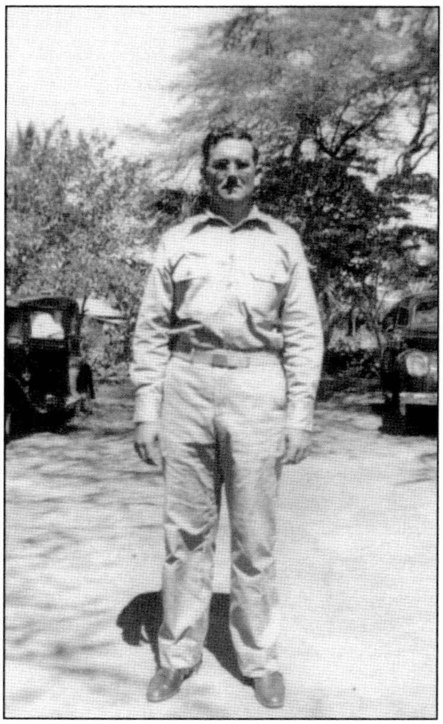

Harry Hughes was known by all on the peninsula as "Mr. Harry." Mr. Harry ran Hughes Grocery store and was well loved by all. He was a good man who loved to visit and swap stories. (Courtesy of the Simpton family.)

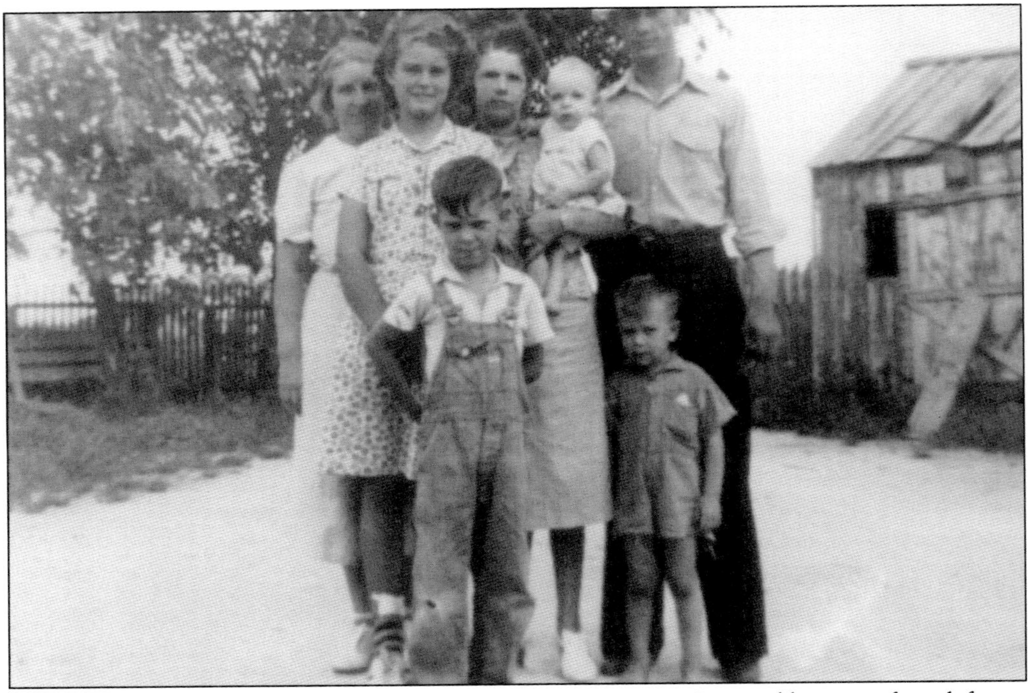

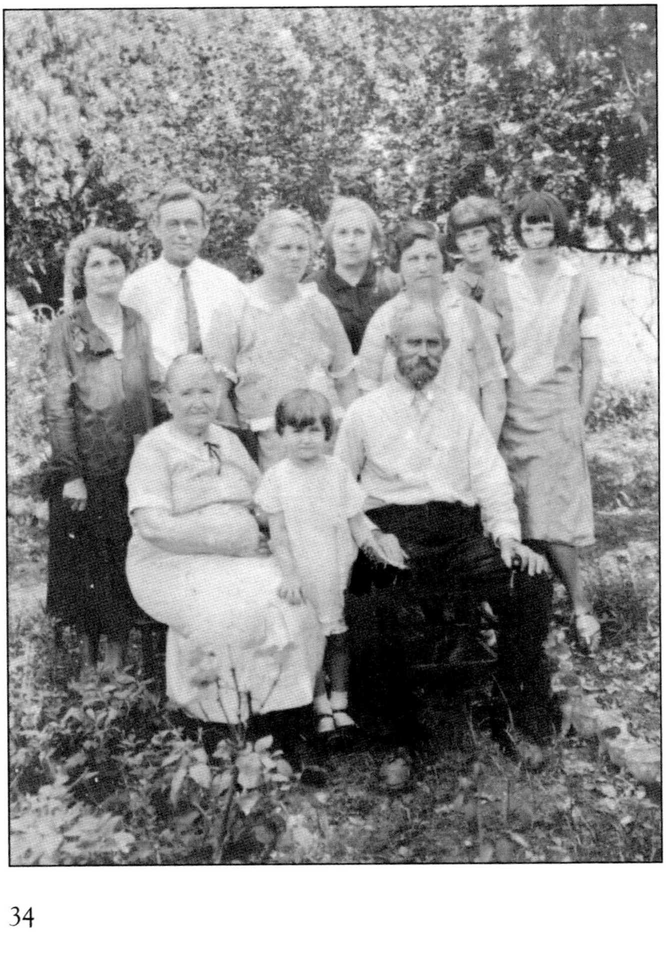

Pictured here are, from left to right (first row) Frank Louis Simpton Jr. and Lyle Eugene Simpton; (second row) Elmira Neola Bouse-Simpton, Josephine Smith-Swift, Wilhemina Simpton-Anderson, Leslie Raymond Simpton, and Charles Alden "Dutch" Kahla. (Courtesy of the Simpton family.)

This is the George Smith family of High Island. Smith acquired the property now identified as Smith Oaks in High Island from John and Mary Ann Brown, the parents of his wife, Charlotte. (Courtesy of Elsie Devers.)

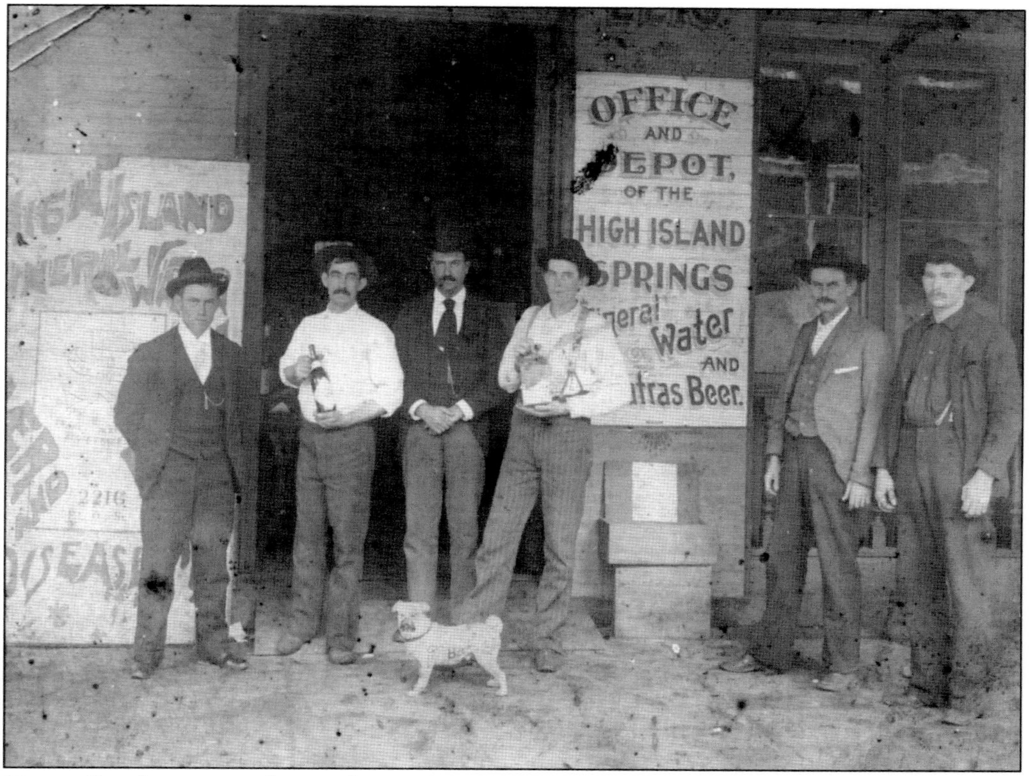

George Smith was most famous for his High Island Mineral Springs Water operation. His first well was dug in 1882. In this photograph, Smith is selling a bottle of mineral water. (Courtesy of Elsie Devers.)

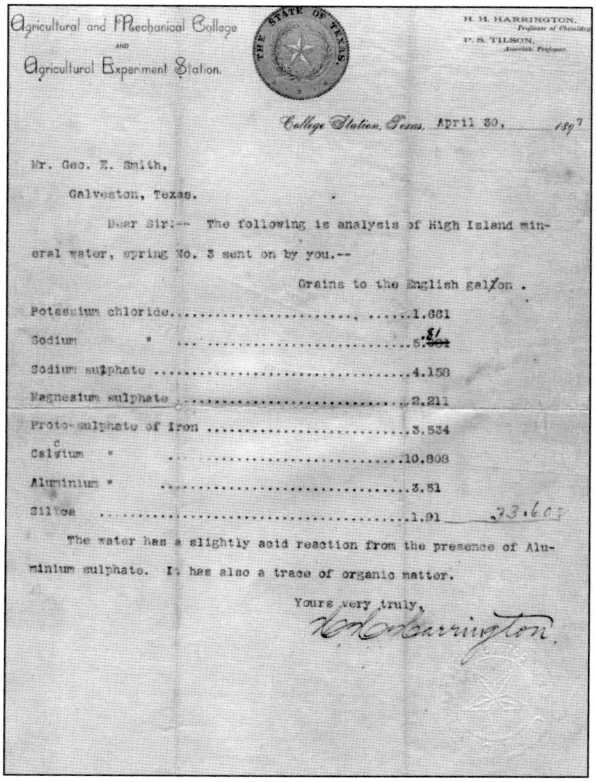

Agricultural and Mechanical College
AND
Agricultural Experiment Station.

THE STATE OF TEXAS.

H. H. HARRINGTON,
Professor of Chemistry
P. S. TILSON,
Associate Professor.

College Station, Texas, April 30, 1897

Mr. Geo. E. Smith,

Galveston, Texas.

Dear Sir:-- The following is analysis of High Island mineral water, spring No. 3 sent on by you.--

Grains to the English gallon .

Potassium chloride..........................1.661
Sodium " 5.81
Sodium sulphate 4.158
Magnesium sulphate 2.211
Proto-sulphate of Iron 3.534
Calcium " 10.808
Aluminium " 3.51
Silica 1.91 33.60

The water has a slightly acid reaction from the presence of Aluminium sulphate. It has also a trace of organic matter.

Yours very truly,
H. H. Harrington.

The ice-cold mineral water, tasting of iron and sulfur, created a boom in High Island for many years. This report from Texas A&M University gives the analysis of the High Island Mineral Water Spring No. 3. Smith received a trademark for his special waters. The mineral waters were proclaimed to "cure Brights Disease, liver and kidney troubles, Catarrah—the cause of consumption, asthma, hay fever, restore hair on bald heads, and remove dandruff on the scalp and all the pimples and blotches from the face." (Courtesy of Elsie Devers.)

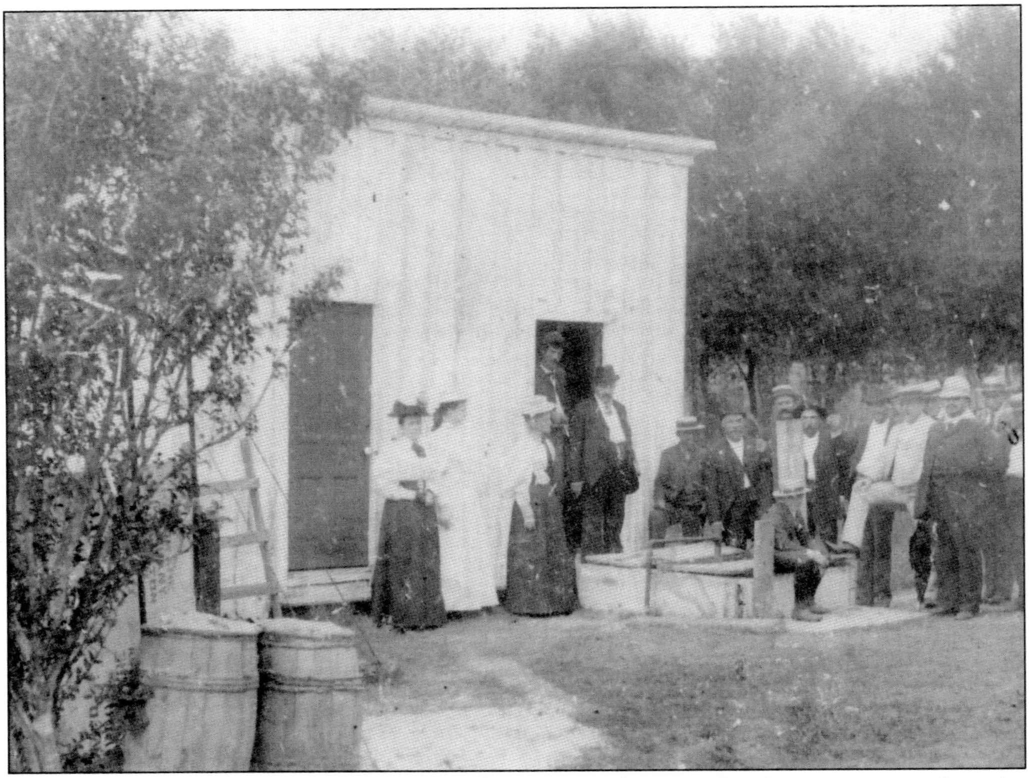

High Island's mineral springs played an important role in the local economy during the late 1800s. This photograph is of the mineral-waters house. George Smith dug several water wells on his property and reported that he had identified 21 distinct waters. (Courtesy of Elsie Devers.)

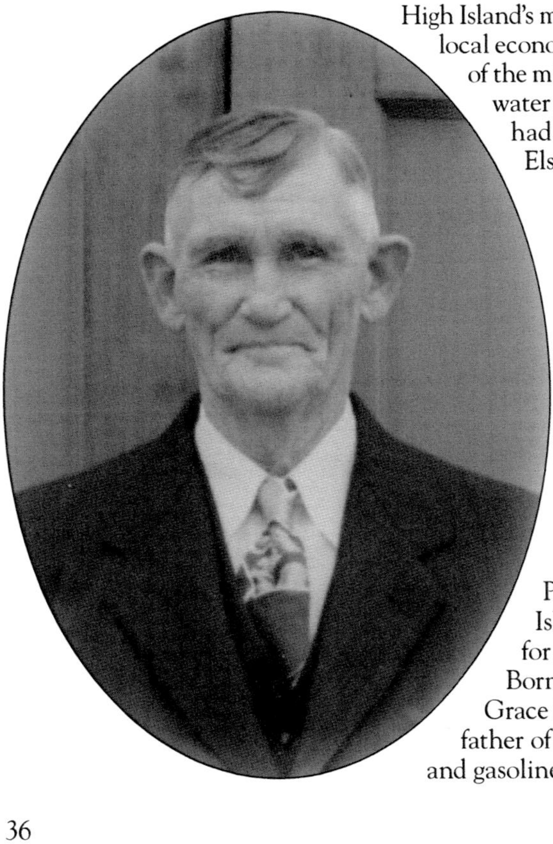

Pictured here is John Samuel Hughes of High Island. Hughes was "Sam" to everyone except for his closest friends, who called him "Buss." Born on December 27, 1872, and married to Edna Grace Smith of High Island in 1917, Hughes was the father of five children and operated a hardware store and gasoline station. (Courtesy of Elsie Devers.)

Three

Making a Living
Farming, Ranching, Bounty of the Sea, and a Little Oil

Early in the settlement of the Bolivar Peninsula, farmers raised sea-island cotton as their principal crop. When that commodity dropped in price, the Bolivar farmers began to grow produce for the Houston and Galveston markets. By 1880, Bolivar had become the Watermelon Capital of Texas. Farmers also raised tomatoes, cantaloupe, and cabbage. Little produce is grown on the peninsula these days. The soil was damaged by severe hurricanes over the past decades, and lifestyle changes make farming a less-than-profitable enterprise. Some families still maintain beautiful gardens in their backyards.

Shrimp, oysters, and fish have always been an important commodity on the peninsula. Warm-water shrimping in the Gulf of Mexico represents the most economically important component of the domestic commercial seafood-harvesting sectors in the United States. Oysters and crawfish are symbols of the famous Gulf Coast seafood.

By 1885, Bolivar was an important cattle region, with a single cross fence at Rollover dividing the peninsula into two cow pastures. In that same year, Bolivar produced half of all the oysters consumed by the Texas market. Many farm families supplemented their livelihoods by tonging and shucking oysters from the reef.

A search for oil in High Island began as early as 1901, as a result of the Spindletop gusher near Beaumont. Some oil was discovered in 1916, but a major find, around the perimeter of the salt dome on High Island, was not hit until 1931. There were as many as 200 flowing wells surrounding the salt dome at one time. There is still some oil activity, with pumps operating to this day.

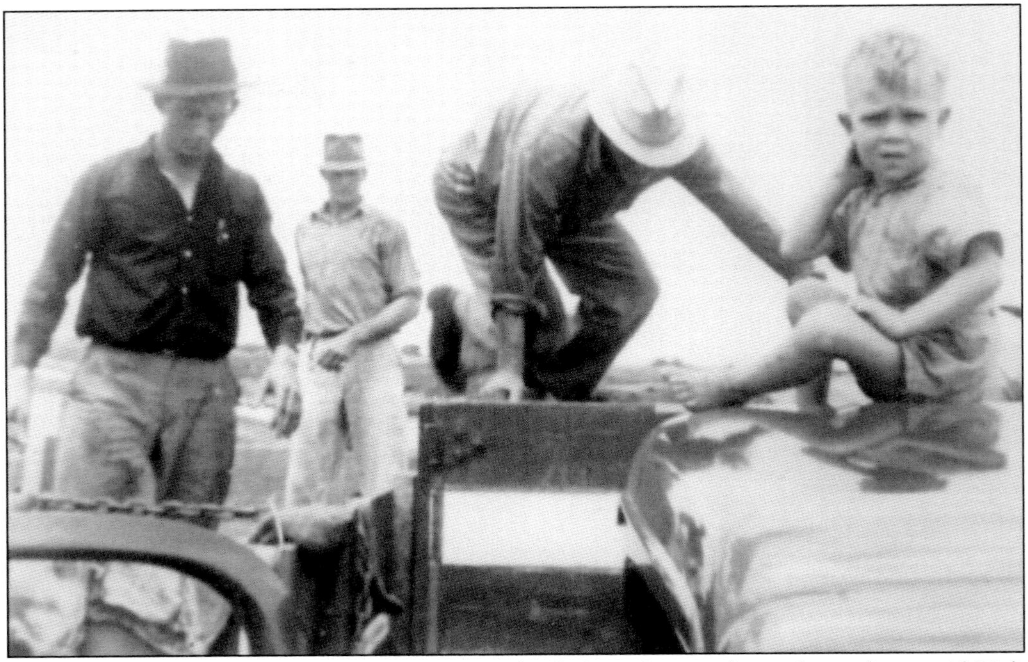

Black Diamond watermelons were grown on the Bolivar Peninsula in the early to mid-20th century. This popular watermelon averages 35 to 50 pounds but can grow much larger. From left to right, Vernon Kahla, Jerry Simpton, an unidentified man, and Lyle Simpton are pictured here at the watermelon farm. (Courtesy of the Simpton family.)

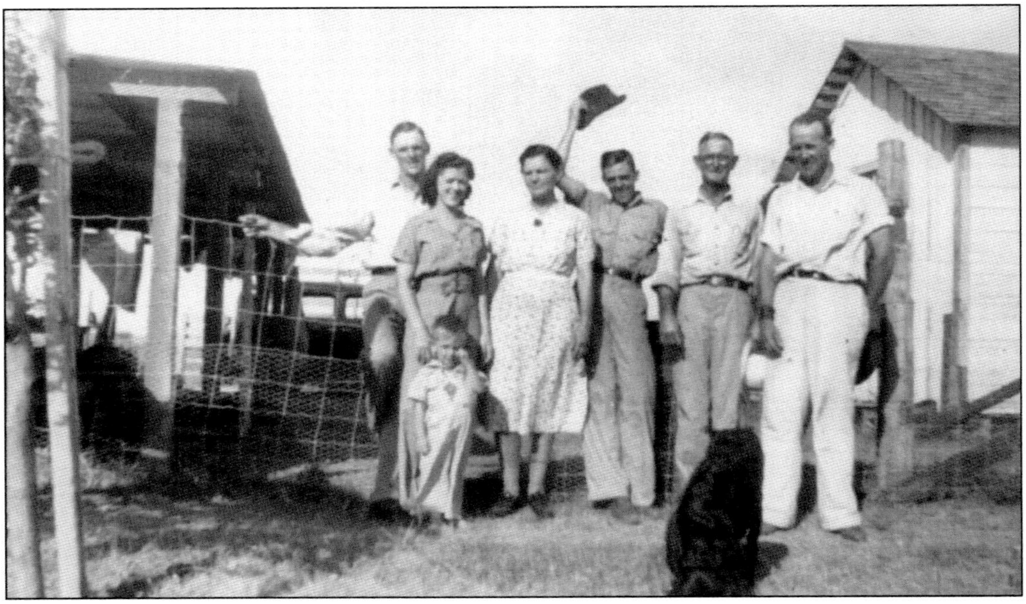

Watermelons were the primary crop on the Bolivar Peninsula for many years. No one really knows why watermelon cultivation came to a halt on the peninsula. Perhaps the hurricanes changed the soil. Or maybe land became more expensive or the hard work of farming was less attractive than it had been. Pictured here at the watermelon farm are, from left to right, Jerry and Eljie Simpton, Annie Laura Simpton, E.B. Brown, Leslie F. Simpton, Dutch Kahla, and an unidentified man. (Courtesy of the Simpton family.)

Before the arrival of railroads or highways on the peninsula, Bolivar farmers had to transport their produce to the market in Galveston by small sailboats. They hauled their harvests by wagon along the beach to Port Bolivar, where they loaded fresh fruits and vegetables into the boats. This boat belonged to J.A. Crenshaw Jr. (Courtesy of Clare Atkinson Wonders.)

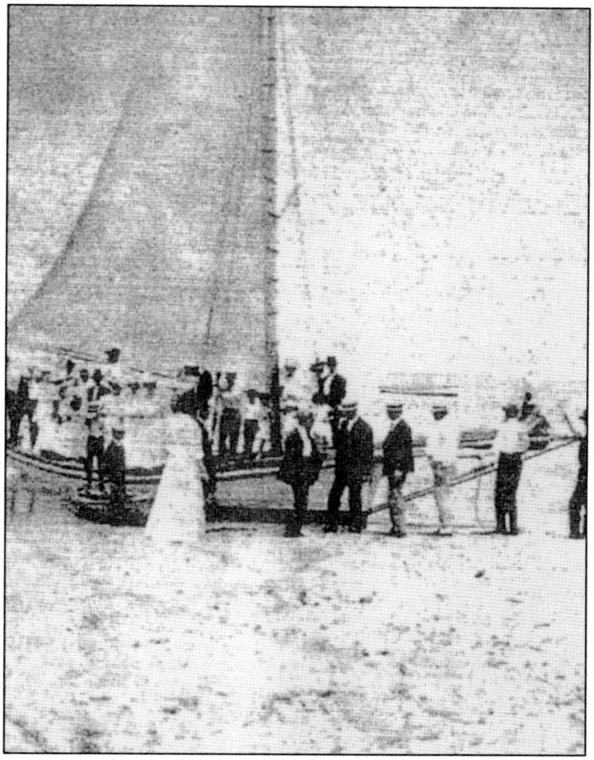

Farmers delivered their produce by horse-drawn wagon before the arrival of motorized vehicles on the peninsula. (Courtesy of Robert and Jerri Bouse.)

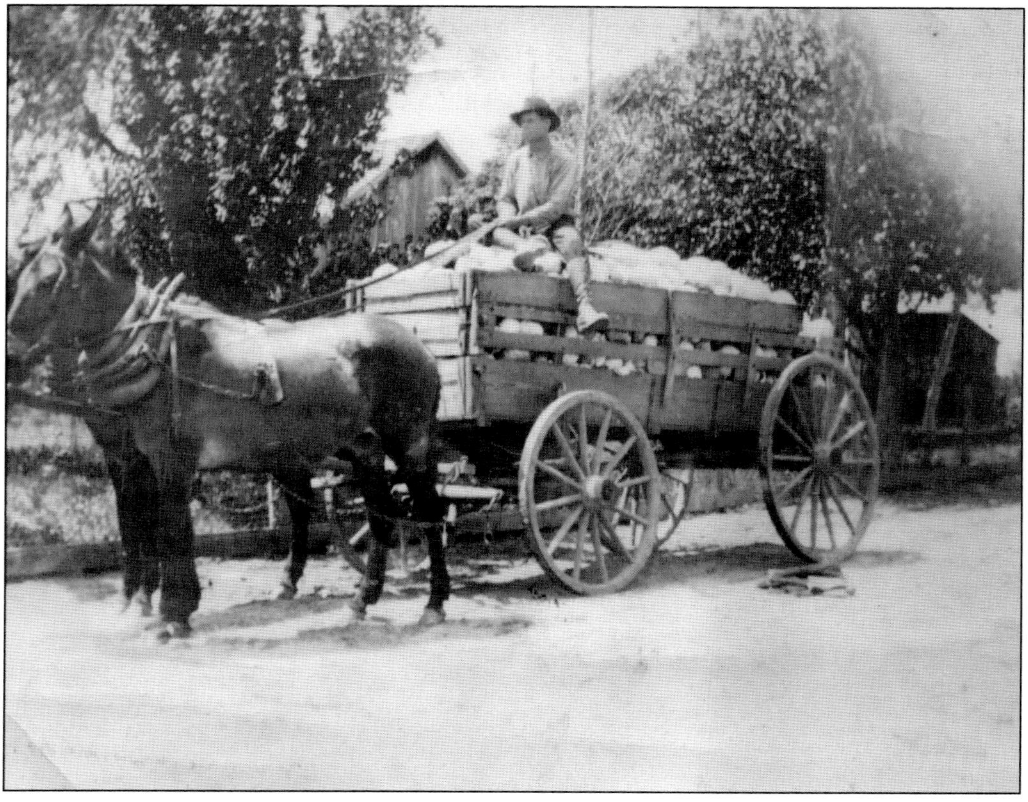

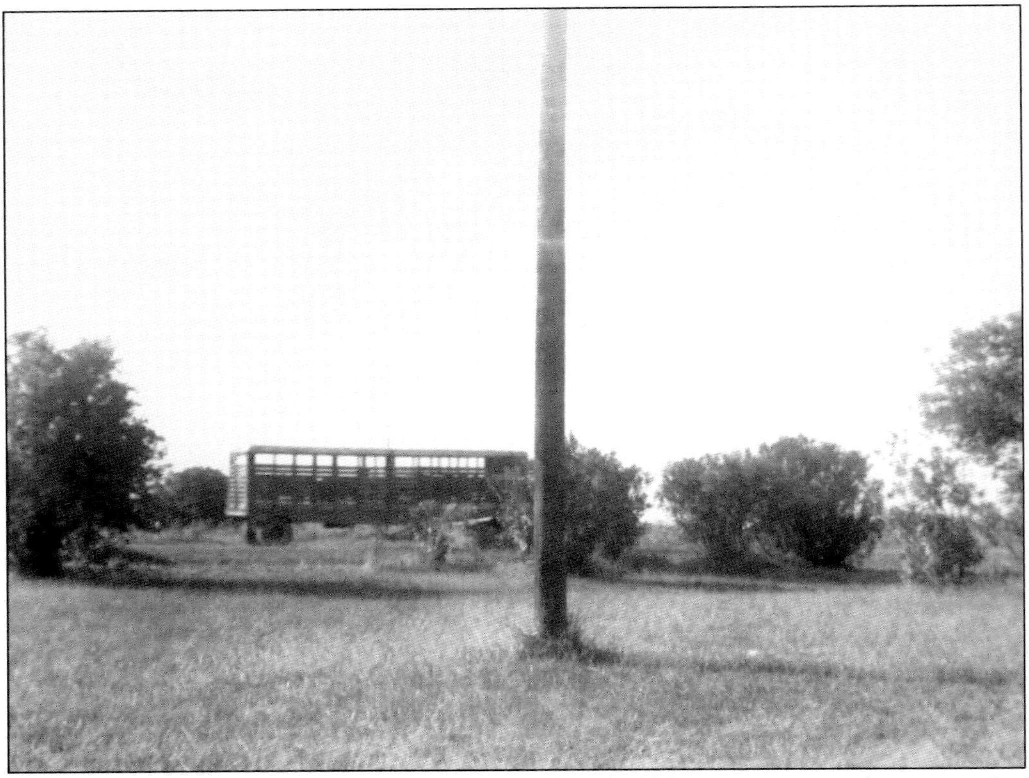

About 1,000 acres on the Bolivar Peninsula were fenced off from cow pastures for watermelon growing by 1880. By 1883, over 200,000 melons were shipped to northern markets. (Courtesy of Margo Johnson.)

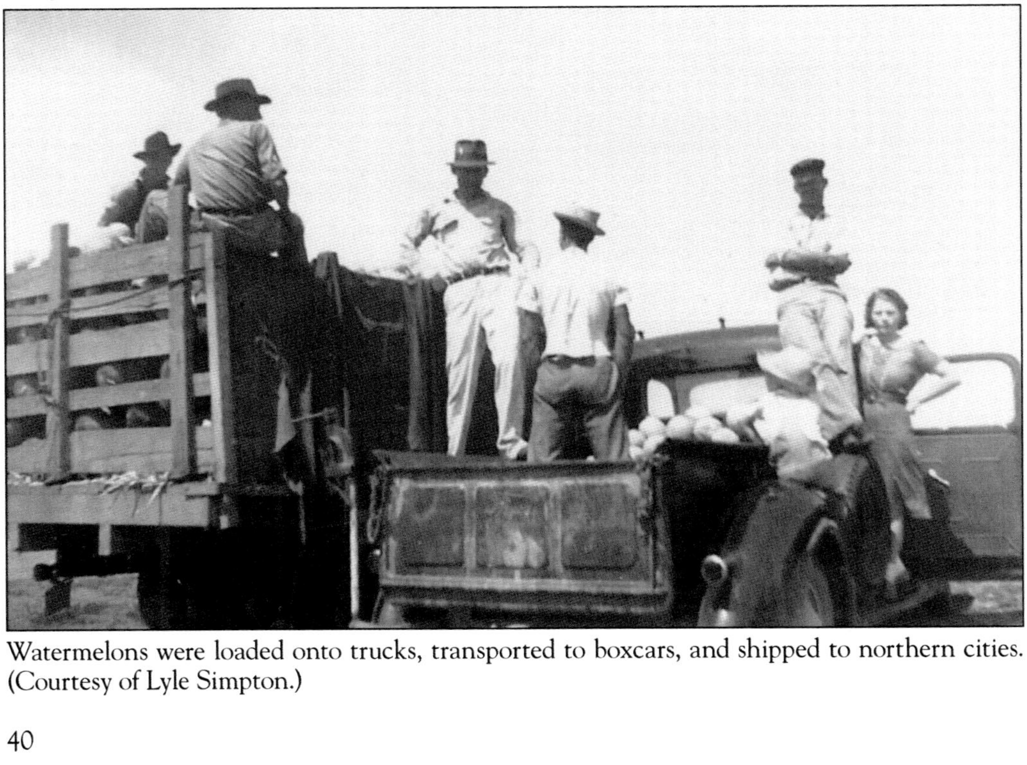

Watermelons were loaded onto trucks, transported to boxcars, and shipped to northern cities. (Courtesy of Lyle Simpton.)

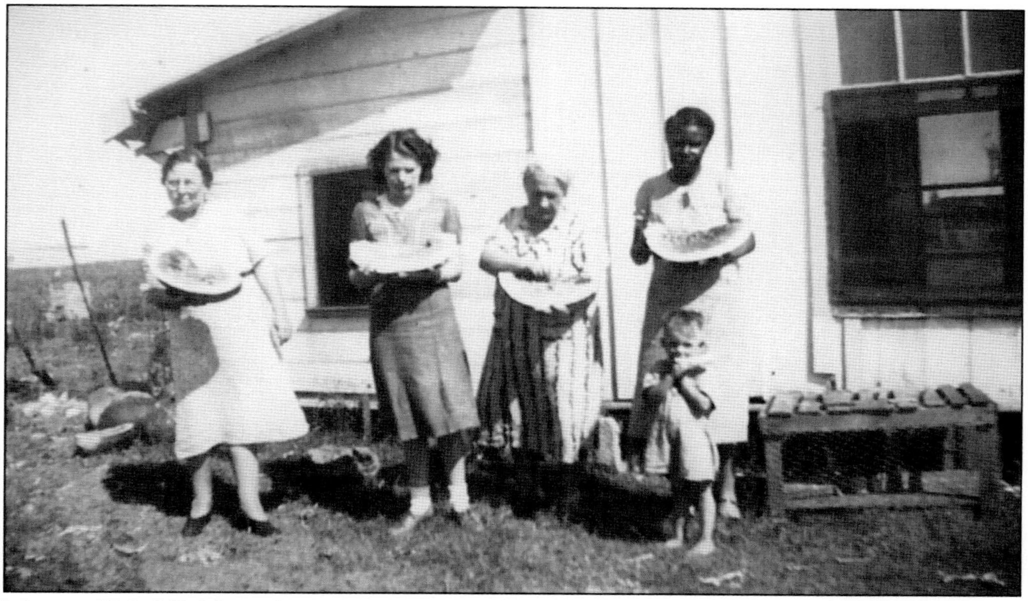

Monroe "Pike" Kahla said, in an interview with Gwendolyn Wingate, "We still raise some fine watermelons. Port Bolivar melons are the best in the world. I got four or five acres of Florida Giants. Bust one of them things early in the morning and get that big old heart out of it." His voice trailed off in a grunt of superlative pleasure. These women are sampling the delicious watermelon at the Simpton watermelon house in Caplen. (Courtesy of Terri Simpton.)

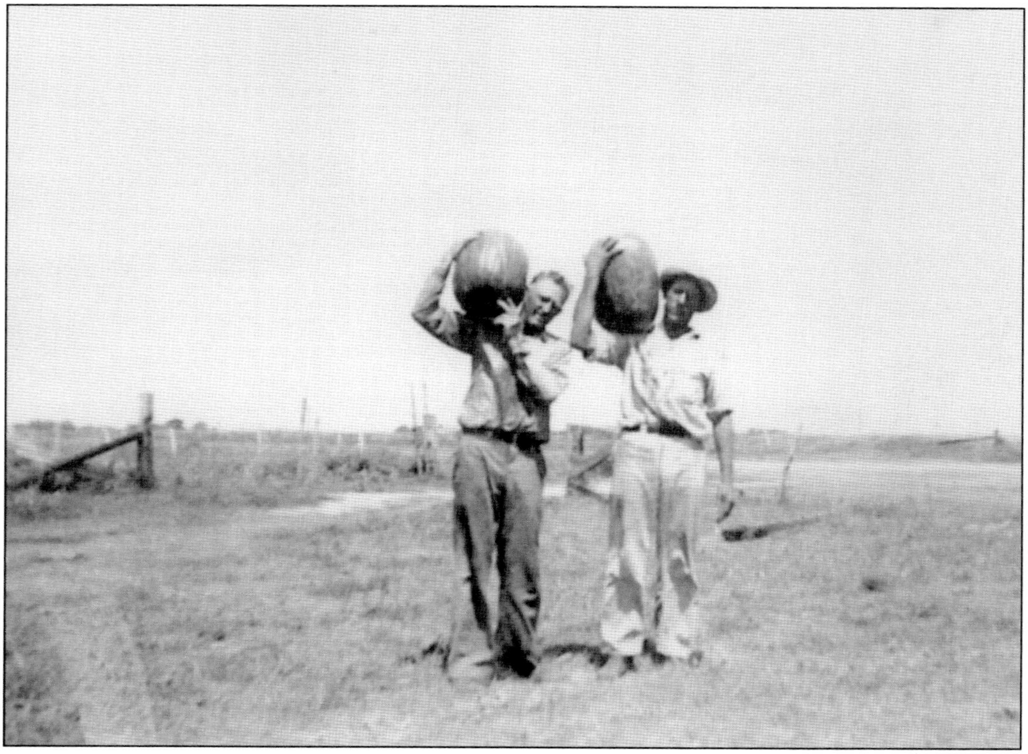

Leslie F. Simpton and Clyde Guidry are carrying watermelons in 1930. (Courtesy of the Simpton family.)

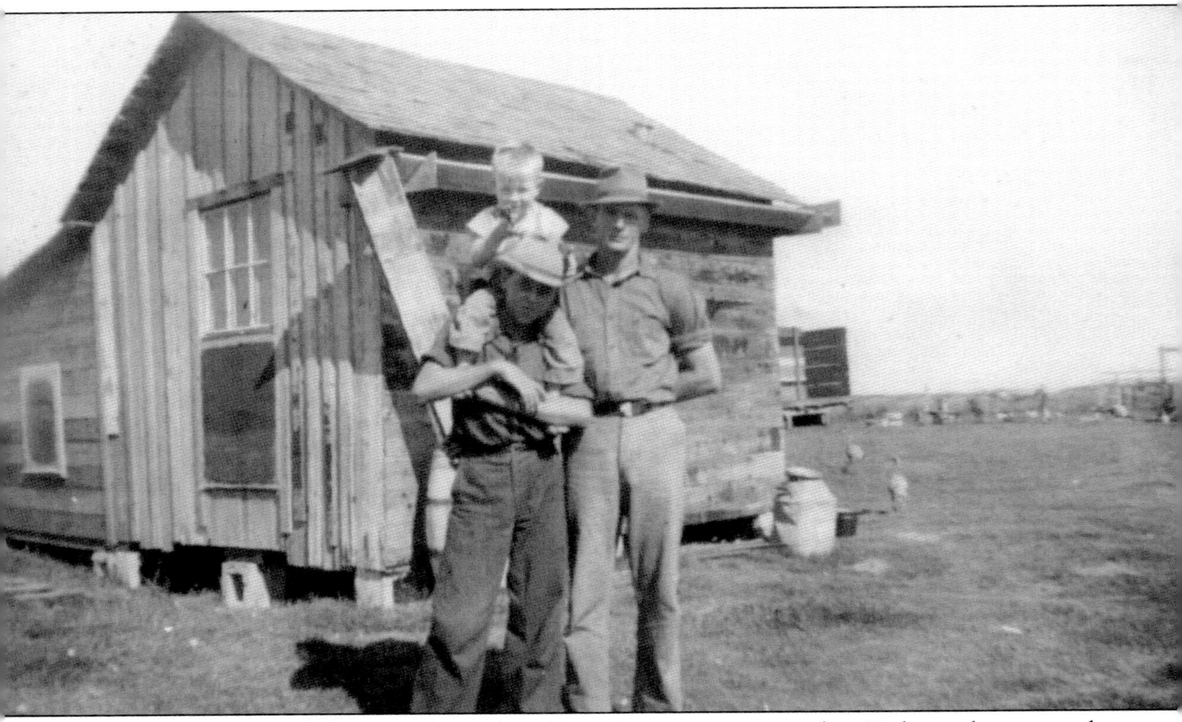

Lyle Simpton (left), E.B. Brown (center), and Jerry Simpton are pictured in Caplen at the watermelon farm. These were the days when the Bolivar Peninsula was known as the Watermelon Capital of Texas. (Courtesy of the Simpton family.)

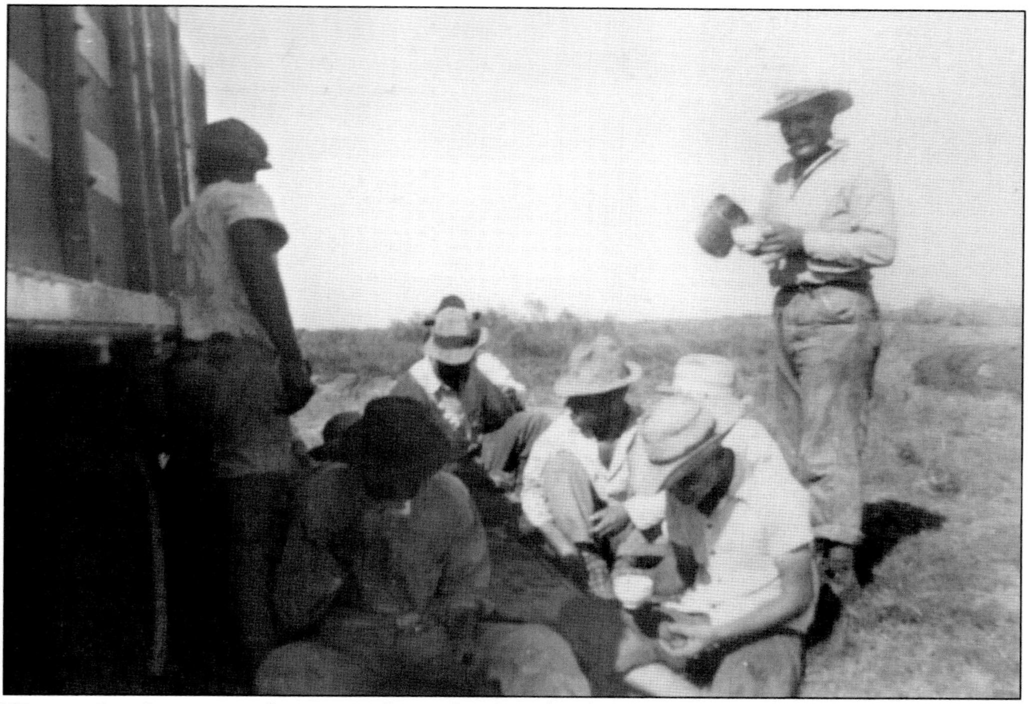

Watermelon farming on the peninsula was hard work. These unidentified laborers at the Simpton Watermelon Farm are taking a coffee break. (Courtesy of the Simpton family.)

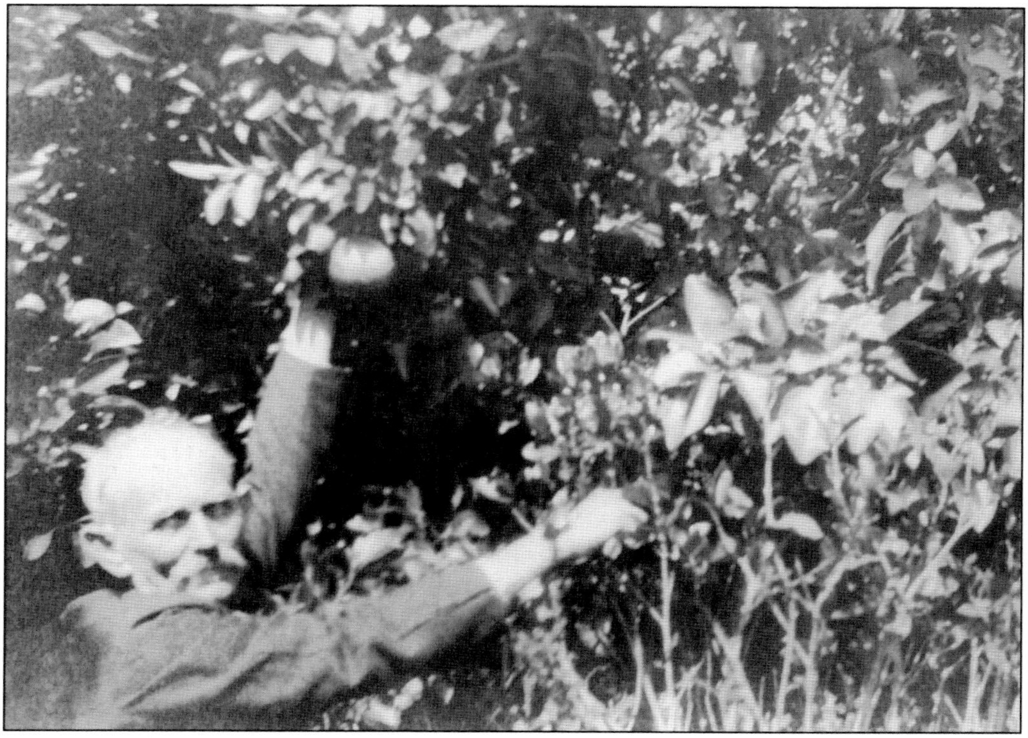

George Smith owned cattle and raised peaches, pears, oranges, strawberries, and cabbage. (Courtesy of Elsie Devers.)

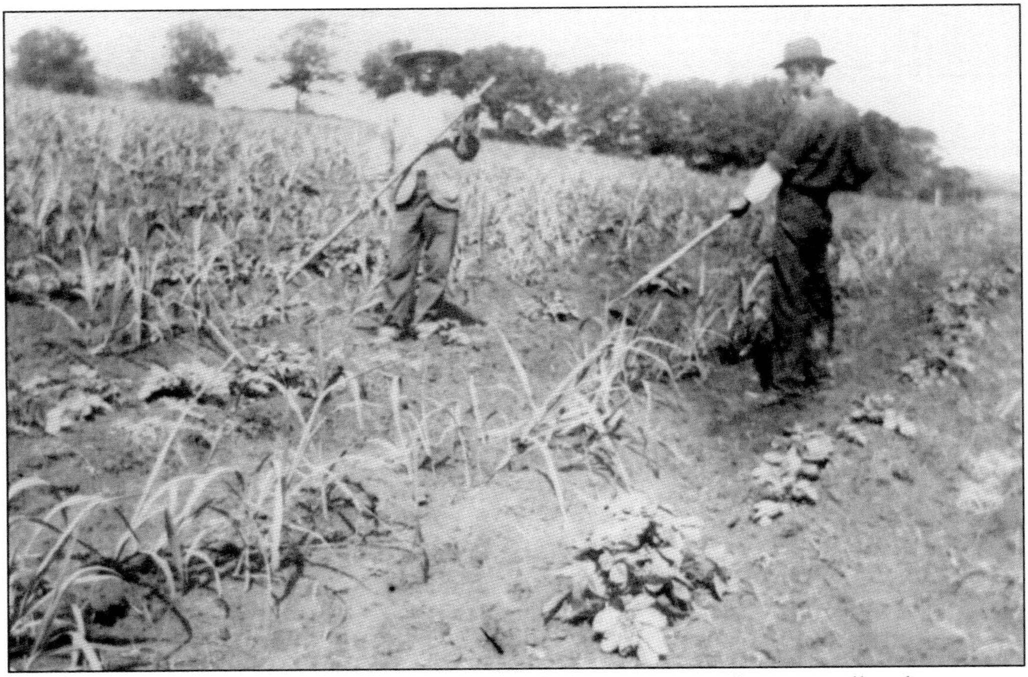

George Smith also raised sugarcane, cotton, and tobacco. He operated a sugar mill and cotton gin on his property in High Island. These men are working sugarcane. (Courtesy of Elsie Devers.)

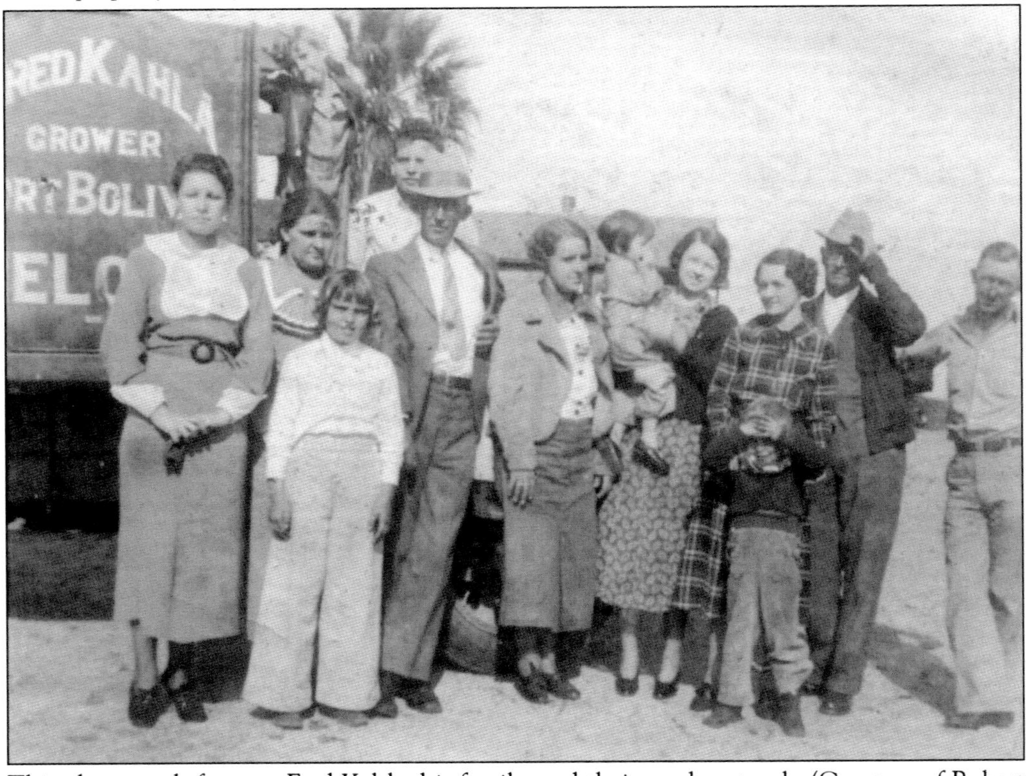

This photograph features Fred Kahla, his family, and their produce truck. (Courtesy of Robert and Jerri Bouse.)

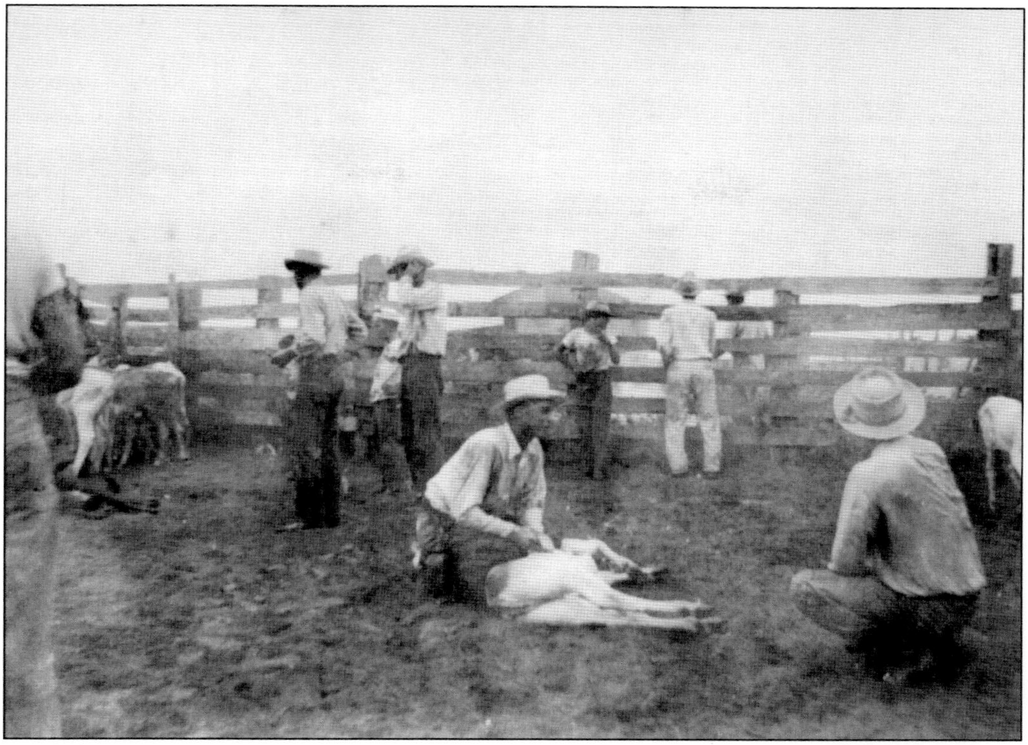

Cattle became an important commodity on the peninsula by 1885. A single fence at Rollover divided the peninsula into two cow pastures. Capt. C.T. Cade had a fenced pasture from the bay to the gulf at Rollover. All of the other cattle ran together on the western side of the peninsula. Cattle even roamed through private yards. (Courtesy of the Bouse family.)

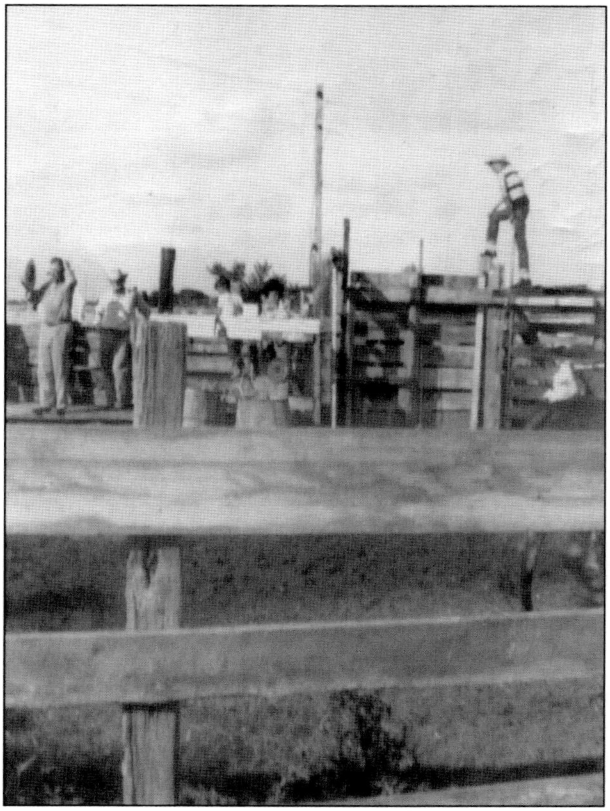

This photograph shows a day of cattle-working at Port Bolivar in 1946. (Courtesy of the Bouse family.)

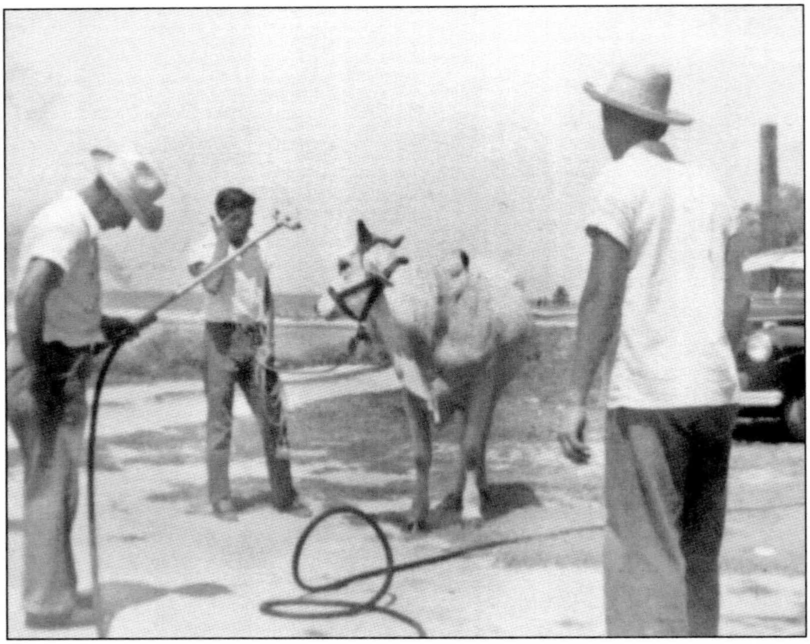

These Bouse family ranchers try out a newfangled piece of equipment. (Courtesy of the Bouse family.)

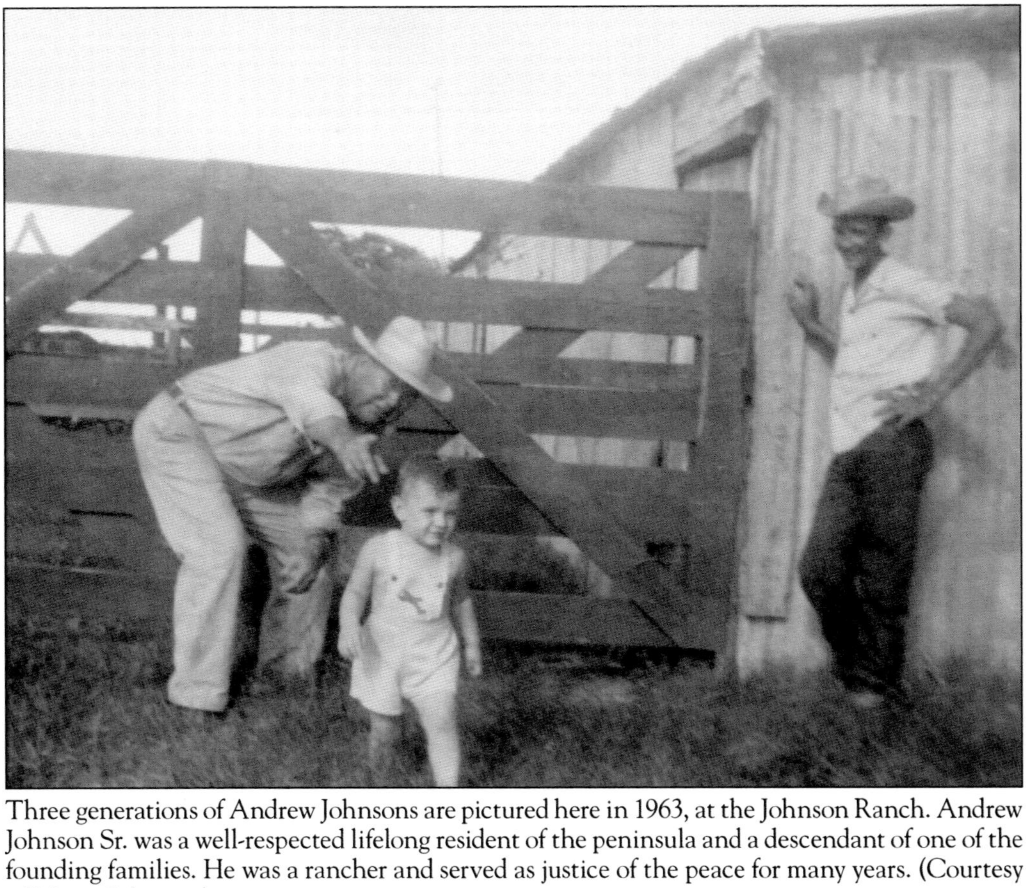

Three generations of Andrew Johnsons are pictured here in 1963, at the Johnson Ranch. Andrew Johnson Sr. was a well-respected lifelong resident of the peninsula and a descendant of one of the founding families. He was a rancher and served as justice of the peace for many years. (Courtesy of Margo Johnson.)

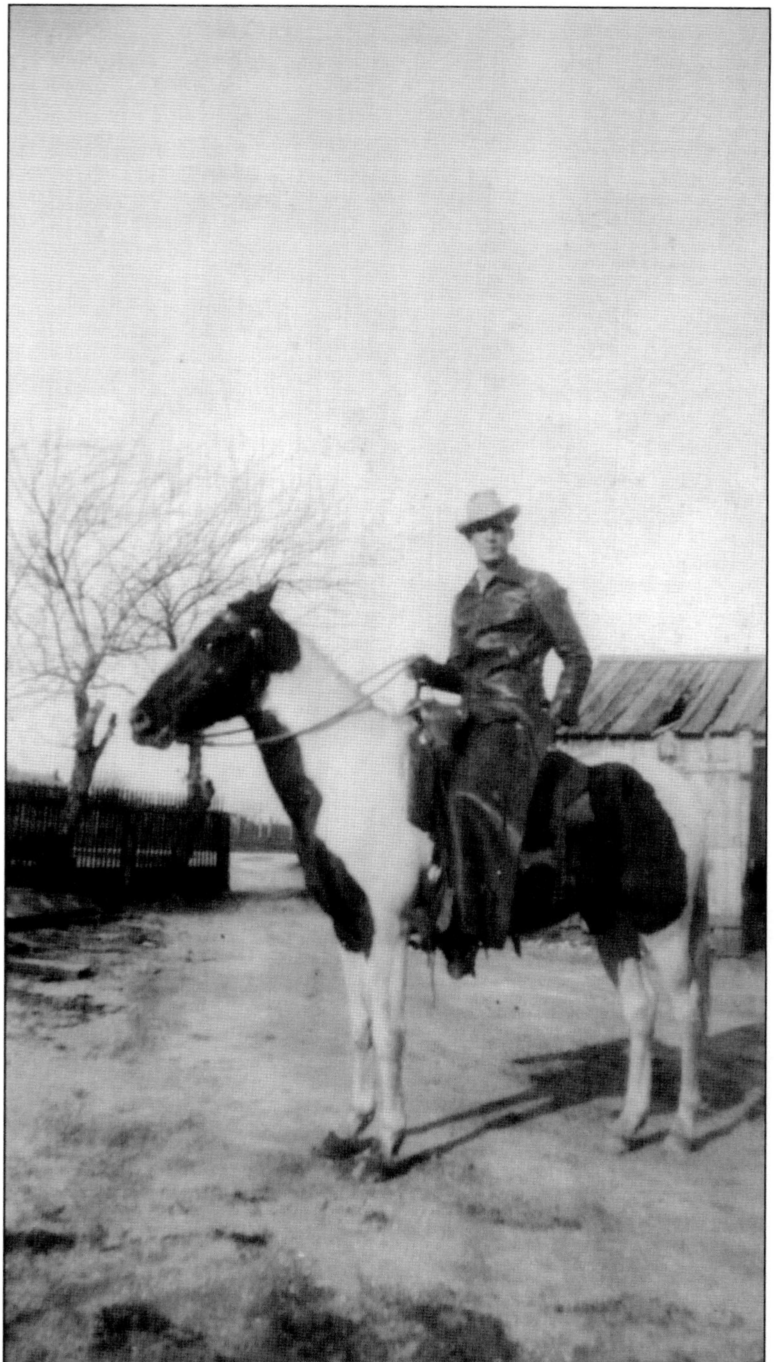

Cowboys herded the cattle to reach the winter salt grass on Bolivar each year. Bolivar was a haven for both cattle and cowboys in the winter. However, in the summer, swarms of mosquitoes and deer flies tormented them to such a degree that few stayed on the peninsula during those months. Some hardy souls like the Kahlas, Simptons, Hamshires, Sullivans, Hughes, and Carrs stayed year-round to battle insects, heat, and frequent storms. Pictured here is Ernest "Jerry" Simpton on horseback in a leather coat and chaps. (Courtesy of the Simpton family.)

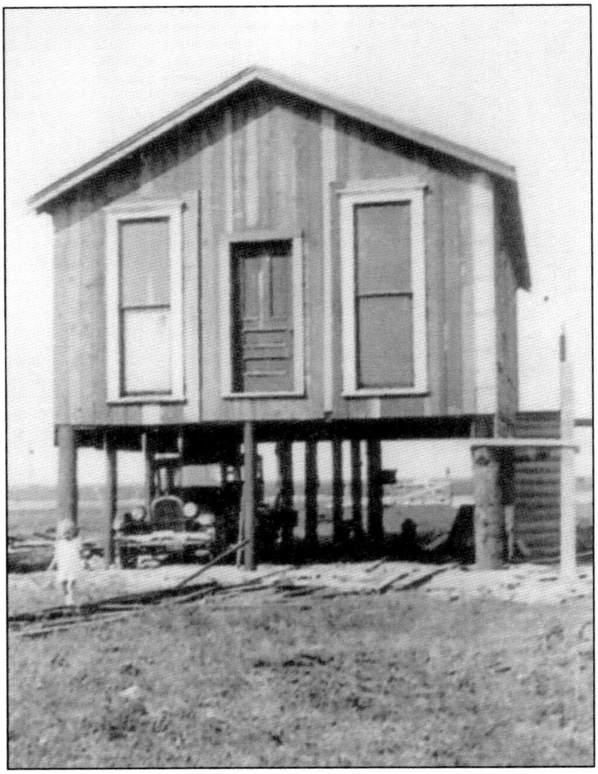

Journalist Gwendolyn Wingate stated, "Those days ended with the coming of barbed wire fences and strings of beach houses on long legs." Pictured here is the Johnson home, built up on stilts, in 1932. (Courtesy of Margo Johnson.)

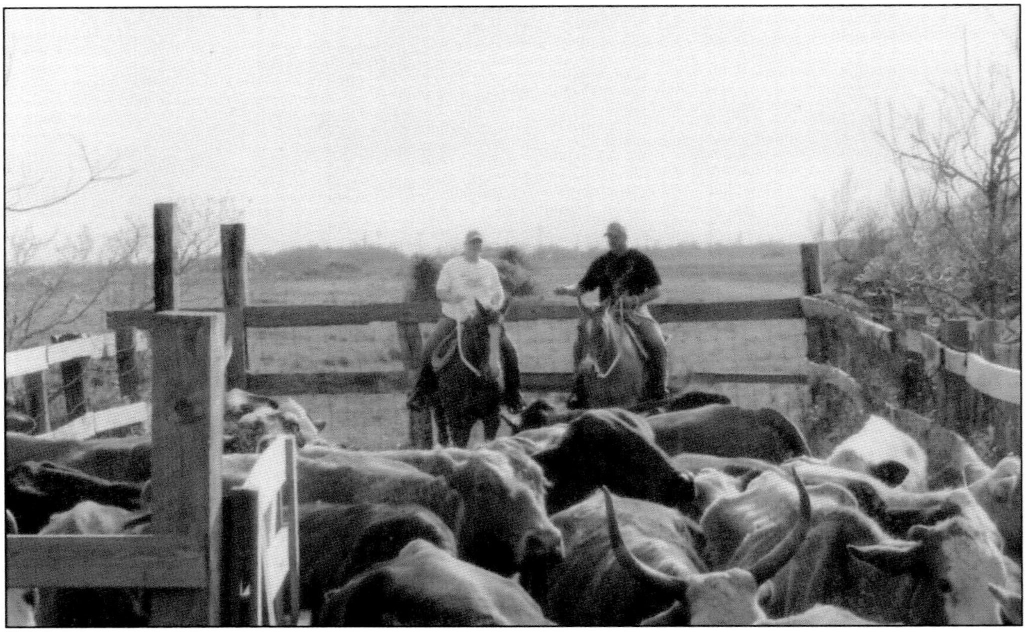

Cattle still graze on the Bolivar Peninsula. They are just not as plentiful as in the early years. Running cattle on the peninsula has all of the hazards of ranching anywhere else, plus a few peculiar to this part of the world: mosquitoes and hurricanes make Bolivar a challenging place to be a cowboy. Pictured here are Darren and Heather Moody, working on the Johnson Ranch in the 1980s. (Courtesy of Margo Johnson.)

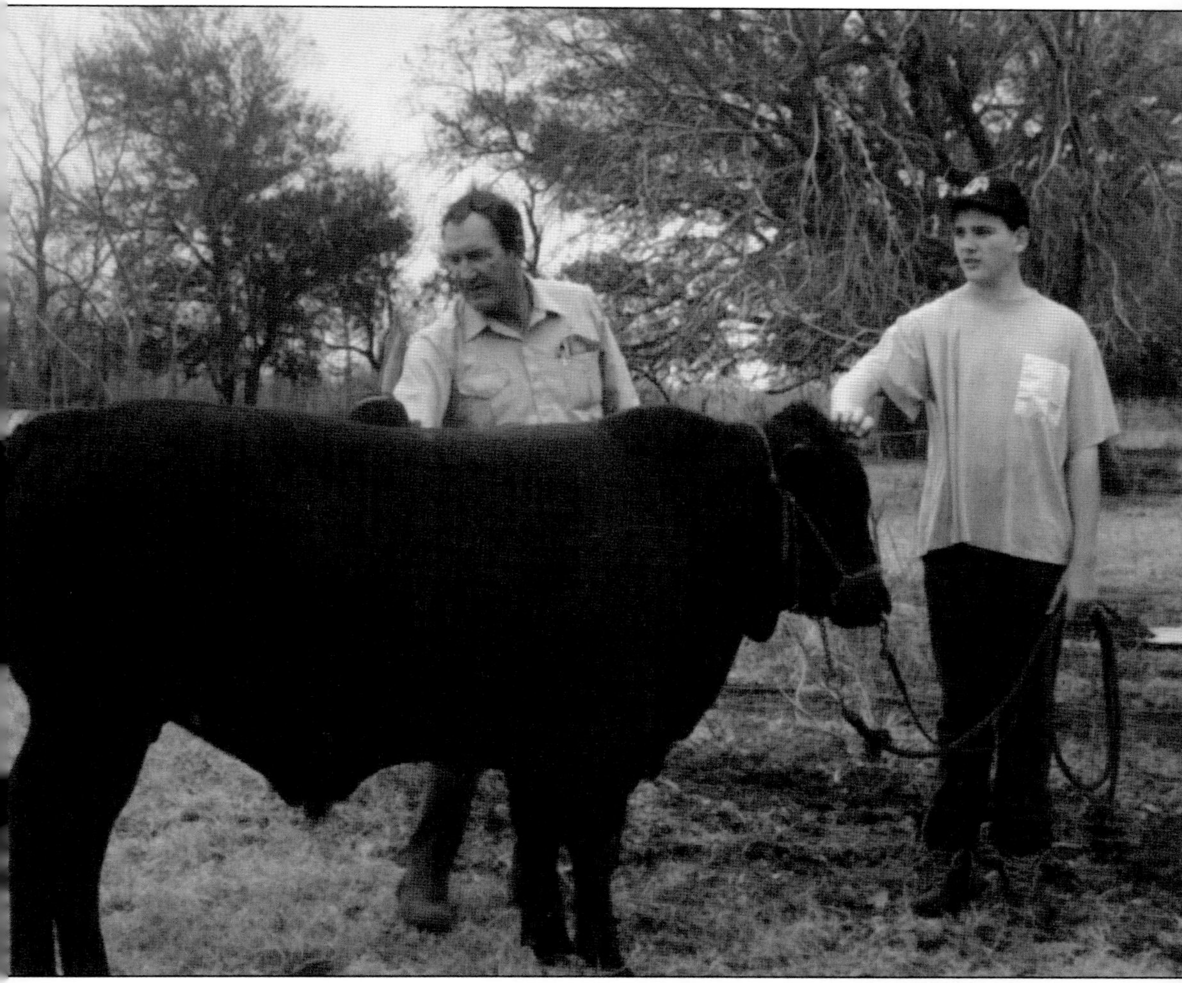

Andrew Johnson Jr. is pictured here in 1985 with Darren Moody and 4-H project Mojo. 4-H has been an important part of the life of young people on the Bolivar Peninsula for decades. Its goal of developing citizenship, leadership, responsibility, and life skills is exemplified in this photograph. (Courtesy of Margo Johnson.)

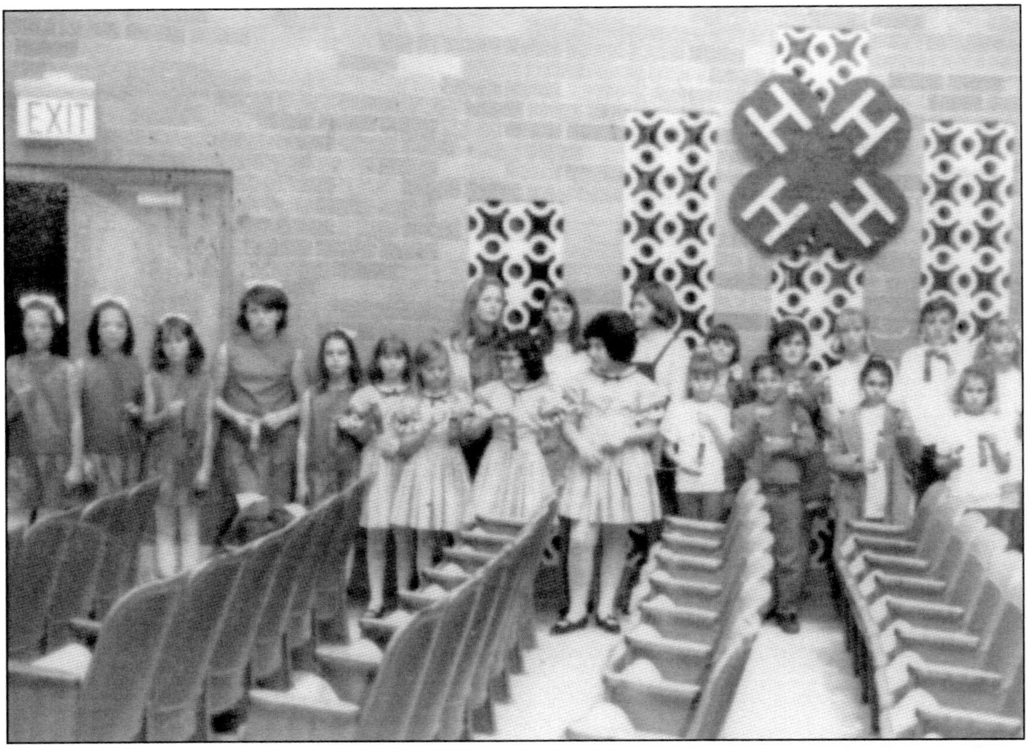

4-H is an important part of the life of youth on the peninsula. This is a group of Bolivar students attending a 4-H competition in Santa Fe, Texas, in 1966. Terri Simpton, one of the participants in the competition, described with great fondness the dress review in which girls designed, made, and then modeled dresses. (Courtesy of Terri Simpton.)

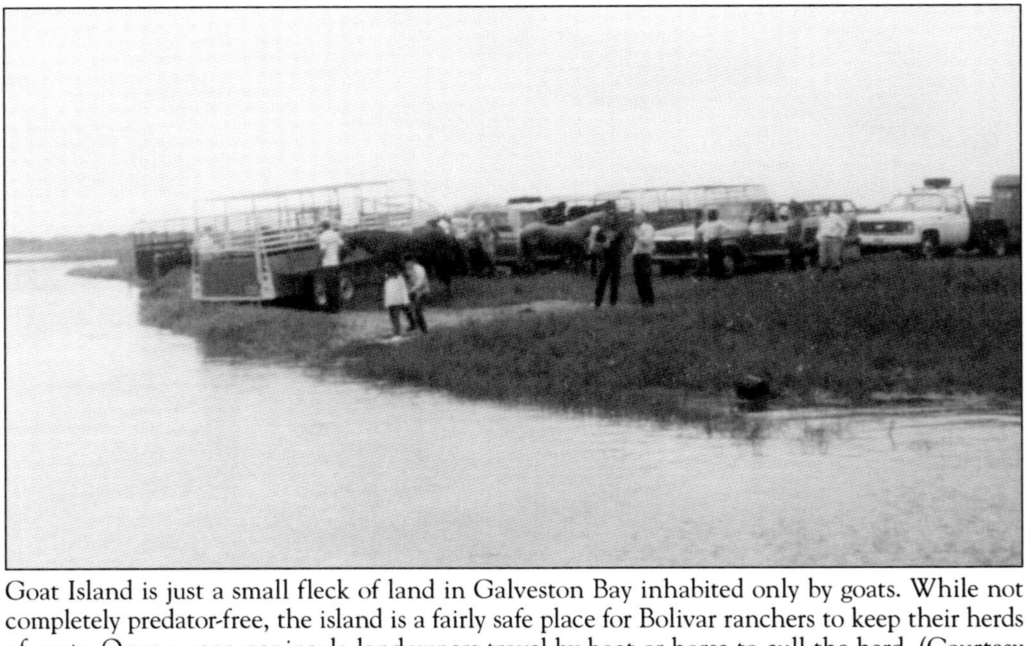
Goat Island is just a small fleck of land in Galveston Bay inhabited only by goats. While not completely predator-free, the island is a fairly safe place for Bolivar ranchers to keep their herds of goats. Once a year, peninsula landowners travel by boat or horse to cull the herd. (Courtesy of Margo Johnson.)

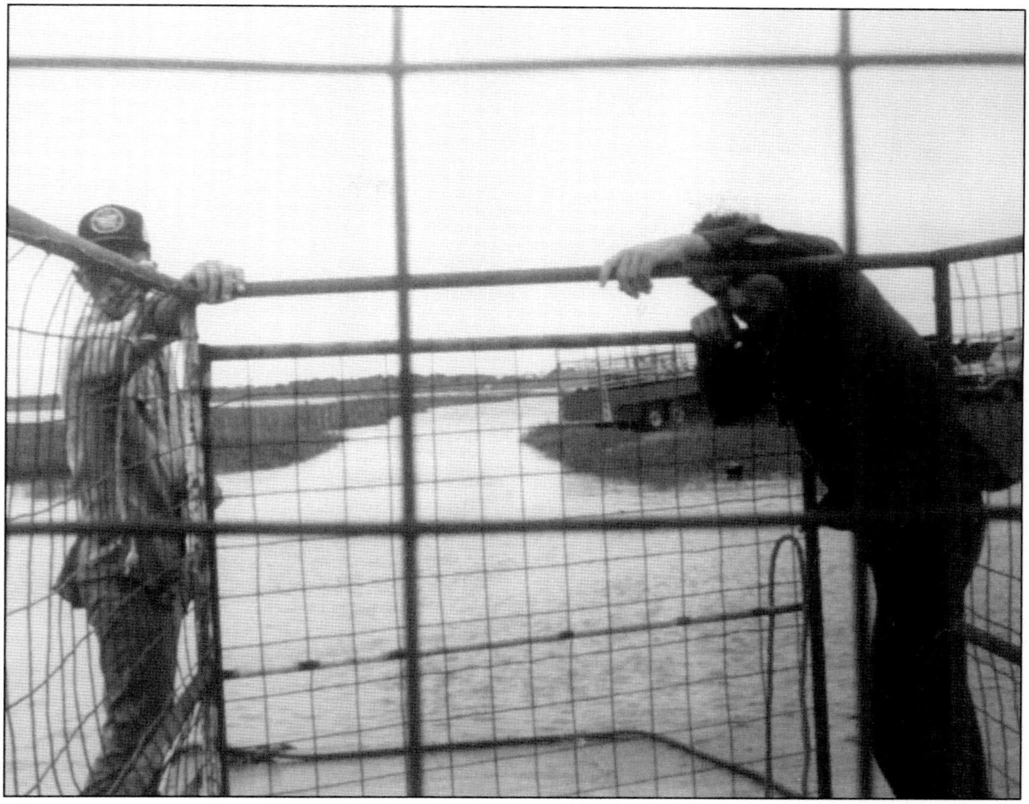

The goat roundup (if one is lucky enough to be invited) is an event not to be missed. Riding horses across the canal, roping contests, and a barbecue at the end of the day are a part of this grand tradition. (Courtesy of Margo Johnson.)

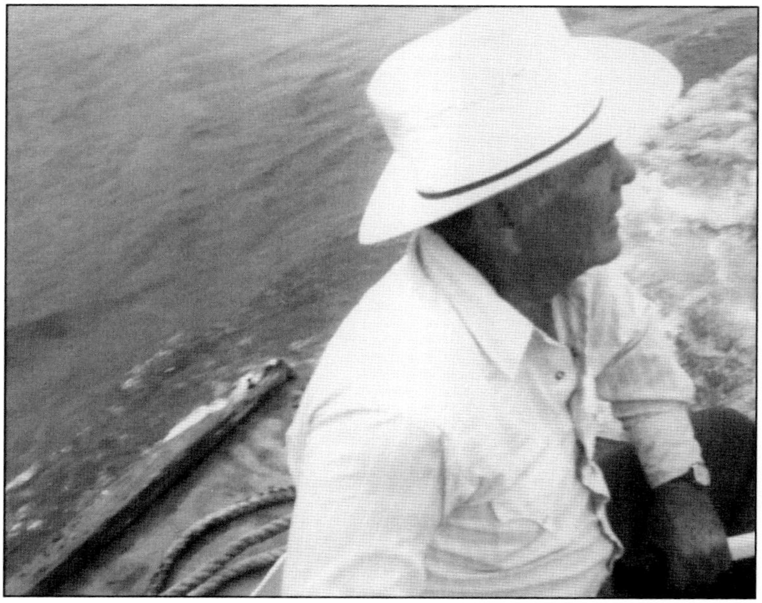

In this photograph, cowboy Joe Bill Kahla looks on as the goat roundup commences. (Courtesy of Margo Johnson.)

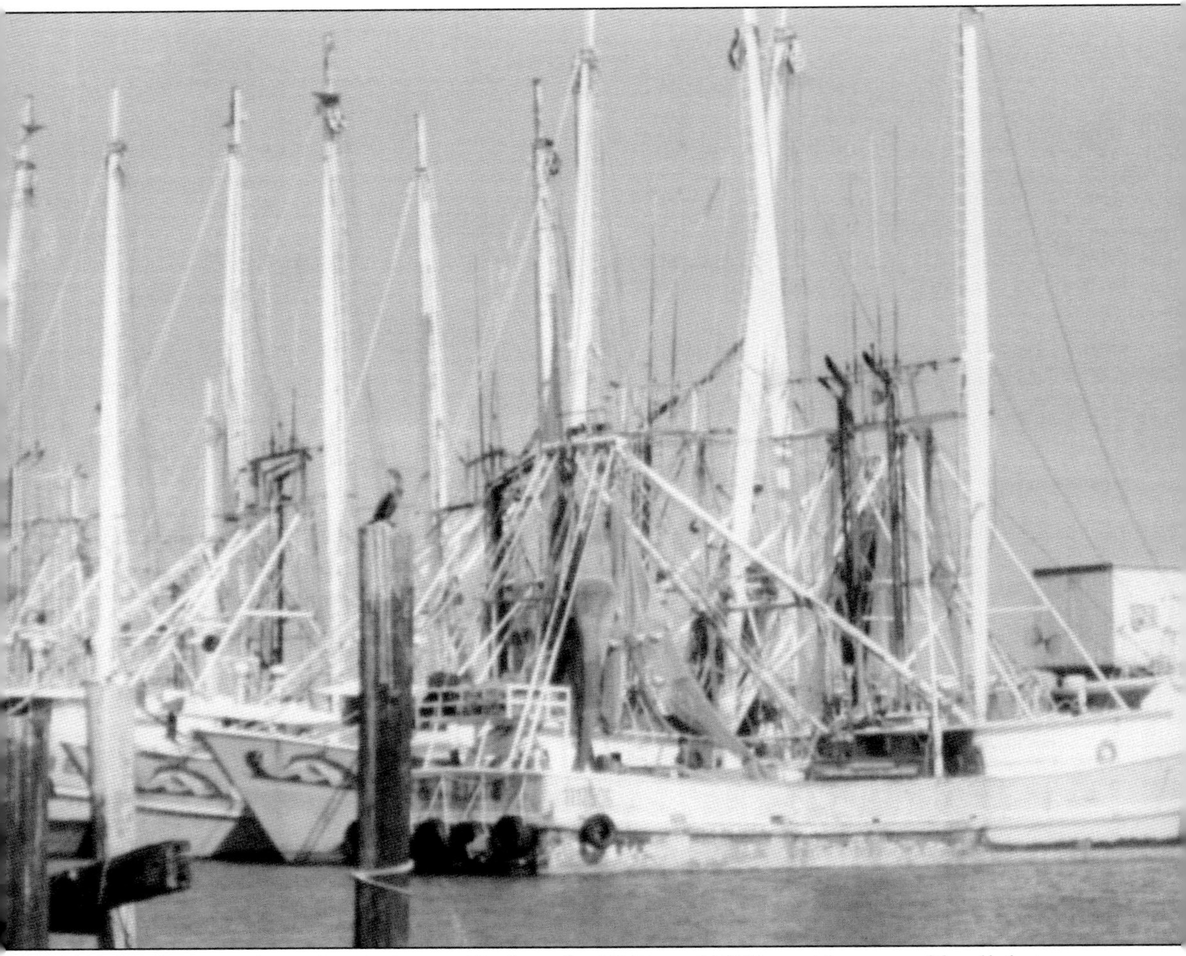

Local waters abound with shrimp. Back in the 1940a and 1950s, residents would pull shrimp nets by hand with a rope before shrimping was regulated. Shrimpers could harvest 1,000 pounds of shrimp from the sea each day. The cost—3¢ a pound. (Photograph by the author.)

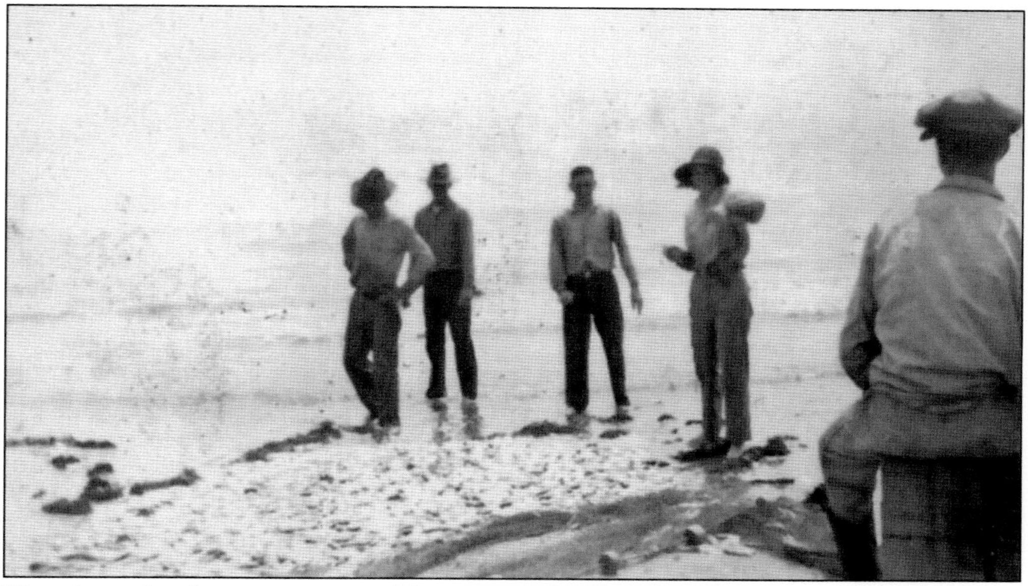

These happy beachgoers are seining. The year is 1947. When the tide was moving (about an hour after high tide and again an hour after low tide), these folks were out with their nets, catching sea creatures great and small. (Courtesy of the Simpton family.)

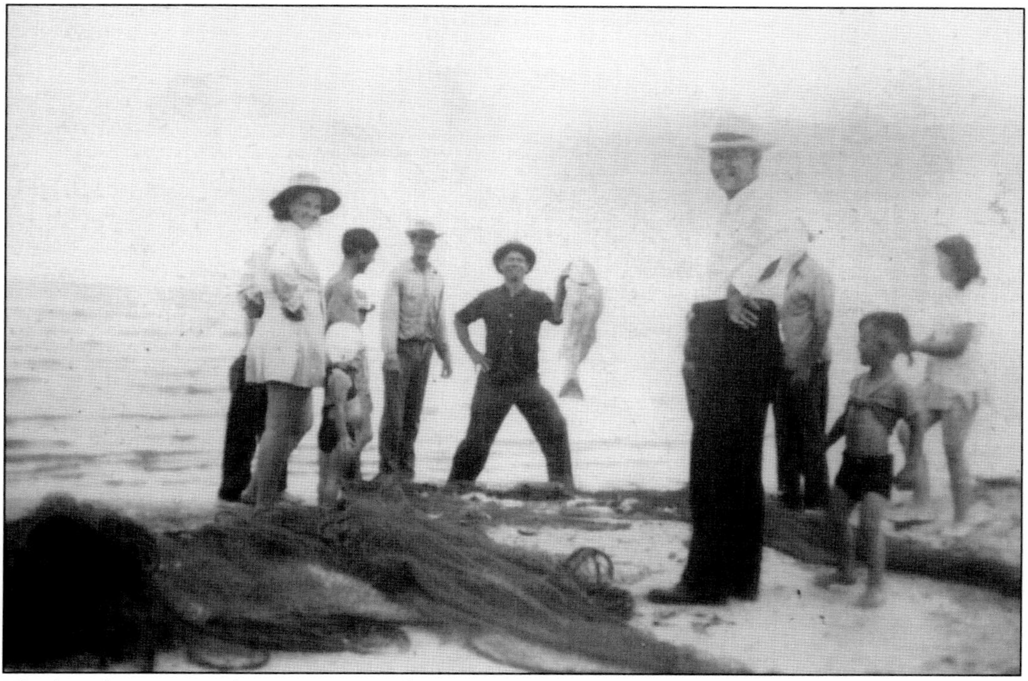

The beach seine is a fun way to spend some time on the beach. The payoff for this group was a big pot of gumbo after the catch. (Courtesy of the Simpton family.)

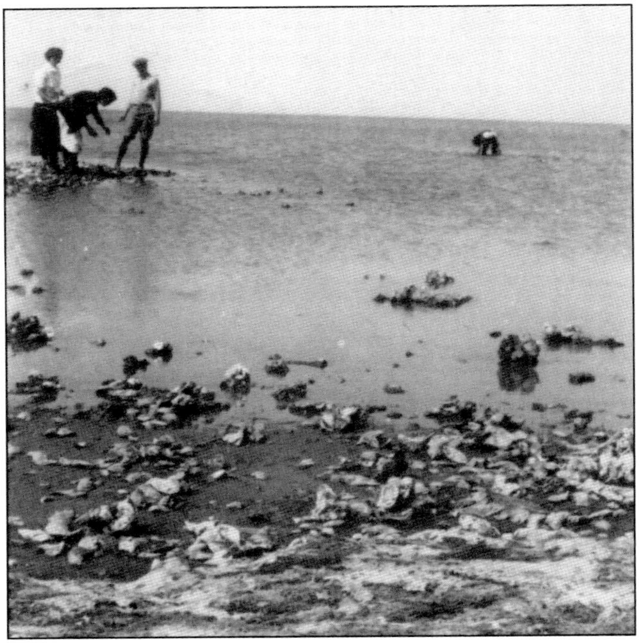

The Bolivar Peninsula produced about half of all the oysters consumed in Texas in 1885. Many farm families supplemented their livelihoods by raking and shucking oysters from the reef. During the cooler months of the year, Bolivar residents waited for low tide, when the waters receded, to approach the large mounds of oyster clusters scattered across the beach. Requiring only heavy gloves and a bucket, oysters are relatively easy to harvest. (Courtesy of Robert and Jerri Bouse.)

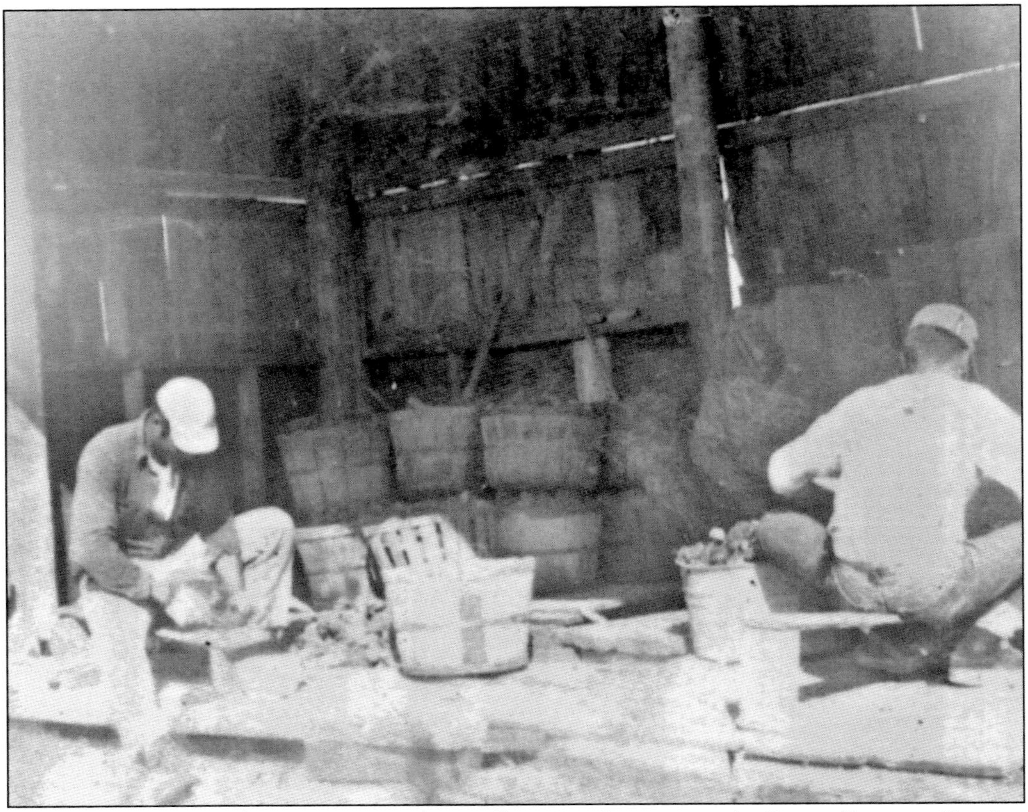

Oysters were sold for $1.25 a quart or $4 a gallon. People came to the Bouse Store on Sunday, and the Bouse men would open the oysters into containers brought by the customers. (Courtesy of Robert and Jerri Bouse.)

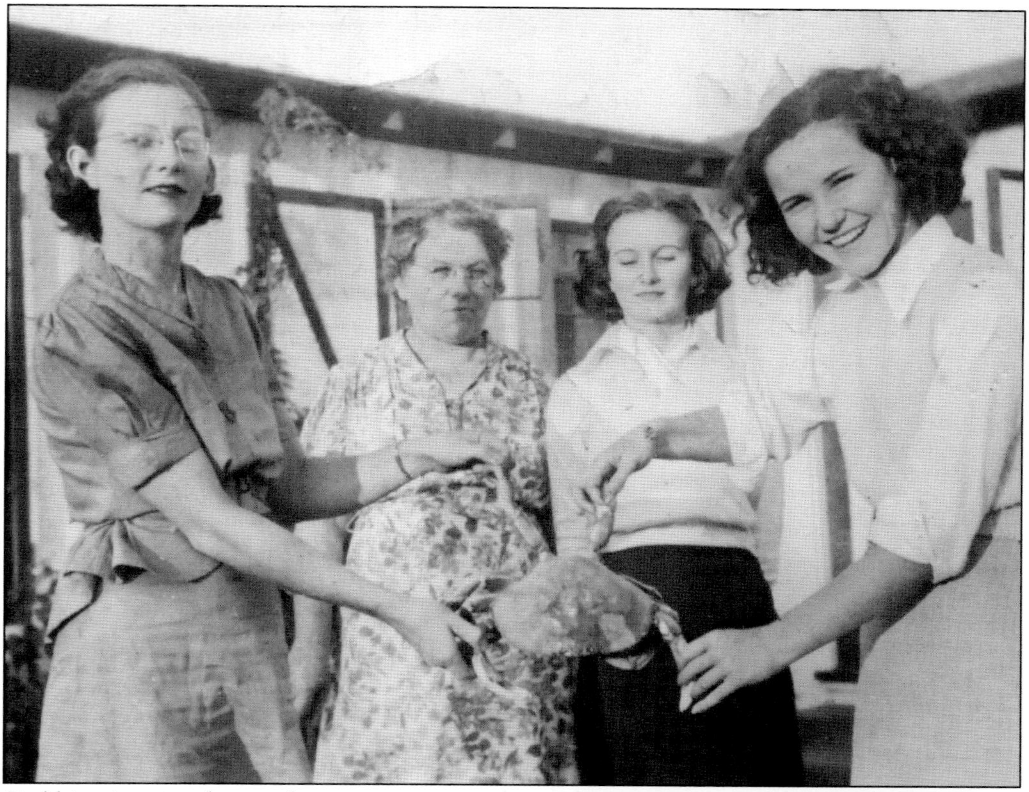

Crabbing is a time-honored pastime on the Bolivar Peninsula. For generations, kids have grabbed a roll of twine and some chicken necks, added a sinker and headed to the jetties or down to the intracoastal to catch a mess of crabs for a lunchtime gumbo. A 1930 article in the *Galveston Daily News* suggests that fishermen supplied shrimp and crabs to the cannery, a "new and promising" industry in Port Bolivar. Most of the workers at the cannery lived in Frenchtown, a small Cajun settlement near the cannery. (Courtesy of Elsie Devers.)

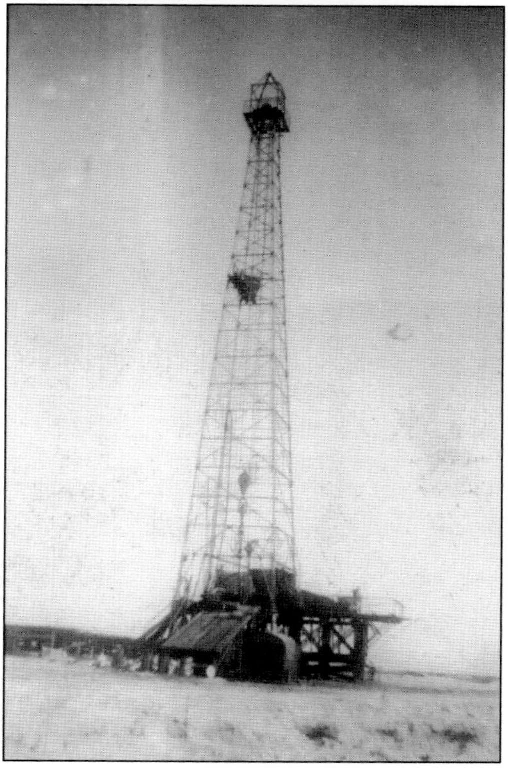

There were several oil discoveries on the peninsula when exploration started after Spindletop in 1901. Because of the mineral springs and salt dome, prospectors felt like there would certainly be oil at High Island. Some shallow wells did produce small amounts of oil but not the gushers that were expected. (Courtesy of the Simpton family.)

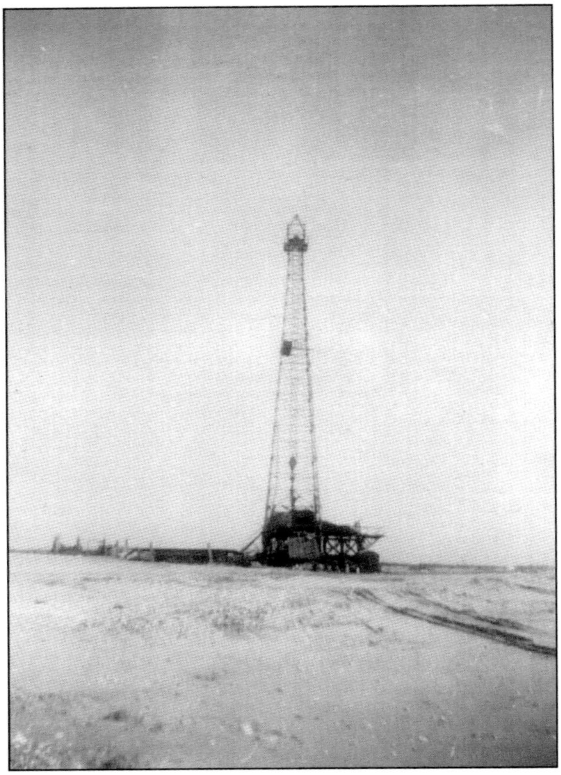

The first test drill at High Island was performed in 1901 in response to the big Spindletop gusher found in nearby Beaumont. It was abandoned without an oil show. (Courtesy of Simpton family.)

Oil was eventually found on High Island. Commercial production began in 1922. In the 1930s, there was a big hit by Young Lee Oil. For several years, High Island was an oil boomtown, having as many as 200 wells. There are still a few pumping wells in the area. (Photograph by the author.)

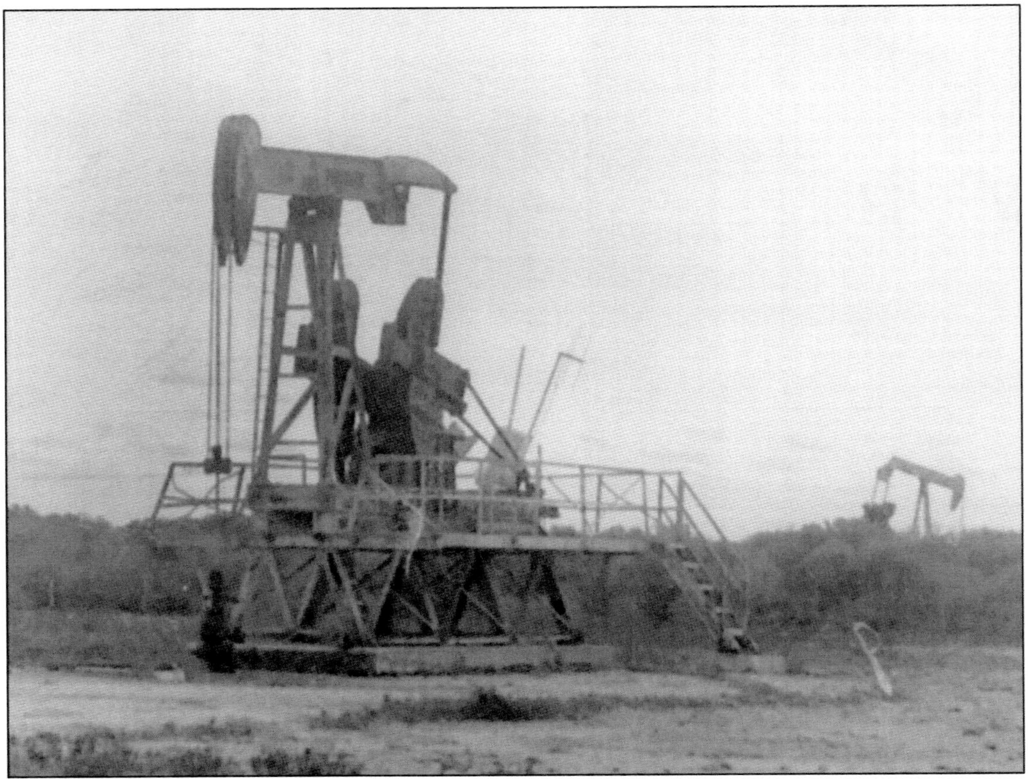

Four

From Pasture to Seashore

Cowboy Boots and Bathing Suits

Motoring down Highway 87 offers an extraordinary view of three seemingly incongruous lifestyles. Only on the Bolivar Peninsula can one spot herds of cattle grazing in salt-grass pastures and tended by third- and fourth-generation cowboys, bikini-clad tourists and weekenders strolling along the beach, and world-class fishermen casting into the surf.

Early settlers of the Bolivar Peninsula made their livings by farming and ranching. The cowboy culture is still well represented on the peninsula. In the first half of the 20th century, weekend rodeos were a mainstay of peninsula social activity. Cowboy boot–clad residents stand side by side with flip-flop-sporting tourists at the Big Store or Stingaree Restaurant.

As a popular tourist destination since the late 1800s, the peninsula sees a population explosion during the summer months. Fishermen, sun-worshippers, birders, and those just looking for a restful week or two come to enjoy the warm gulf water and mellow lifestyle.

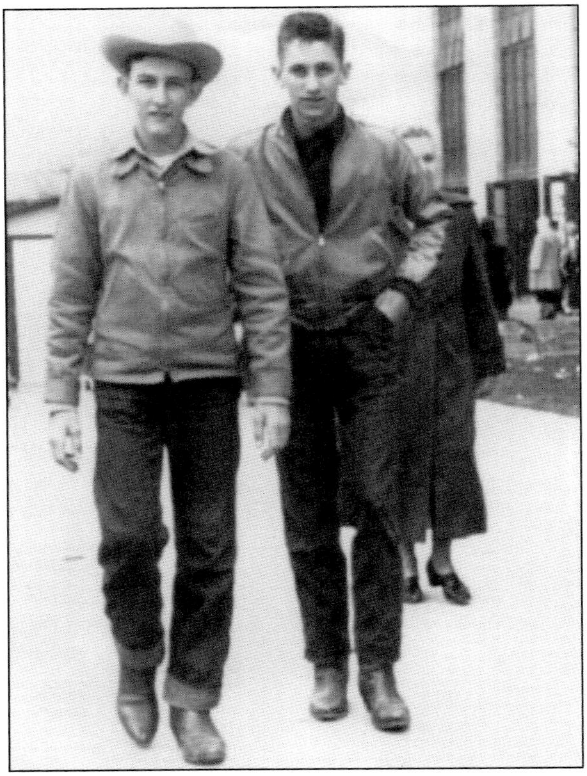

Lifelong friends Andrew M. Johnson Jr. (left) and Skippy Miers are pictured here strolling through Galveston in 1950. Johnson, part of the third generation of the earliest settlers on the Bolivar Peninsula, was born in 1935. The Johnsons lived, farmed, and ranched on Bolivar for over a century. Most at home on a horse, Johnson ranched for over 40 years, founded the Salt Grass Cattle Company in the late 1960s, and started surveying in the 1970s. (Courtesy of Margo Johnson.)

Andrew Johnson was known in church and community productions as the "Traveling Troubadour." His rich baritone voice and guitar were always a favorite part of any program. Johndon is pictured here on his horse Ranger in 1947. (Courtesy of Margo Johnson.)

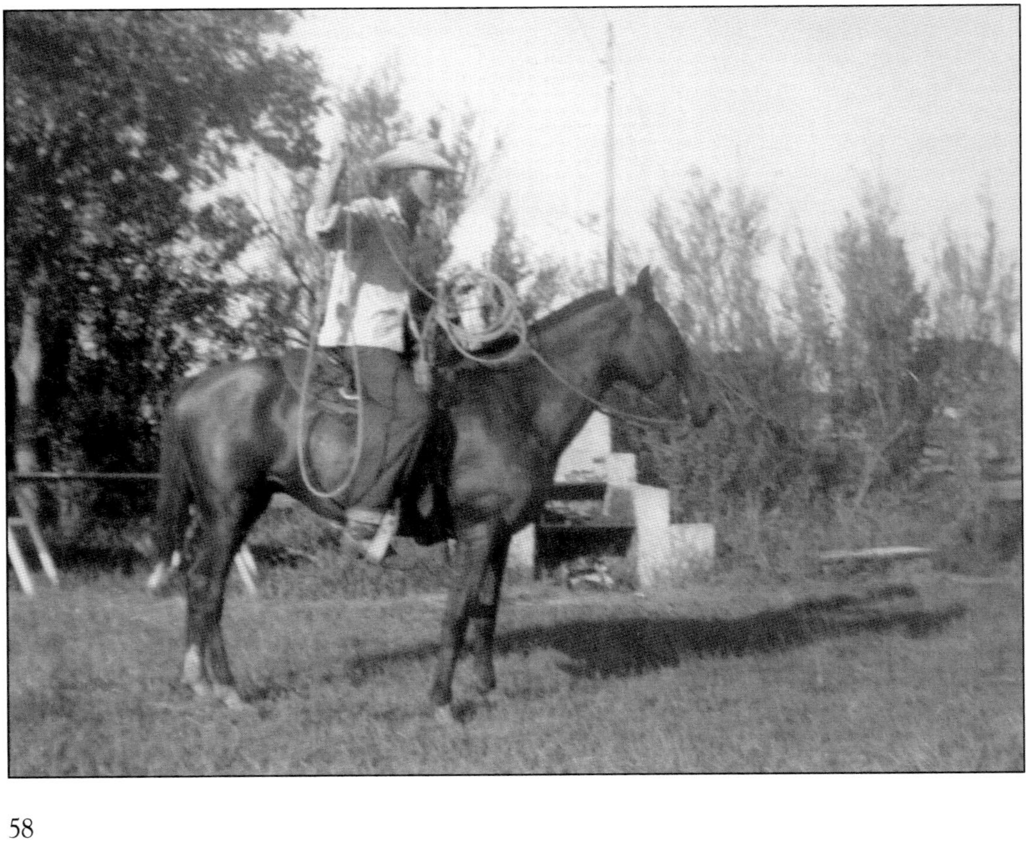

Earl Ray Bouse is a born cowboy. (Courtesy of the Simpton family.)

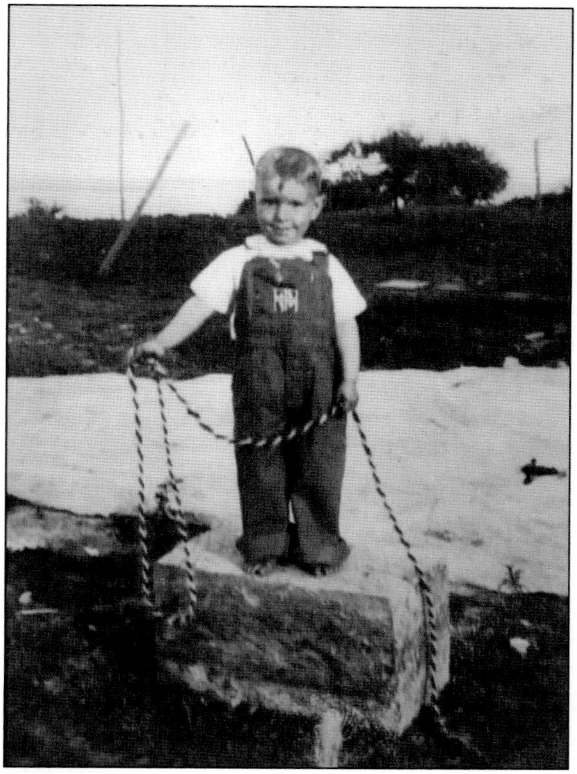

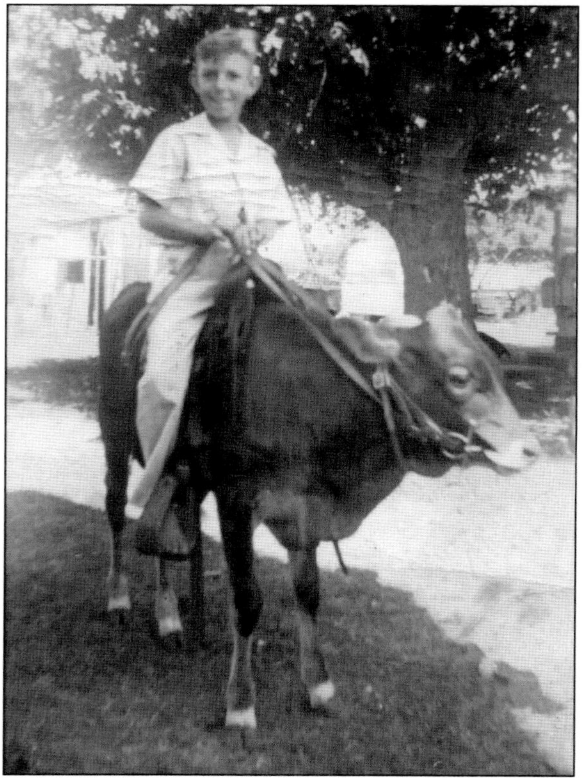

A very young Earl Ray Bouse takes a ride of a different kind. (Courtesy of the Bouse family.)

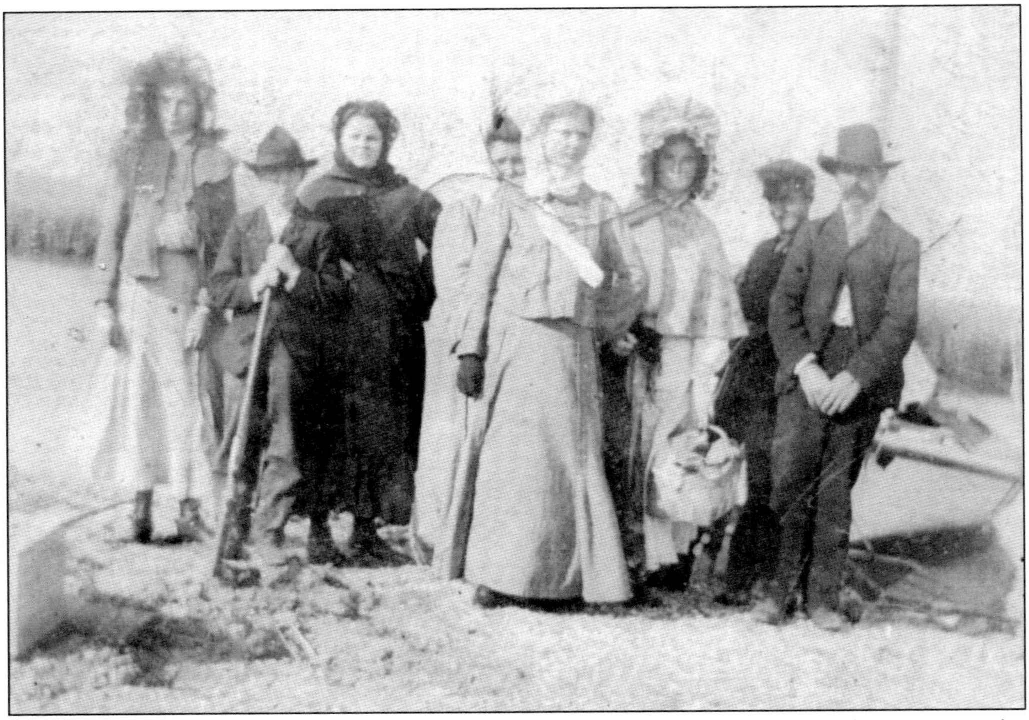

This late 19th-century photograph exemplifies the pioneer spirit of the Bolivar Peninsula. (Courtesy of Elsie Devers.)

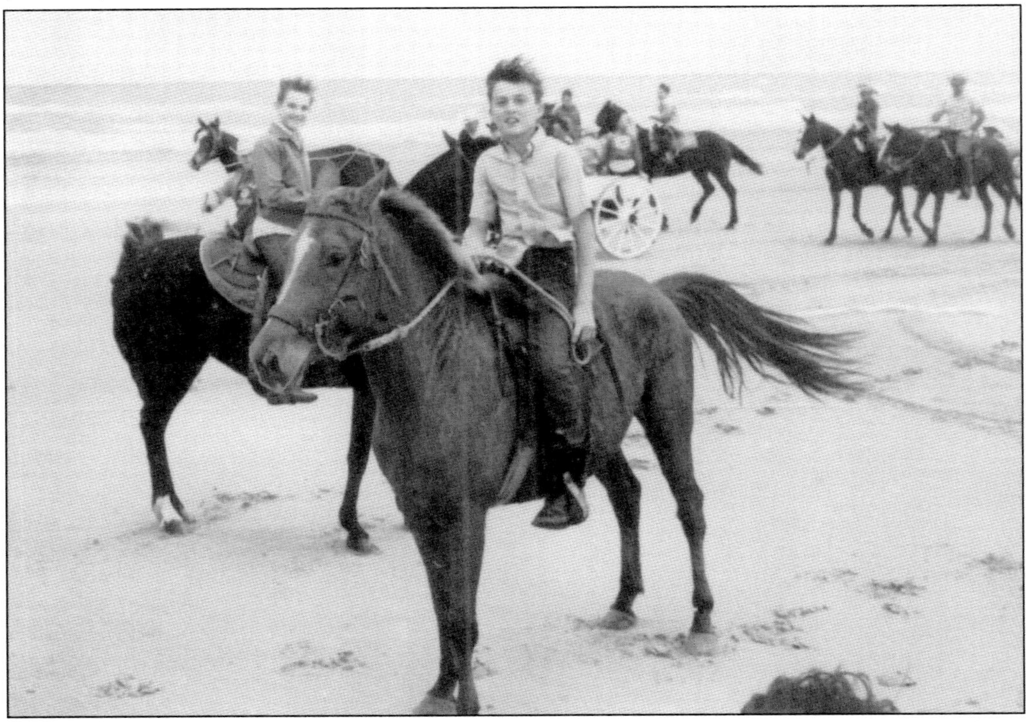

Frank Senseney (foreground) is pictured here on a beach trail ride with a group of fellow students in the mid-1960s. (Courtesy of Rhea Senseney.)

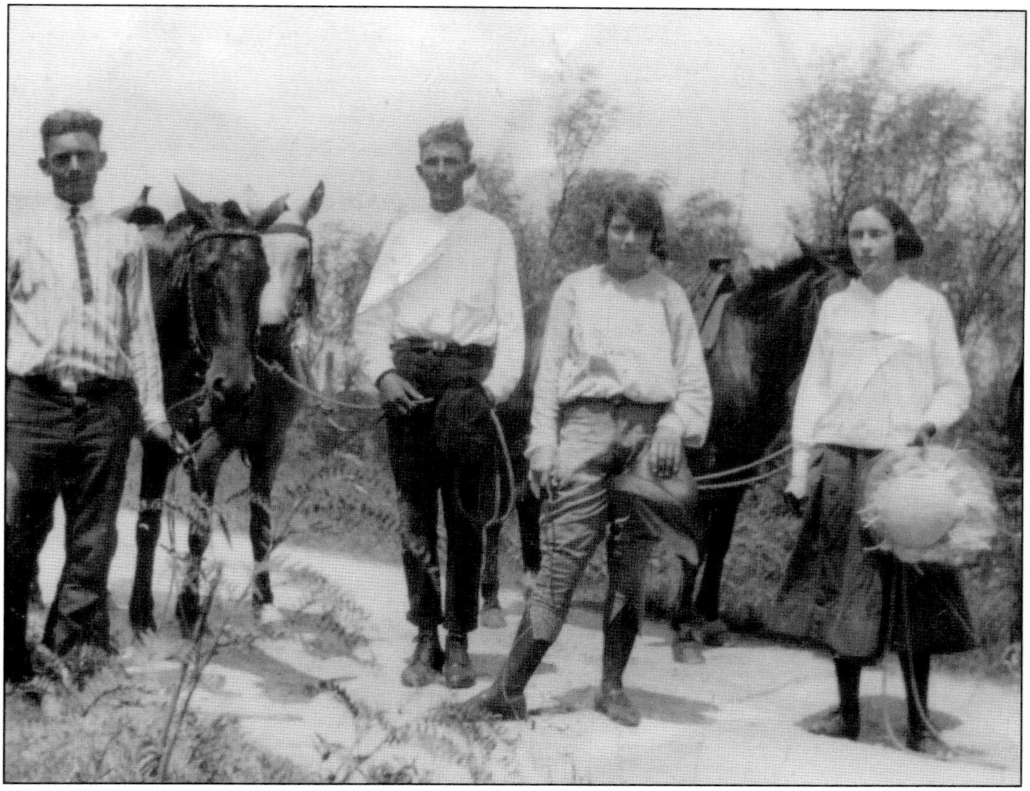

Horses have always been an important part of the Bolivar Peninsula. While not nearly as plentiful today as at the time of this photograph, a few prized horses can still be spotted in the area. (Courtesy of Robert and Jerri Bouse.)

The Simpton Rodeo Arena is pictured here. Beginning in the early 1920s, rodeos were popular around the country, and local cowboys liked to show off their stuff on weekends. Such events as calf roping, bronc and bareback riding, bull riding, and barrel racing were regular events at small rodeos across the country. The Simpton Rodeo was a staple of Bolivar Peninsula entertainment and a popular meeting place on weekends. (Courtesy of Terri Simpton.)

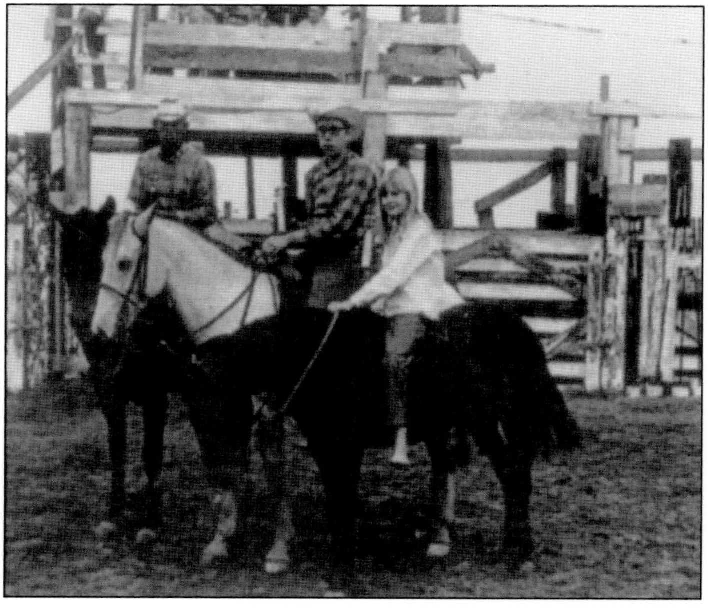

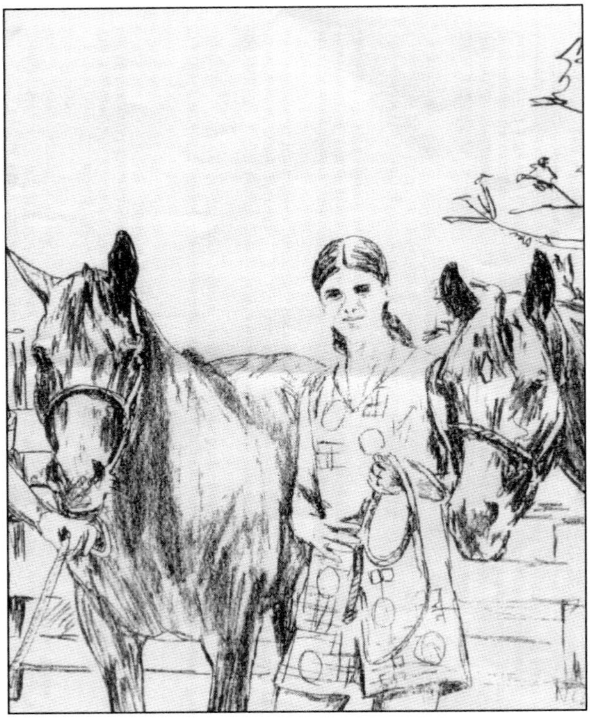

Father O'Malley, popular priest of Our Mother of Mercy Catholic Church in Port Bolivar, sketched an original image for each Sunday's church bulletin. This bulletin advertises the rodeo coming to the Simpton Rodeo Arena. Old-time church members have been quoted as saying that "the church was built with barbecues, bazaars, gumbo cook-offs, and rodeos." (Courtesy of Terri Simpton.)

Pictured here is Father O'Malley, priest of Our Mother of Mercy Catholic Church. The occasion was a church festival. (Courtesy of Terri Simpton.)

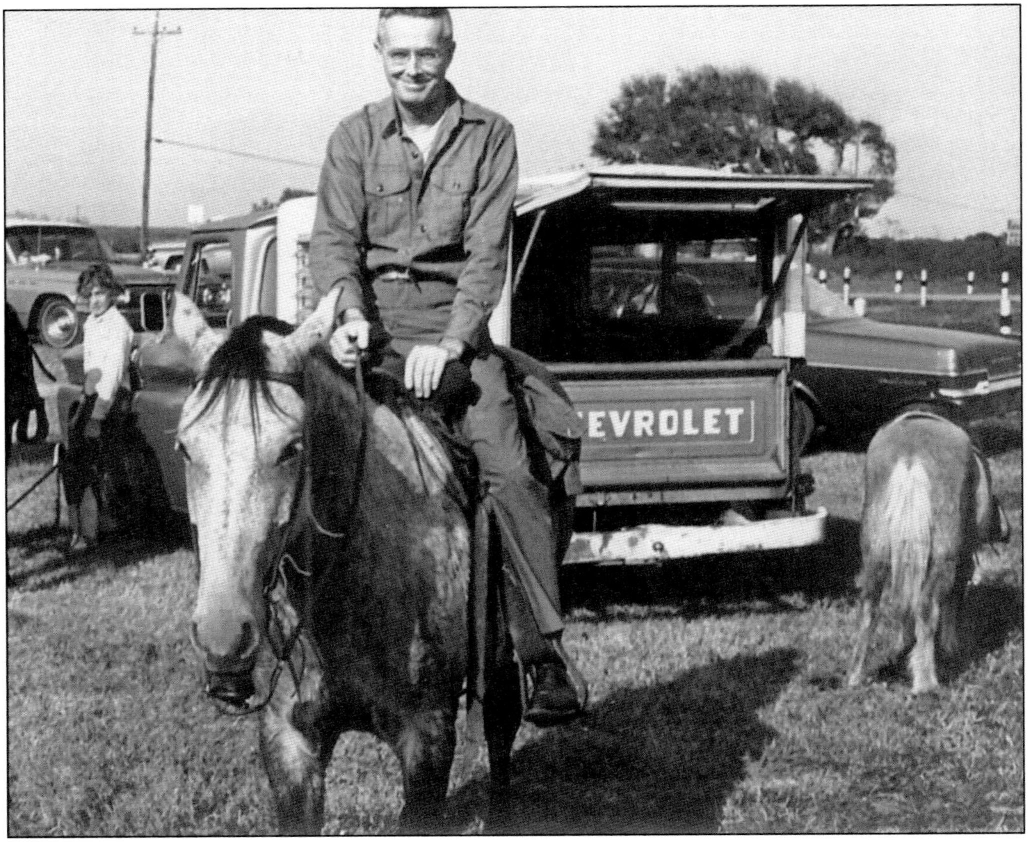

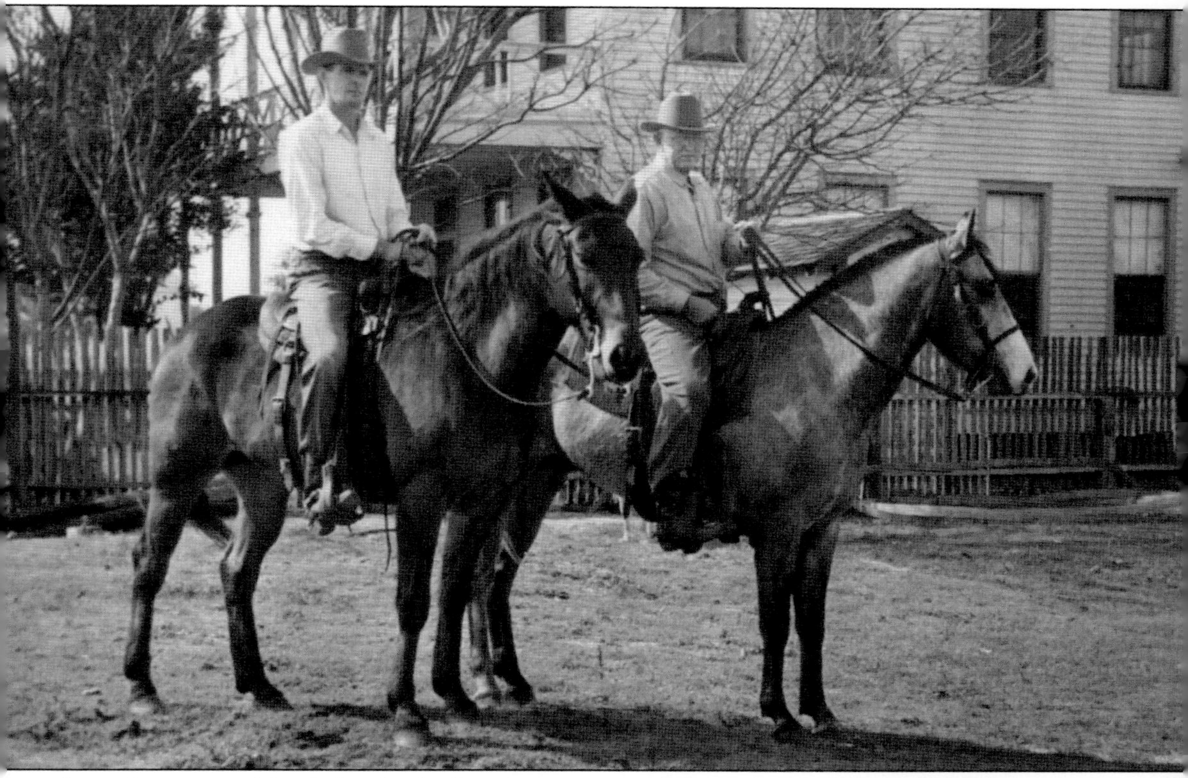

Jerry Simpton and his father, Leslie Fern Simpton, are shown riding beside the Kahla/Simpton house in Port Bolivar. The horses are named Todd and Half Hitch. Jerry ran the Bolivar Rodeo for years. It was located right across the street from this house on Madison Avenue. (Courtesy of the Simpton family.)

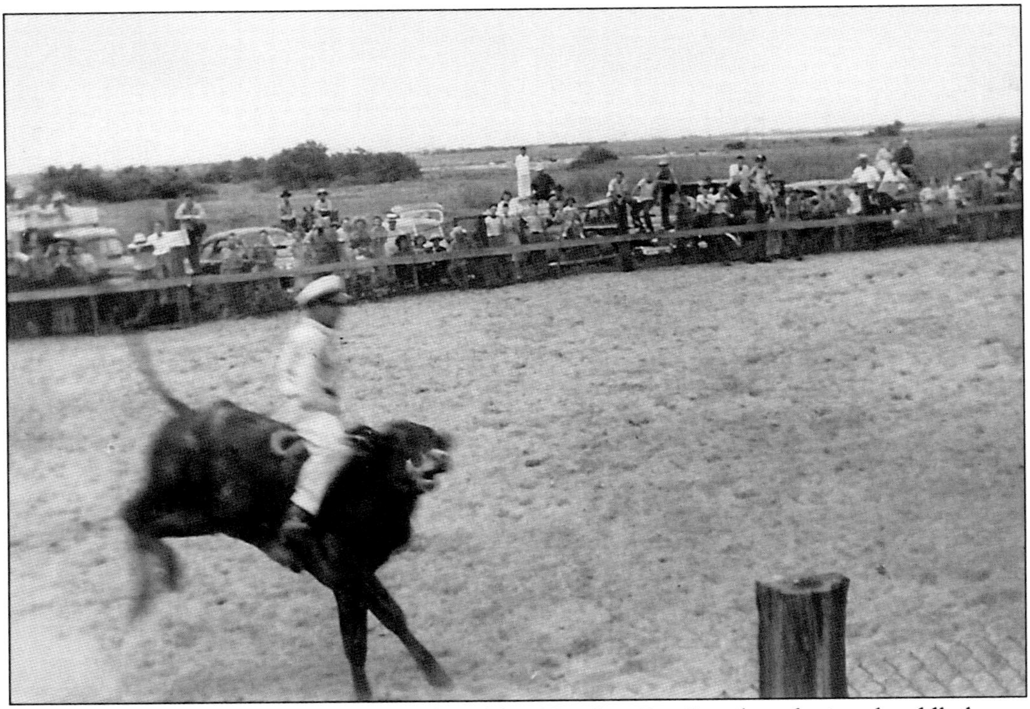

Pictured here is the Bolivar Rodeo. Bob Kahla, "Cowboy Poet" and professional saddle bronc rider, recounts tales of such events as wild mare milking and goat roping at rodeos up and down the Bolivar Peninsula. (Courtesy of the Simpton family.)

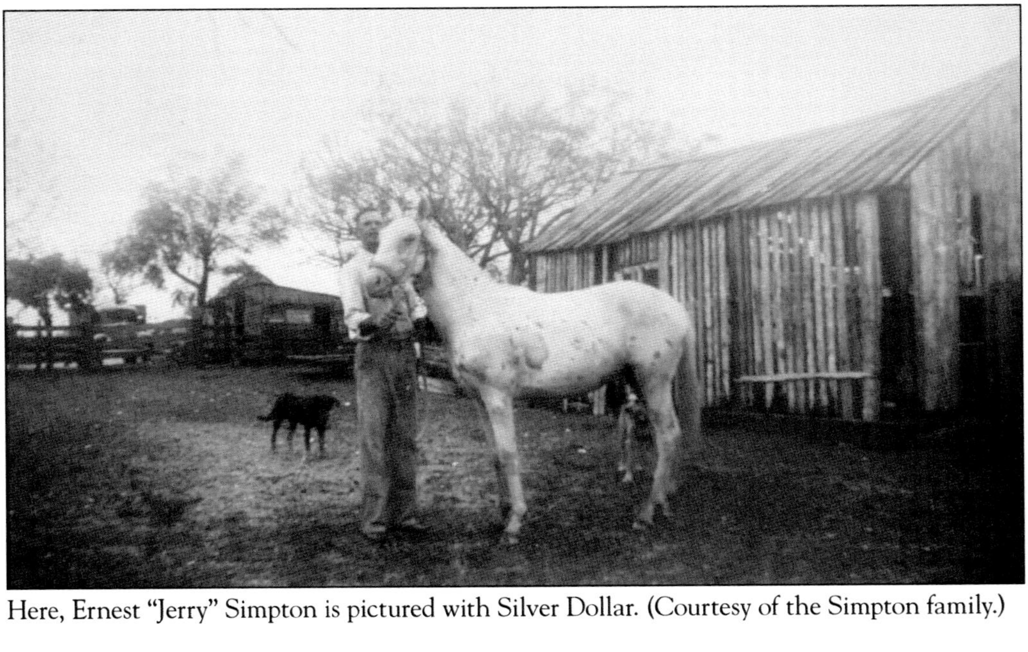

Here, Ernest "Jerry" Simpton is pictured with Silver Dollar. (Courtesy of the Simpton family.)

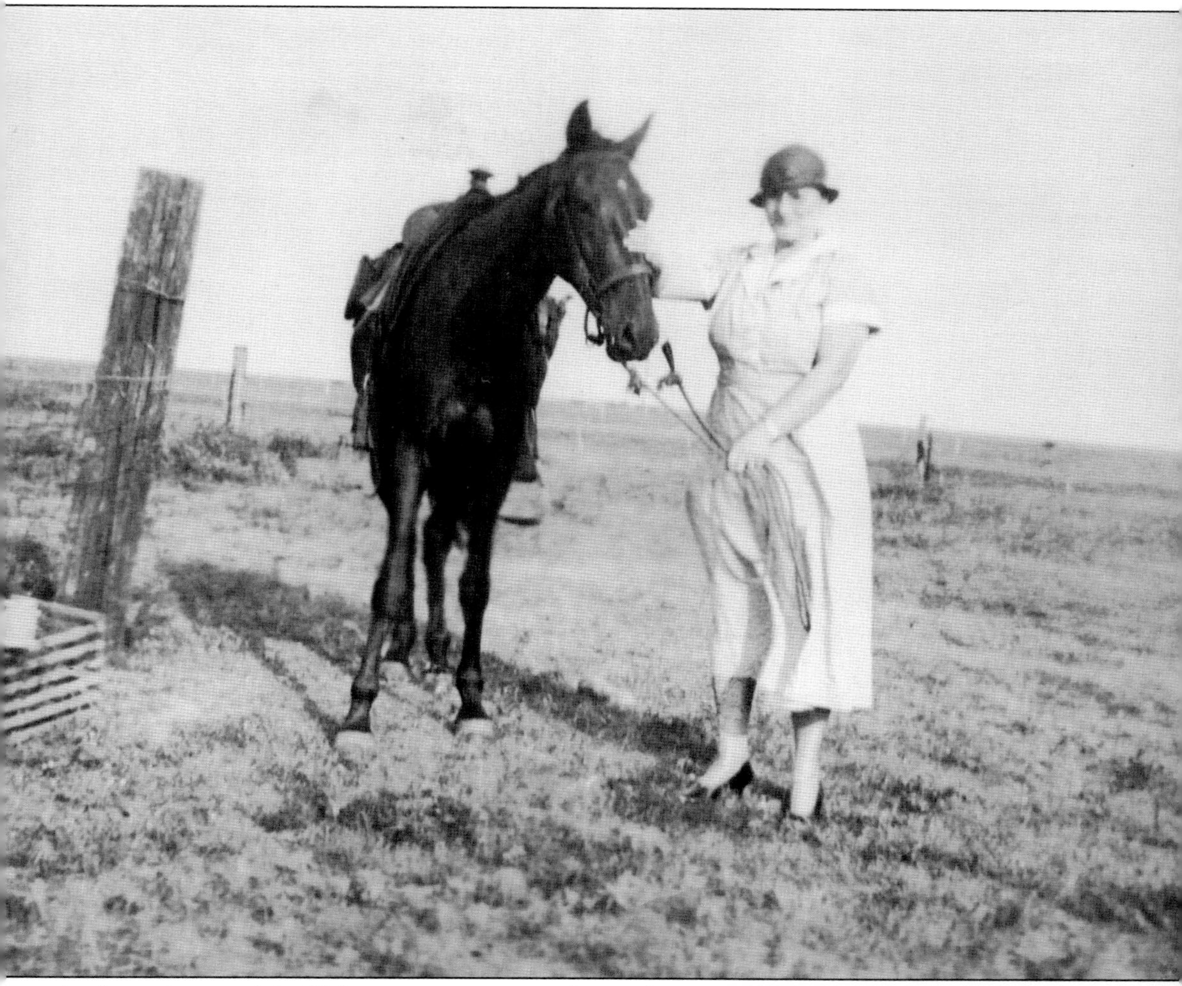

In the early part of the 20th century, women and men alike traveled the peninsula on horseback. Pictured here is Verdia Johnson in 1933. Verdia wrote to her mother during the 1943 storm: "We are in the thick of a hurricane. Things got so bad we just had to hold on to each other." She reports that many homes had been blown off their blocks, trees were down, and the schoolhouse and Methodist church were flattened. "The worst thing that happened was when a dredge boat (the Dredge Galveston-Dallas Co.) went to pieces on the jetties. Andrew (Johnson) and Mr. Myers pulled men out of the water, put them on horseback, and brought them in to Mrs. Myers and I. They had drifted to our beach. We gave them coffee, whiskey, soup . . . got eight of them in bed with dry clothes on. They had been in the water since 12:30 the night before and it was then Wednesday at 10:00 am." (Courtesy of Margo Johnson.)

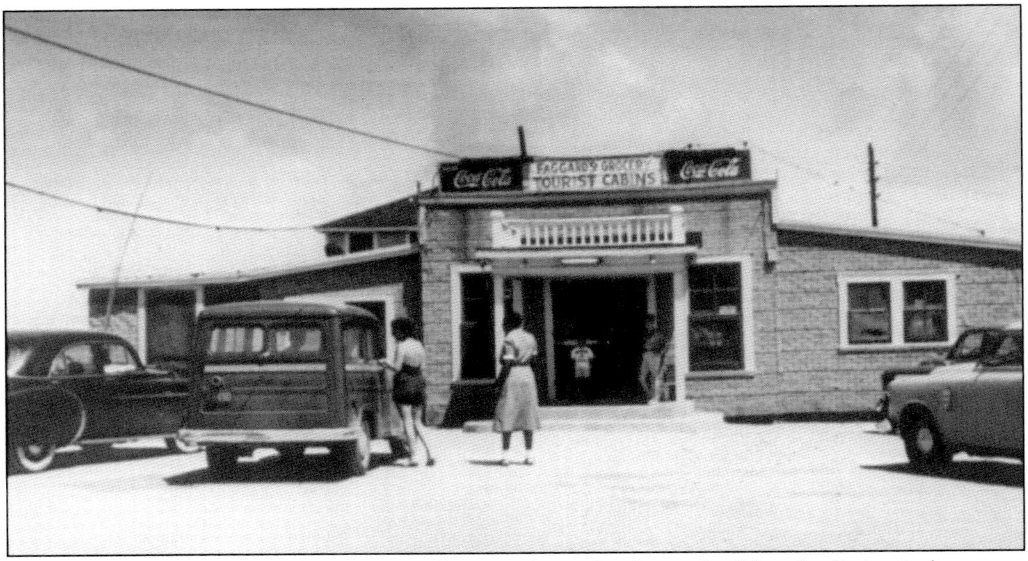

Part of the charm of the Bolivar Peninsula stems from the dissimilar lifestyles living in harmony on this small barrier formation. Alongside cowboys are an array of people coming for a day or a month to enjoy the warm water and good fishing. The entrepreneurial Faggard family rented tourist cabins to beachgoers in the first half of the 20th century. This photograph was taken in the mid-1940s. The availability of wonderful sea bathing, boating, beach cabins, fishing, shelling, and sunbathing made the Bolivar Peninsula a haven for tourists. A telephone booth, located to the side of the parking lot, was the only direct line to Beaumont in the 1940s. Otherwise, callers would have to call the operator, and she would "plug them in." (Courtesy of Shan Faggard.)

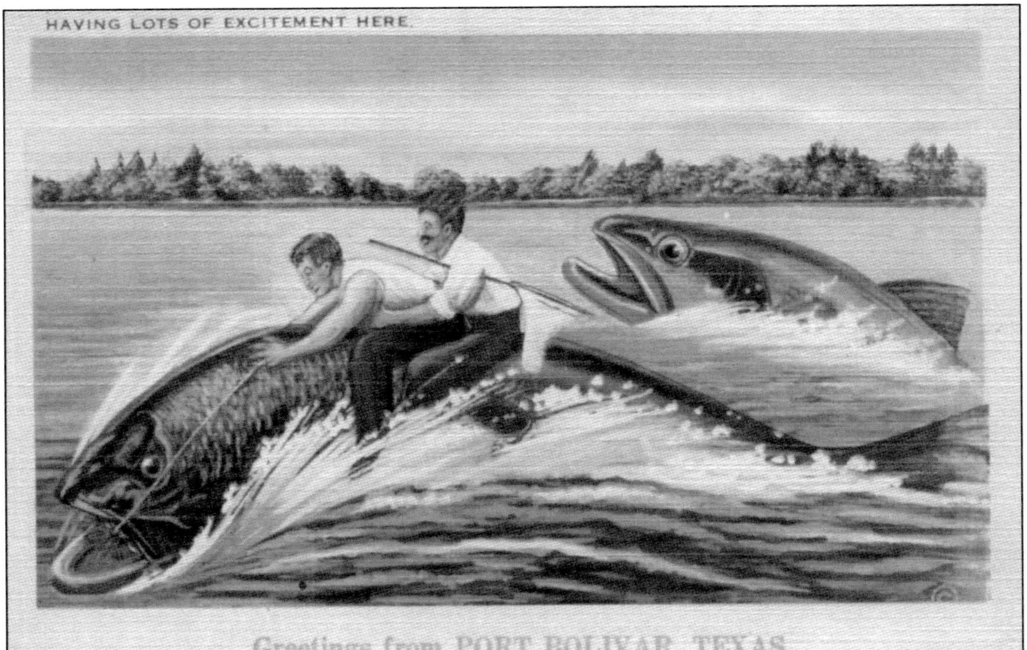

This postcard sends greetings from popular tourist destination Port Bolivar, Texas, and notes that visitors are "having lots of excitement here." (Courtesy of Ralph Stenzel.)

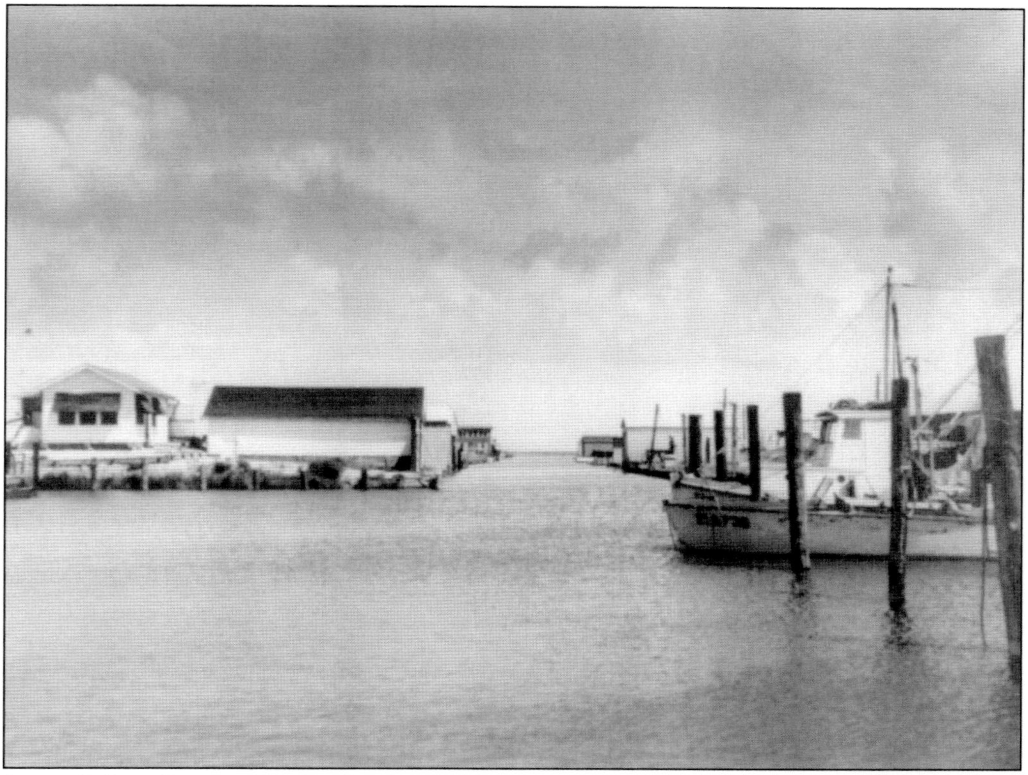

Faggard's Boat Basin was a popular place for fishermen to launch their boats. Faggard's boat, the *Step and Fetch It*, was moored here. (Courtesy of Shan Faggard.)

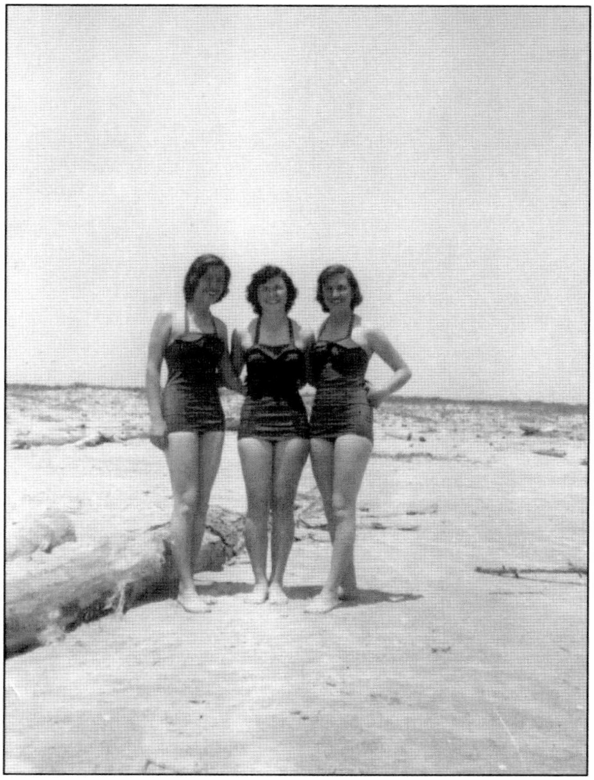

Paula (left), Cora Beth (center), and Pauline Johnson are enjoying a sunny day on the beach around 1960. (Courtesy of the Bouse family.)

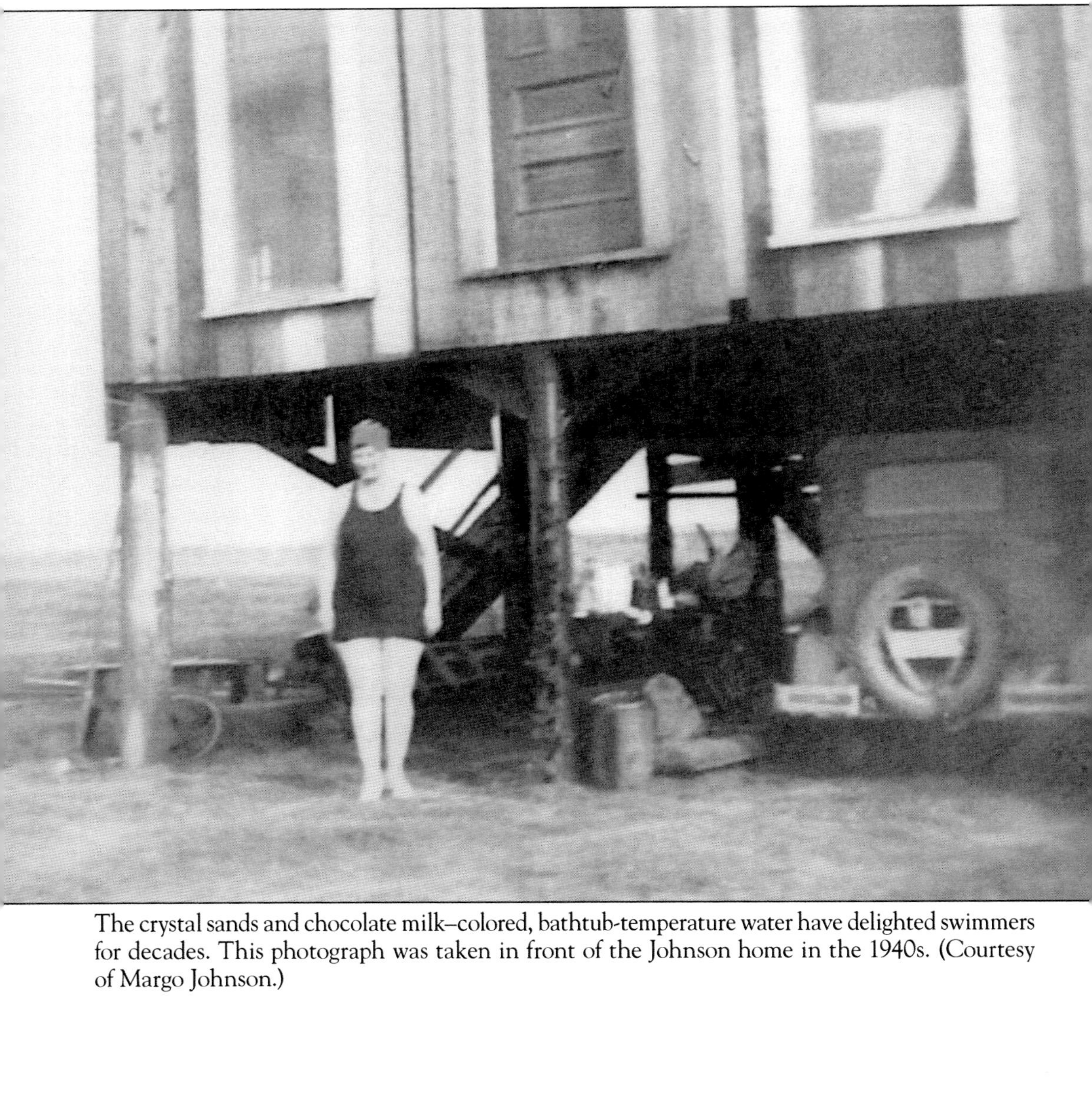

The crystal sands and chocolate milk–colored, bathtub-temperature water have delighted swimmers for decades. This photograph was taken in front of the Johnson home in the 1940s. (Courtesy of Margo Johnson.)

The Bolivar Peninsula has been popular with East Texans since the late 1800s. Many folks from Beaumont have made the peninsula their vacation spot for decades. Charles Schmucker and his sister Ruth are pictured here visiting the peninsula in 1932. (Courtesy of Linda Elissalde.)

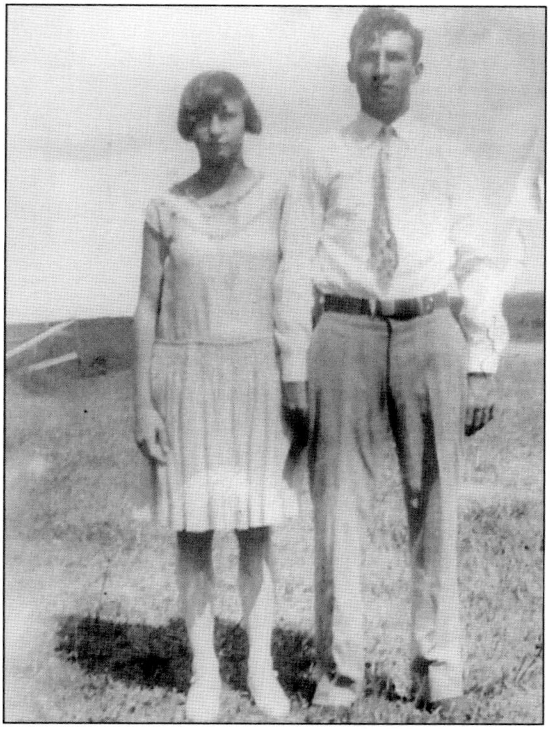

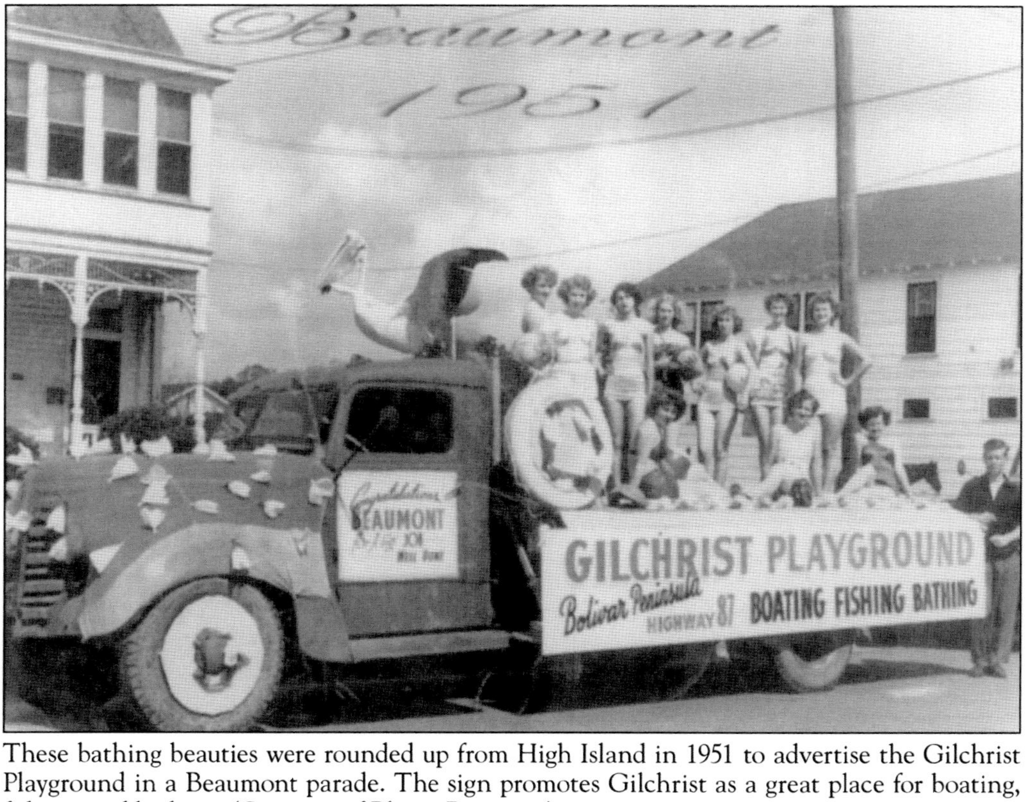

These bathing beauties were rounded up from High Island in 1951 to advertise the Gilchrist Playground in a Beaumont parade. The sign promotes Gilchrist as a great place for boating, fishing, and bathing. (Courtesy of Blaine Brigance.)

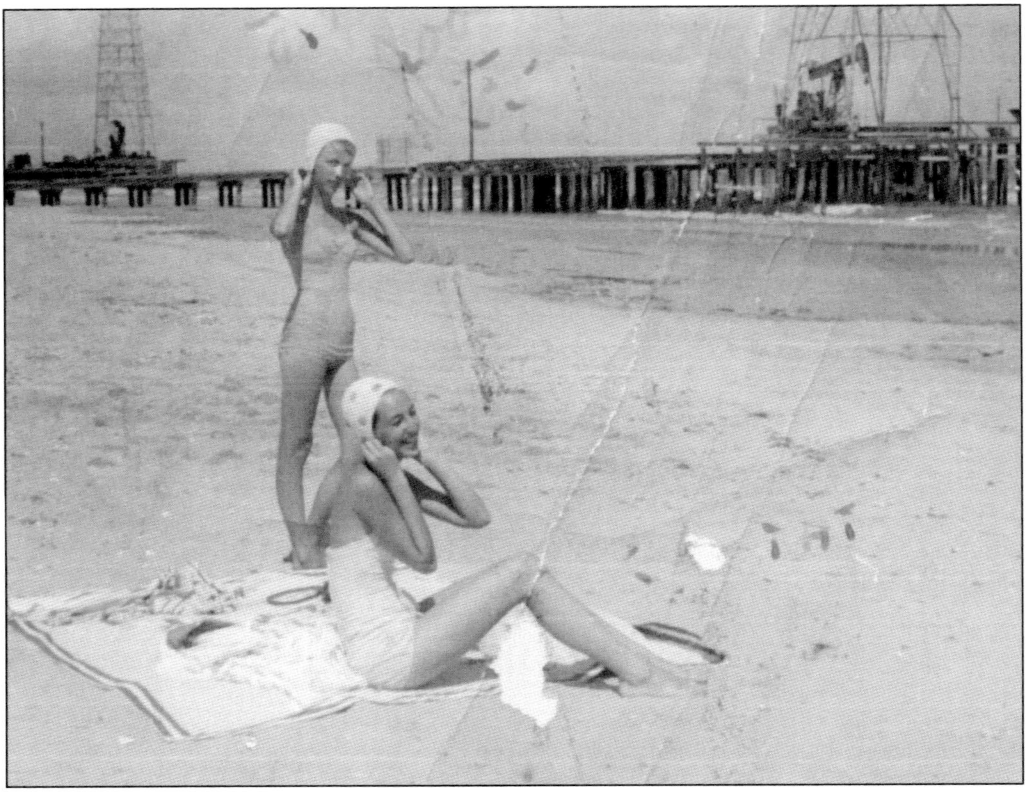

High Island teenagers enjoyed beach days down past the intersection of Highways 124 and 87 in the 1940s and 1950s. In those days, the music came from the radio blasting through the windows of the car parked on the beach. Notice the oil pumper and derrick in the background off the pier. (Courtesy of Elsie Devers.)

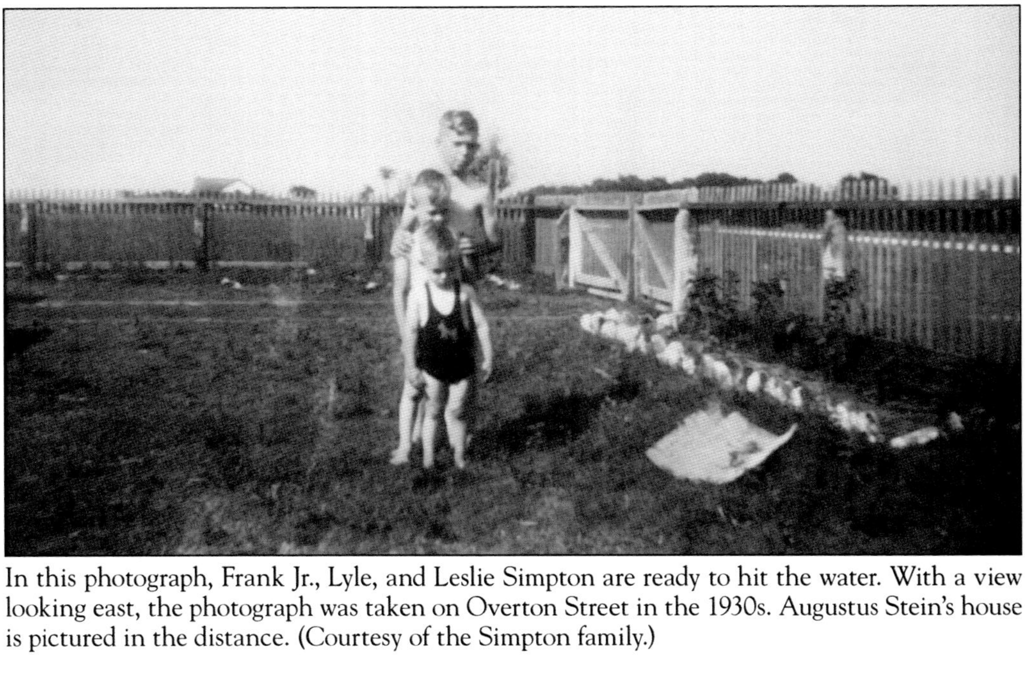

In this photograph, Frank Jr., Lyle, and Leslie Simpton are ready to hit the water. With a view looking east, the photograph was taken on Overton Street in the 1930s. Augustus Stein's house is pictured in the distance. (Courtesy of the Simpton family.)

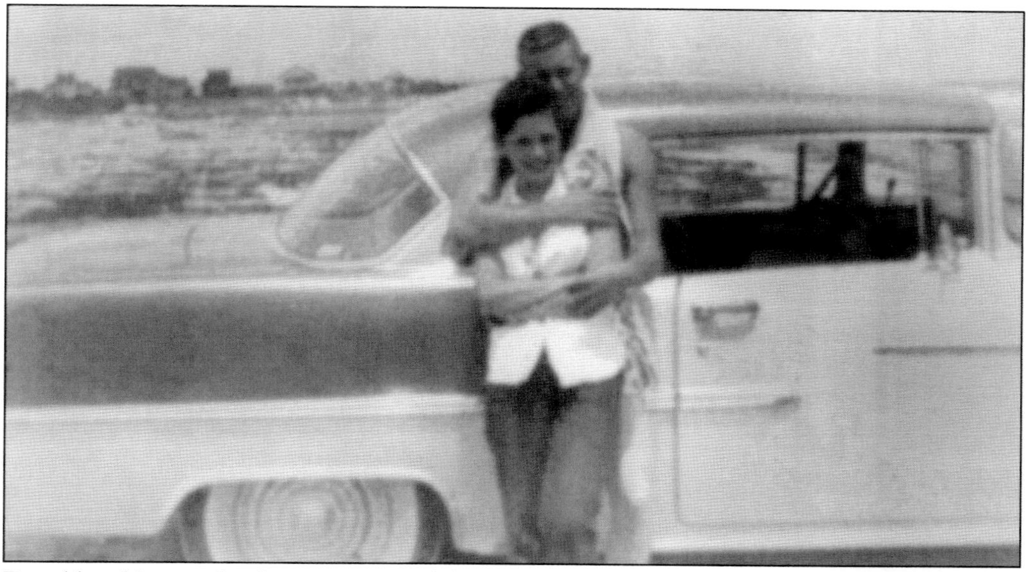

Donald and Jimmie Lee LaCour motored down for a beach trip in 1957. Donald's family owned a cabin on Bolivar, on the bay side near Bluewater Bait Camp. The entire family would spend the whole summer there. In those days, most of the women in the family did not work outside the home. When the children got out of school in May, they would head out to the beach with all of the aunts and cousins. The men would come down when they could. This family has wonderful memories of huge family meals, their grandfather's shrimp boat, crabbing, and many hours spent searching for the perfect seashell. (Courtesy of Donna LaCour Broussard.)

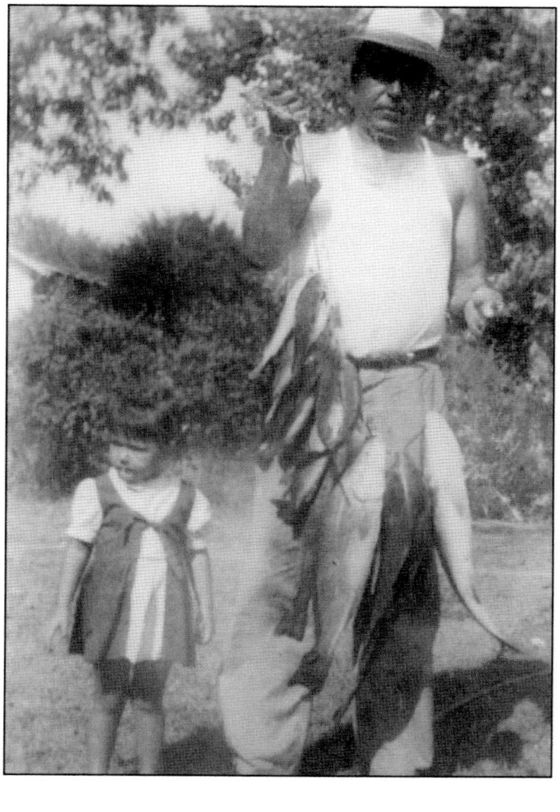

Joann Roberts and her uncle Harold Roberts display their catch of the day in 1956. Fishing enthusiasts Harold and Birdie Roberts owned a cabin at Smith Point in the 1950s, which was enjoyed by their extended families. The Roberts family enjoyed wade fishing at "the pocket," located between the lighthouse and the base of the Bolivar Jetties, at Rollover Pass, and in the surf. (Courtesy of Rae Sullivan.)

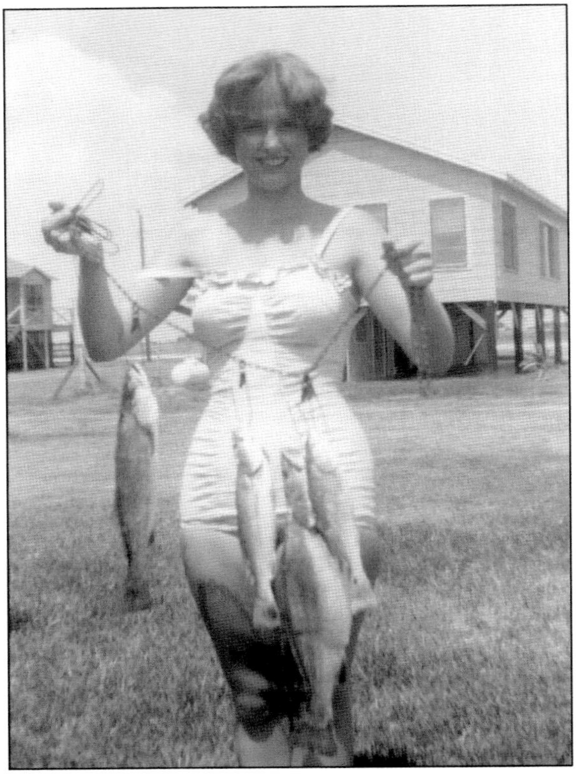

Gay Thames is pictured here with her catch in August 1958. On that day, Thames went fishing with Charlie Schmucker and his daughter Linda. It is remembered with some chagrin that Thames is the only one to have caught fish that day. (Courtesy of Barbara Gordon McNeill.)

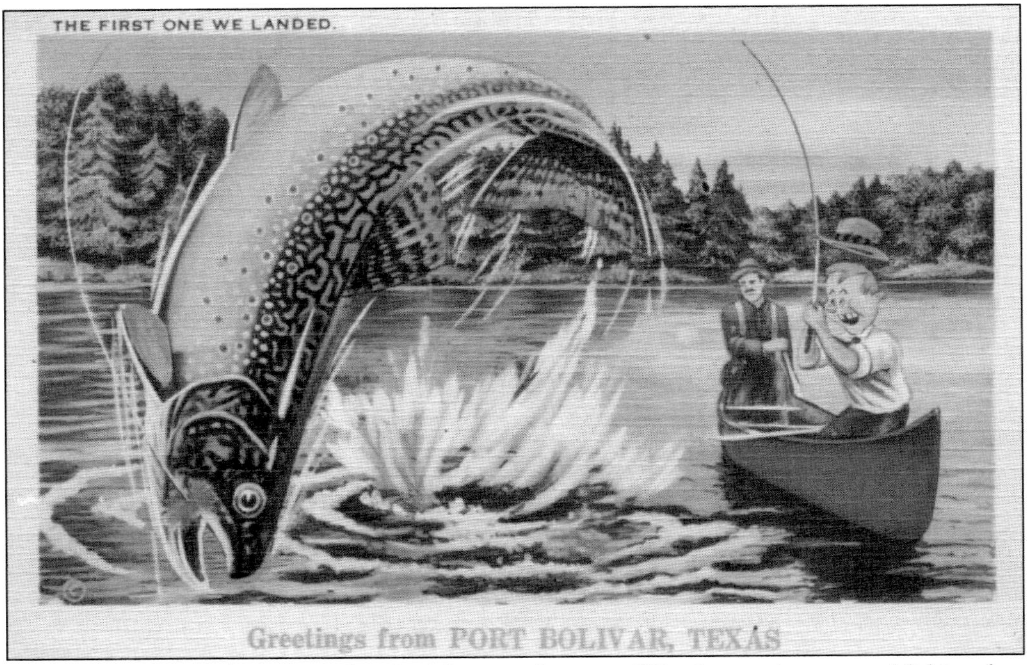

The Bolivar Peninsula is a paradise for fishing enthusiasts. Whether anglers are surf fishing, bay fishing, fishing from Rollover Pass, or off the jetties, the fish are always running. Rollover Pass is the most popular fishing hole on the peninsula. Almost any time of year, any time of day or night, people of all ages can be found pulling in the big one at Rollover. (Courtesy of Ralph Stenzel.)

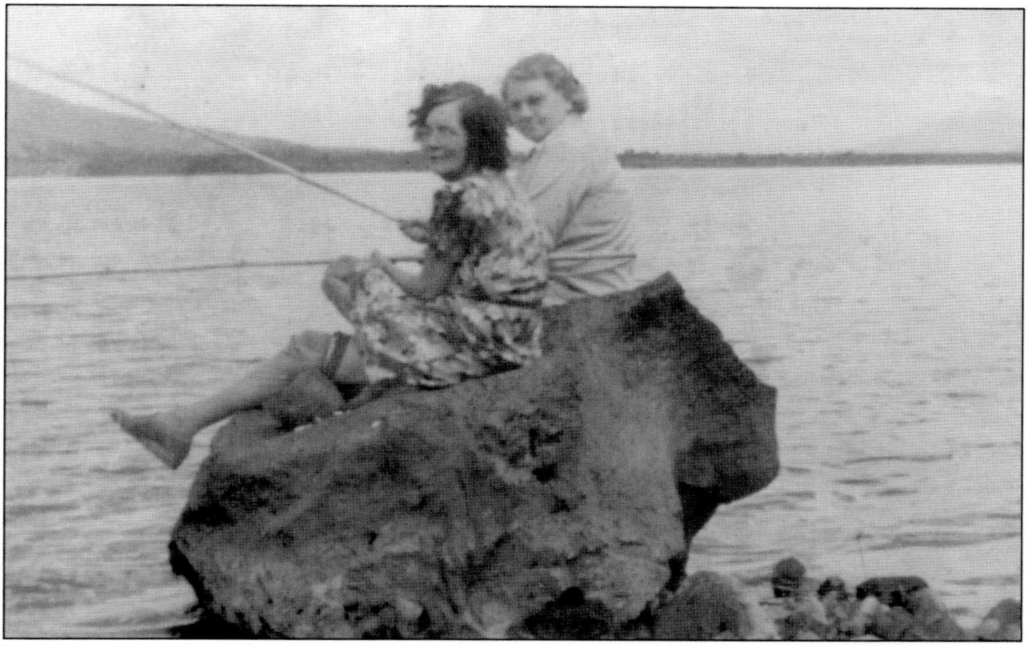

Jetty fishing is outstanding on the Bolivar Peninsula. Construction on the twin jetties began in 1874 to provide a deepwater channel to Galveston. Completed in 1898, the jetties are constructed of huge blocks of granite and serve as a paved walkway for the first 200 feet. The jetties provide an excellent platform for fishing and crabbing. Fishermen can continue walking out on the rocks for almost a mile in pursuit of their catch. Jetty fishing is particularly fabulous during the flounder run in the fall. (Courtesy of Elsie Devers.)

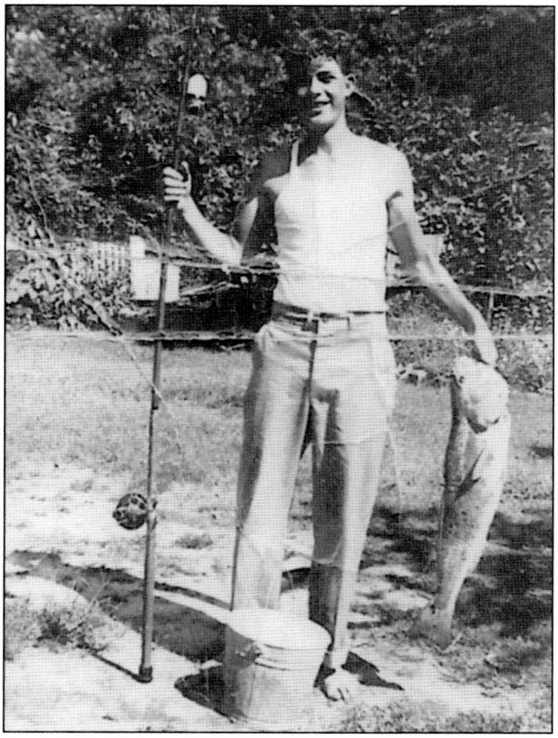

This fisherman is one of a multitude of folks who have spent countless carefree days fishing on the Bolivar Peninsula. Fishing is good all over the peninsula, but particularly at Rollover Pass, which is considered one of the premier fishing spots on the upper Texas coast. Rollover is free and easy to get to; no special equipment is necessary. And the camaraderie among fishermen at Rollover is great. (Courtesy of Terri Simpton.)

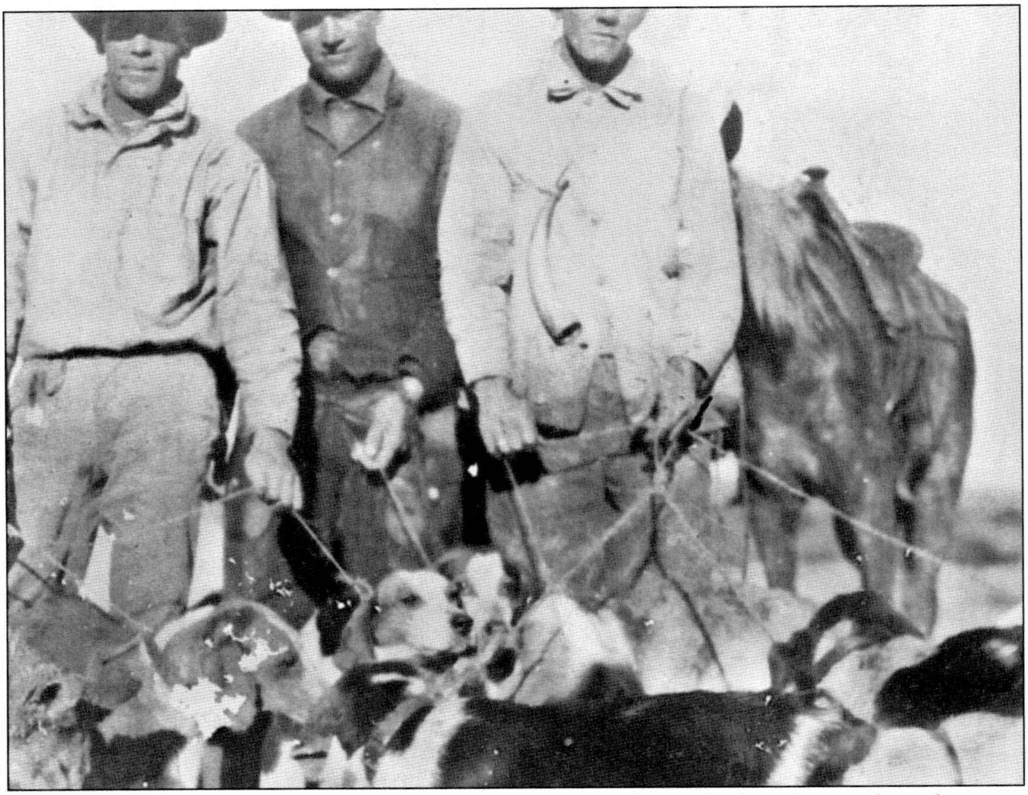

Hunting dove and waterfowl in the marshes of Bolivar Peninsula has been a popular pursuit for centuries. In early days on the peninsula, wild ducks and geese would come in flocks of thousands on cold rainy days. These unidentified hunters, pictured here around 1940, had a successful day of hunting. (Courtesy of Terri Simpton)

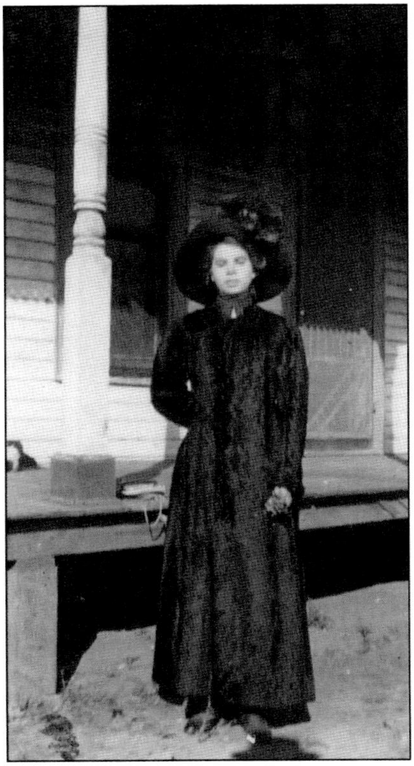

A beautiful Genevieve Kahla is pictured here in a long black coat. Family members are not sure if the coat is made of velvet, mink, or muskrat. What is known is that family members, and other Bolivar residents, trapped muskrats for extra cash. The animals were abundant in the coastal marshes of southeast Texas. During the early 1900s, High Island was a primary collection point for muskrat hides. (Courtesy of the Simpton family.)

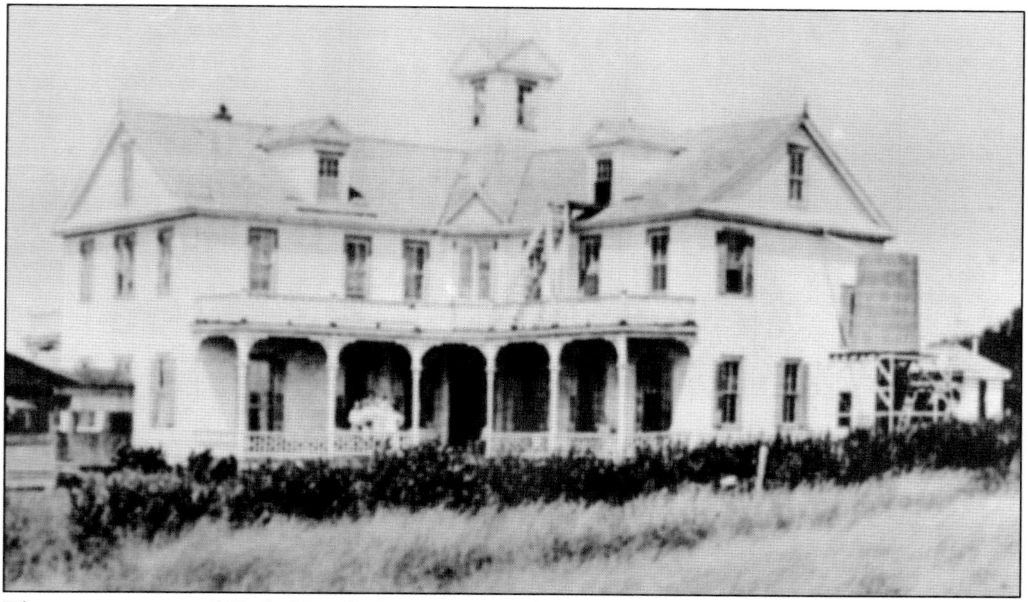

The construction of High Island's Sea View Hotel in 1897 by C.T. Cade marked the beginning of resort life on the Bolivar Peninsula. Fabulous parties, mule-drawn wagons to the beach, and mineral baths brought guests from Beaumont and across the state. Note the cupola on top, raised cistern, barn on the right rear, and dance pavilion on the left. The hotel had a balcony in front, and the one in the back overlooked the gulf. An early article in the *Beaumont Enterprise* describes the hotel as having "ornate chandeliers hung from the ballroom's 20-foot ceiling as couples swirled to Big Band music by 6-10 piece bands." (Courtesy of Melanie Wiggins.)

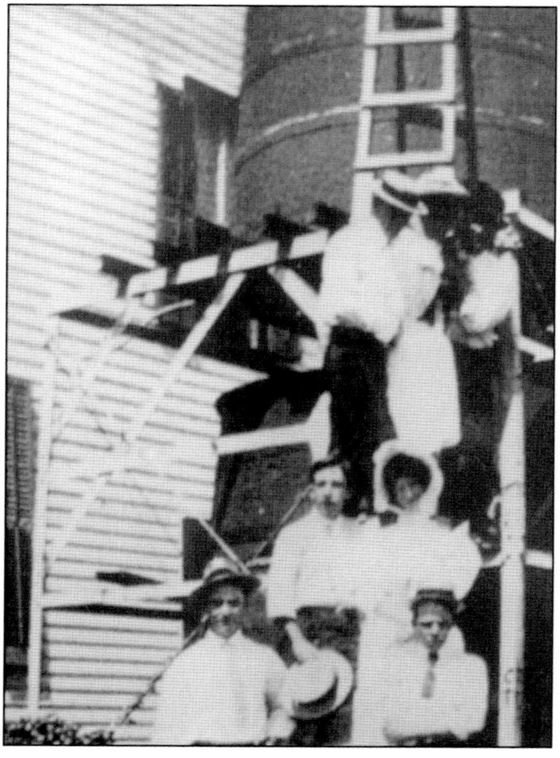

The group posing next to the Sea View cistern sometime between 1897 and 1900 includes Kitty Cade (at bottom), Margaret Cade (above Kitty), and other friends. The 1900 storm ended the golden age of this kind of luxurious tourism on the peninsula, though the hotel was not destroyed. The Sea View was subsequently the headquarters for oilmen during the oil boom and is rumored to have been taken over by the Coast Guard during World War II to house its "horse patrol," which watched for enemy submarines in the Gulf of Mexico. (Courtesy of Melanie Wiggins.)

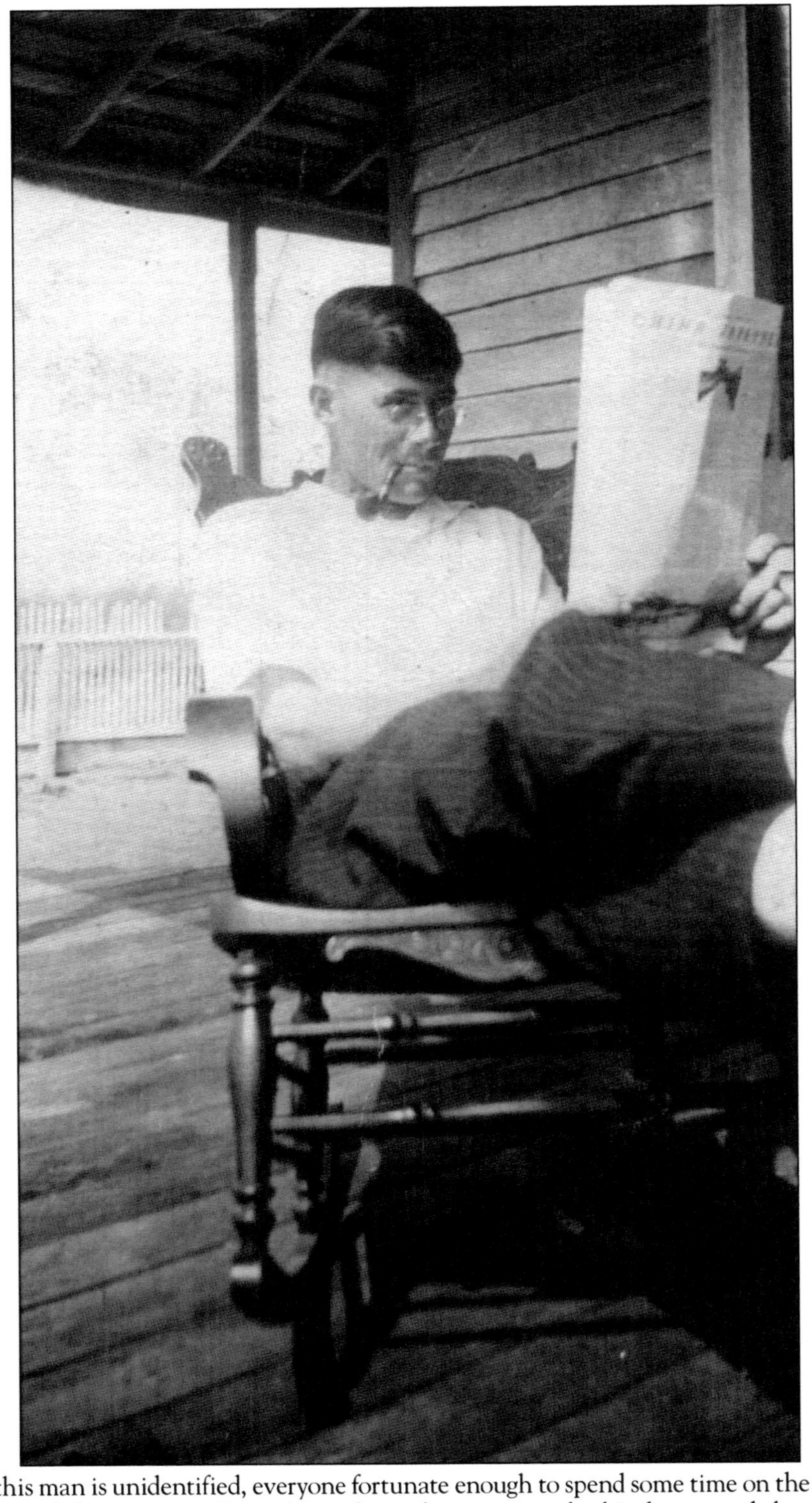

Though this man is unidentified, everyone fortunate enough to spend some time on the peninsula is familiar with his position. Something about the sea air and a big front porch lends itself to relaxing and reading in a rocking chair. (Courtesy of the Simpton family.)

Five

TRANSPORTATION

BY LAND AND BY SEA

Like everything else on the Bolivar Peninsula, getting around is just a little bit different and exciting because of the terrain, location, and climate (including some very intense hurricanes). Travel around the peninsula has always been an adventure.

Traveling to and from a barrier formation naturally requires a trip across the water—either by boat or bridge. The history of Bolivar Peninsula travel includes horse-drawn carriages, pirate ships, passenger trains, ferries, sailboats transporting watermelons across the bay, ferryboats, and Model Ts.

One of the events that made the Bolivar Peninsula a popular tourist destination was the advent of the Gulf & Interstate Railroad (G&I). Many stories have been told about the train and its contribution to building the tourism industry on the peninsula. Of course, the train also played an important role in the growth of industry on the peninsula.

Like much of the population of America in the mid-20th century, Bolivar Peninsula residents had a love affair with the automobile. As would be expected, many families had their photographs taken with a prized automobile as a backdrop. Service stations, usually attached to a small grocery store, were meeting places for residents. Several of those facilities are explored in this chapter.

And finally, in this chapter, the history of the intracoastal canal (the Gulf Intracoastal Waterway, GIWW), sometimes referred to as the 1,000-mile miracle, is examined. From the early settlers who recognized the advantages of inland waterways to the vast network of protected waterways that now exist, the intracoastal canal has been an important element in areas of national defense, industry, fishing, and recreational boating. Running the length of the peninsula and all the way to the Northeast, the Intracoastal Waterway is an integral part of the history of the Bolivar Peninsula.

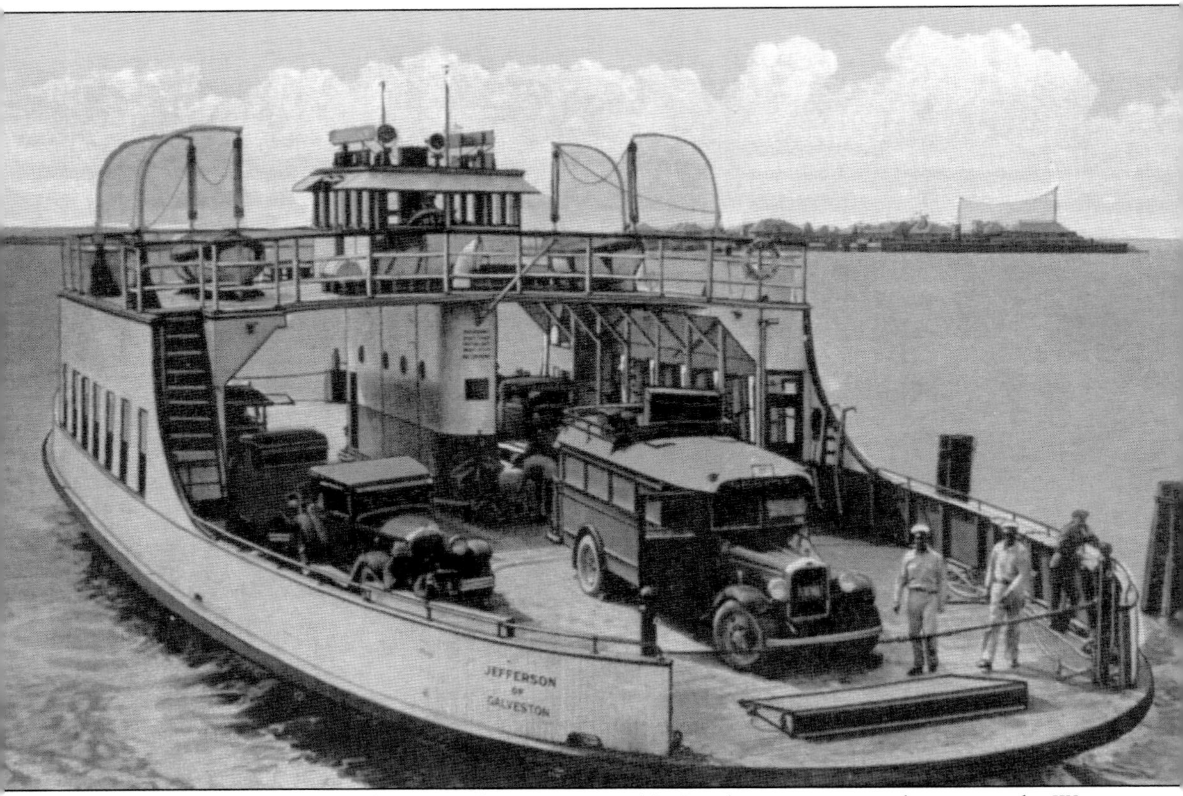

The Bolivar ferry marks the start of many memorable family vacations on the peninsula. Warm gulf breezes, squawking seagulls, and dancing dolphins set the scene for a fun-filled, sun-warmed time on the beach. (Courtesy of Ralph Stenzel.)

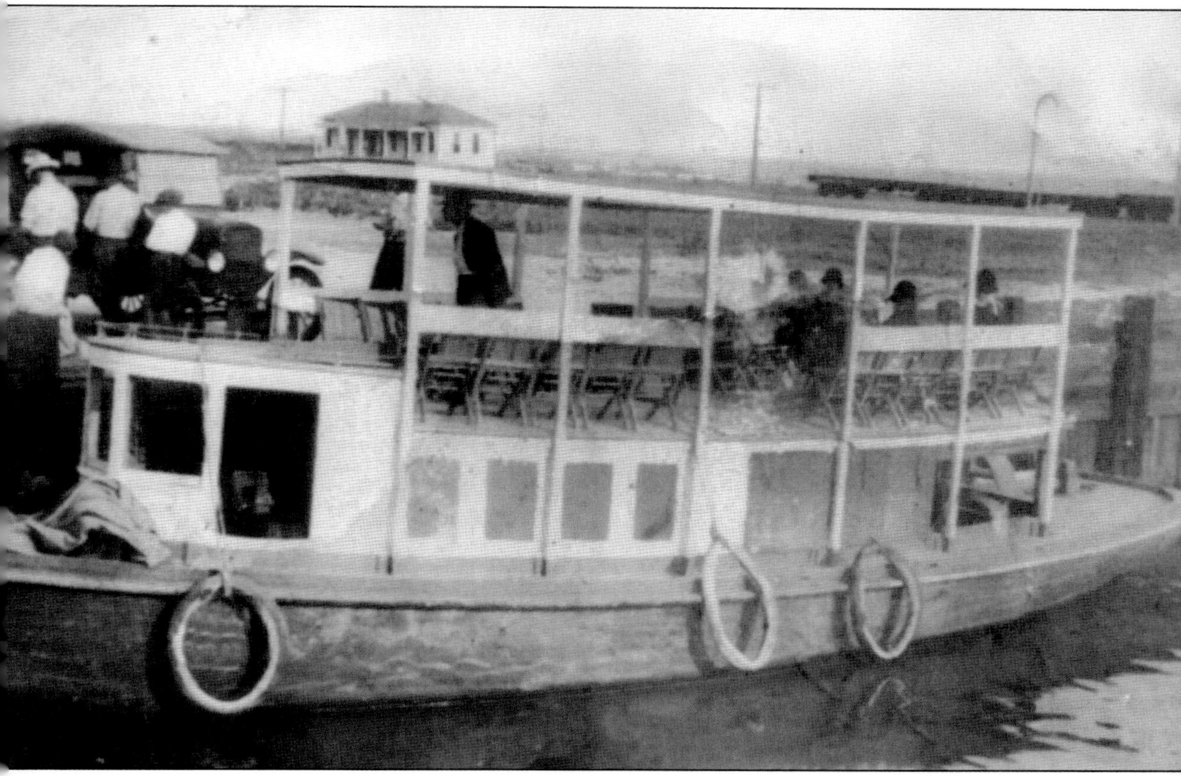

According to the Texas Department of Transportation, ferry service has been a part of the Texas transportation system since the 19th century, when the *Tarpon* began operating from Galveston. The first regularly scheduled ferry service between Bolivar and Galveston was established in 1929 by a private company. Pictured here is the *Silver King*, in an image dated "before 1932." Notice the single automobile, a Model T, on the top deck and the folding chairs on the deck beside it. The *Silver King* and the *Pelican*, both primarily passenger ferries, delivered bread and mail on certain days. (Courtesy of the Simpton family.)

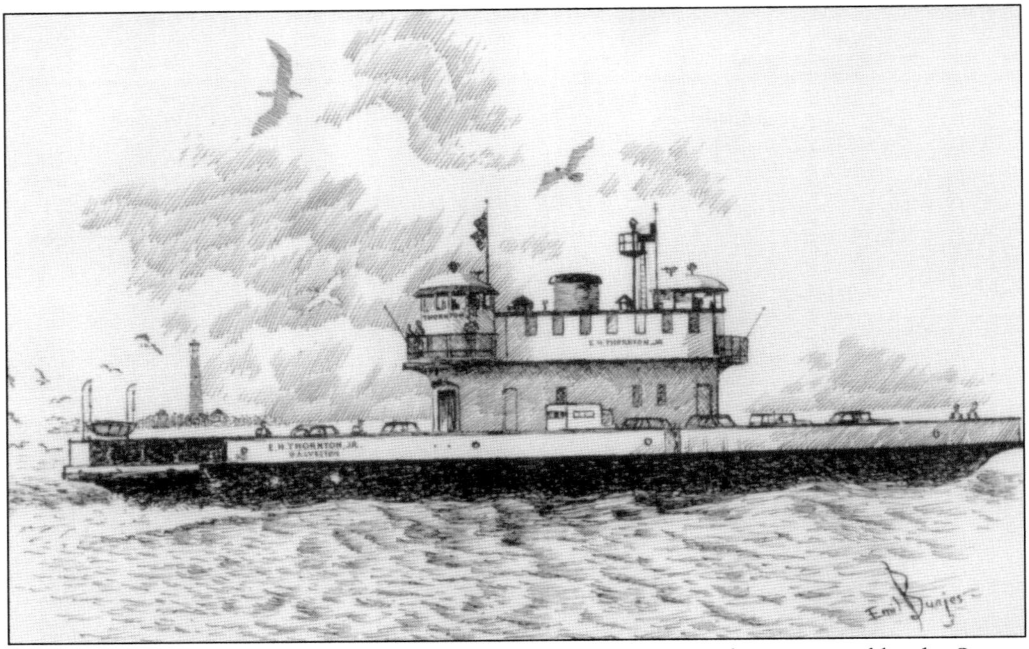

The first ferry operated by the State of Texas left Port Bolivar on July 1, 1934. For a brief time, to ease congestion, there was a 25¢ fee for the ride. However, the ferry has been operated toll-free since 1949. The Texas Department of Transportation reports a record-breaking day for ferry travel on July 3, 1994, when 43,472 people boarded the ferry in Galveston for the 2.7-mile trip across to Bolivar. (Courtesy of the Galveston County Museum.)

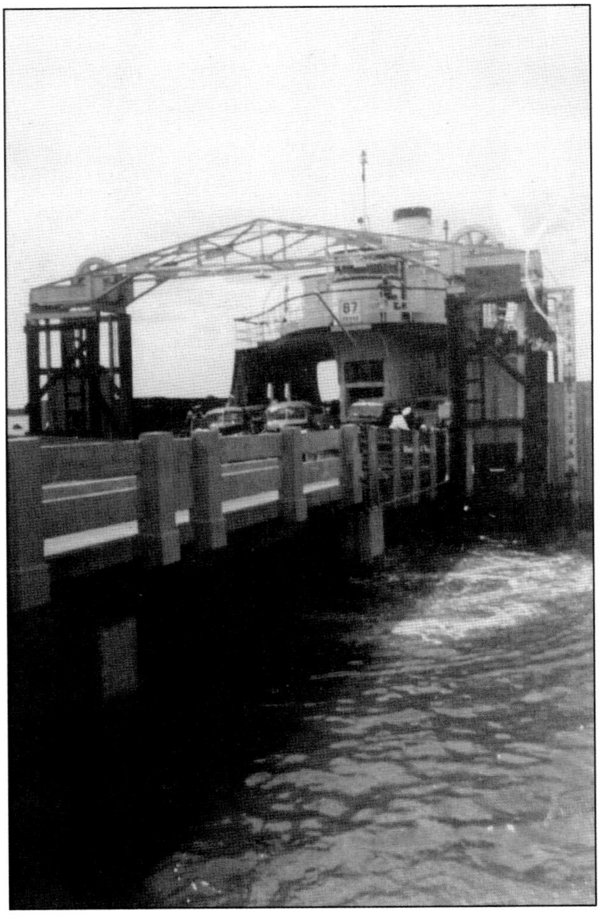

The Galveston–Port Bolivar ferry is the bridge between two segments of State Highway 87. The free ferry service provided by TxDOT is the only way motorists can cross the waterway between Bolivar Peninsula and Galveston Island. The 2.7-mile trip takes approximately 18 minutes to cross one of the busiest waterways in the world. (Courtesy of Galveston County Museum.)

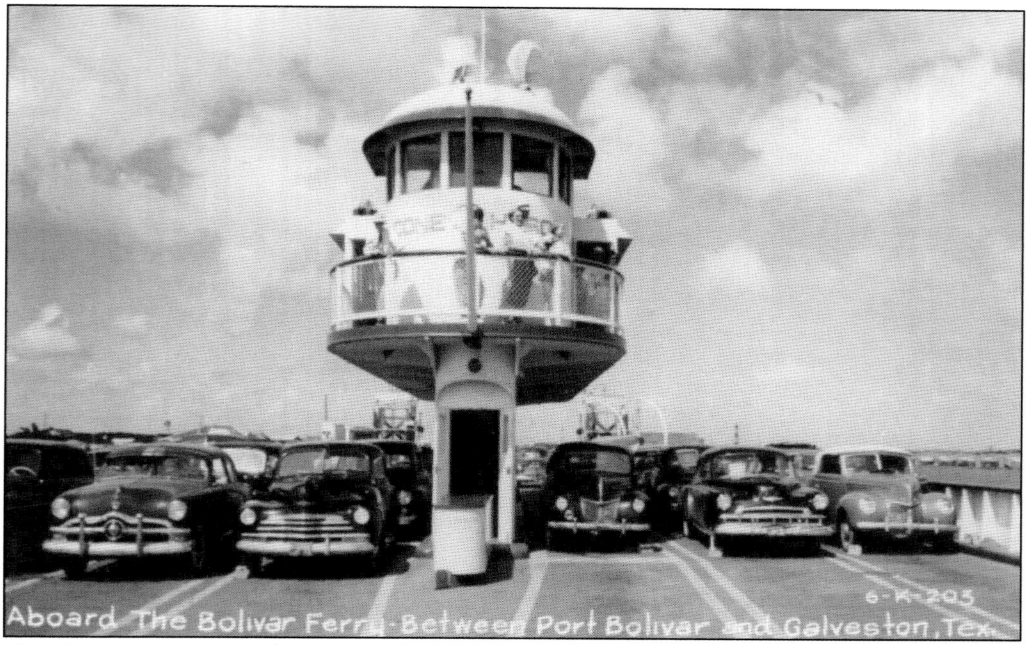

The ferry system originally consisted of three vessels—*Cone Johnson*, *E.H. Thornton Jr.*, and *R. S. Sterling.* Currently, the vessels are *Robert C. Lanier, Gibb Gilchrist, Dewitt C. Greer, Ray Stoker, Jr., and Robert H. Dedmam.* The newest ferry, *John W. Johnson*, made its maiden voyage on Wednesday, August 1, 2012. All of the boats are named after former Texas Transportation Commission members, except one. The *Gibb Gilchrist* was named for a man who served as state highway engineer twice during his career. (Courtesy of Ralph Stenzel.)

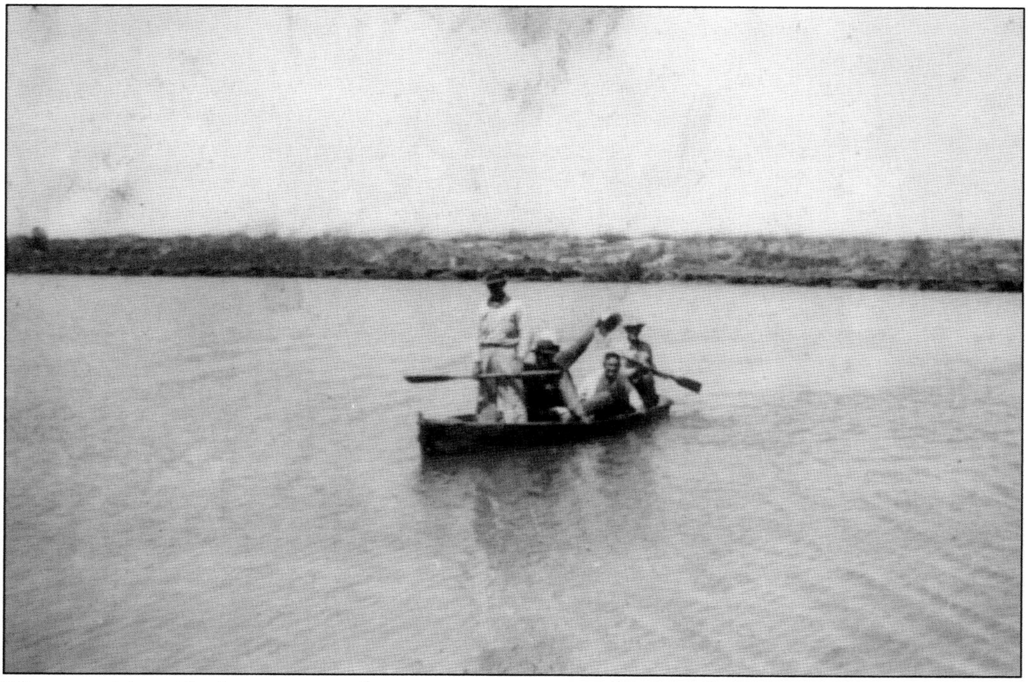
These unidentified men are taking a canoe across the canal in 1930. (Courtesy of the Simpton family.)

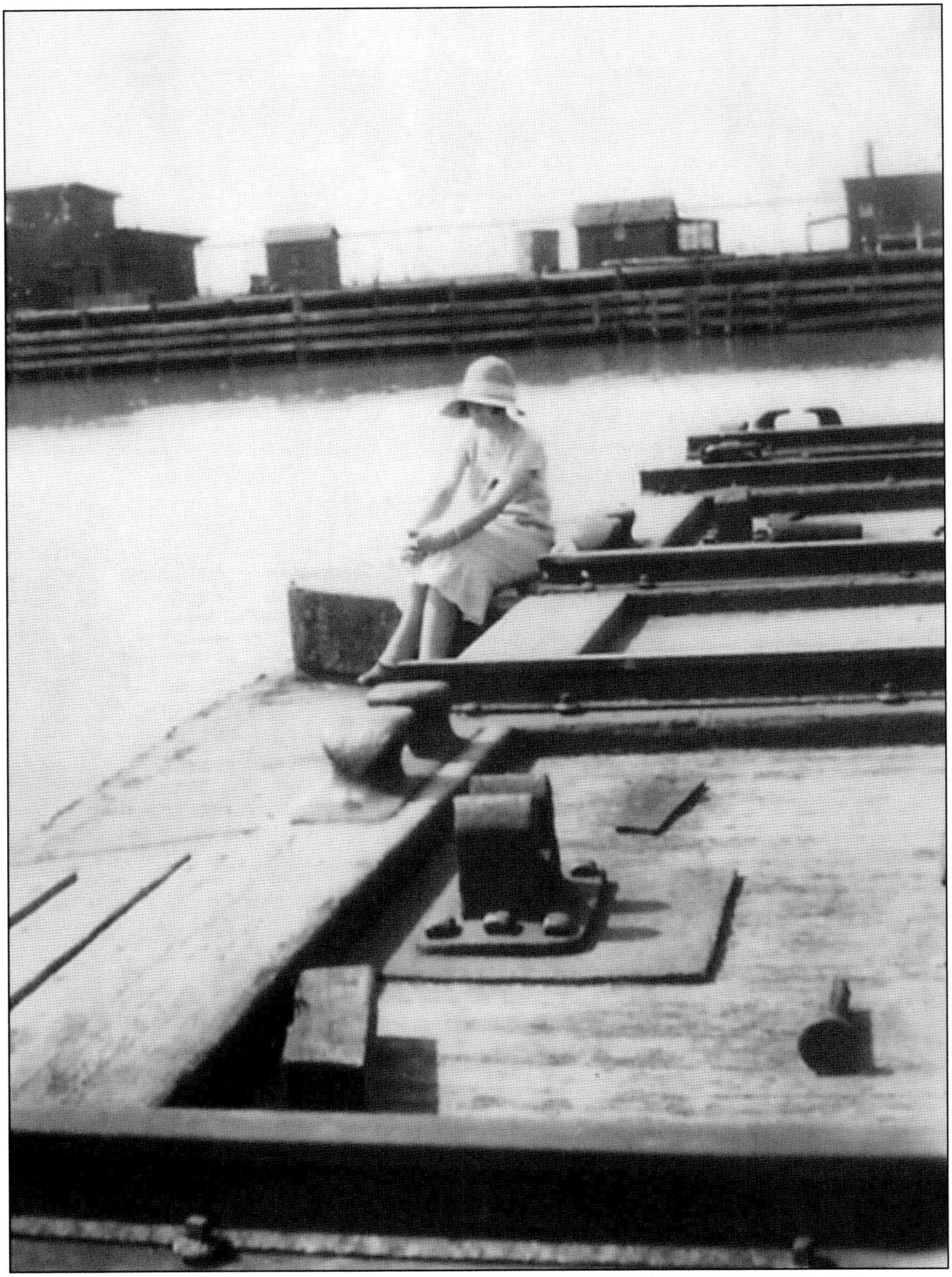

The romance of the rails is a part of the history of America. Nowhere is this notion of romance, the colorful life on the move, more evident than in the stories of the railway on the Bolivar Peninsula. Created in 1894, the Gulf & Interstate Railway company was the first railroad on the peninsula. The first excursion on the railroad is described in wonderful detail by George E. Smith in an article for the newspaper. In this photograph, Myra Bouse sits on the rail tracks at the far west end of the Bolivar Peninsula. (Courtesy of the Simpton family.)

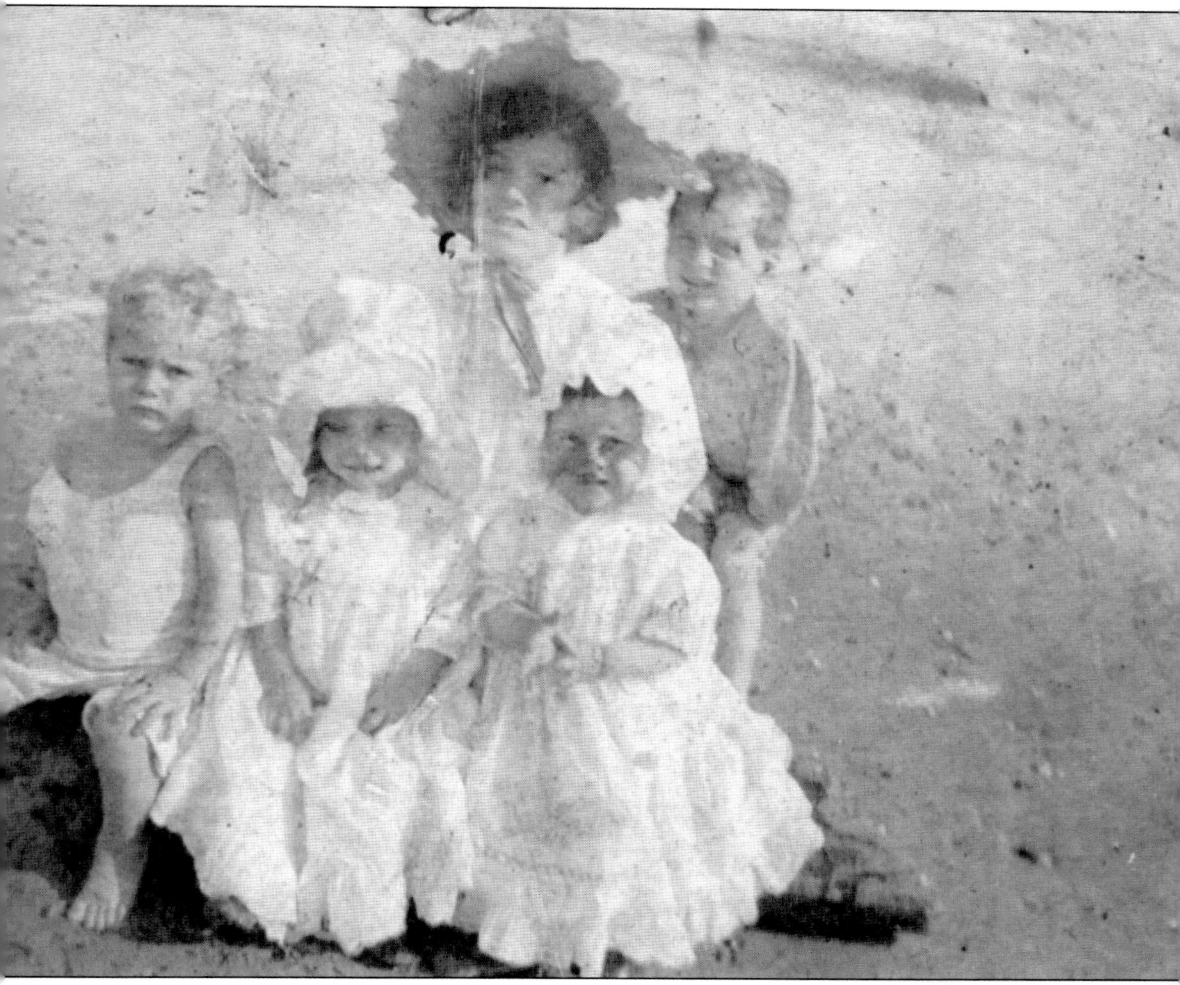

The first documented trip on the G&I from Beaumont took two hours. The passengers enjoyed three brand-new cars. Happy passengers were reported to have been treated to a feast of barbecued meat, homemade bread, sour pickles, catsup, and George Smith's famous mineral water. This family is pictured having a picnic on the beach. (Courtesy of Elsie Devers.)

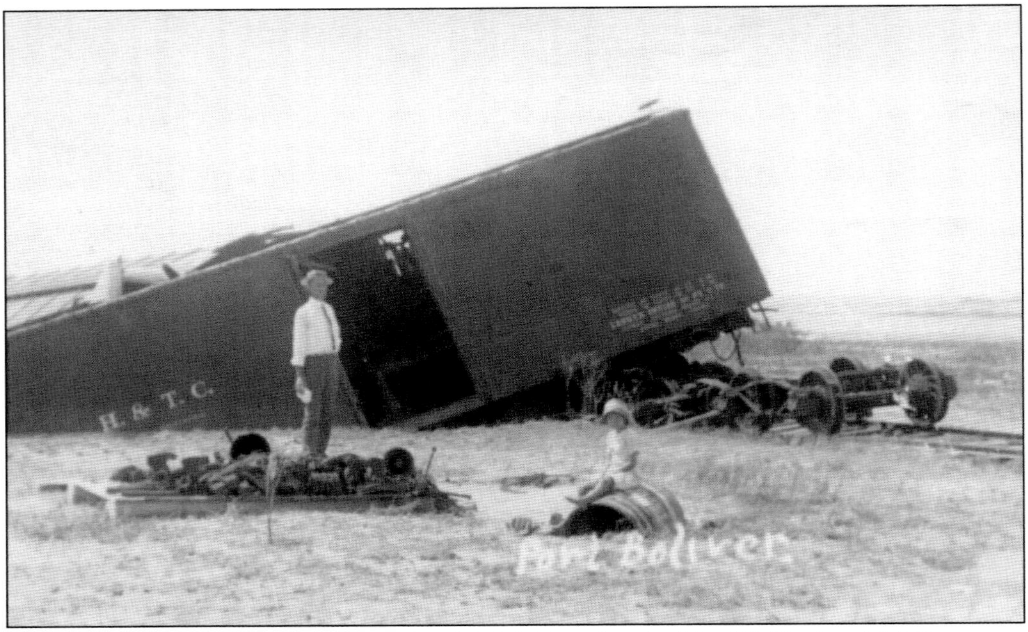

A devastating hurricane hit on September 8, 1900. Train No. 1 of the G&I Railroad left Beaumont at 7:00 a.m. that day to make the 85-mile run to Port Bolivar and was caught in the storm. The 28 miles of track between High Island and Port Bolivar were washed away. Beaumont, Galveston, and Port Arthur held bake sales, dances, and concerts to raise the funds needed to reconstruct the track wiped out by the storm. (Courtesy of Ralph Stenzel.)

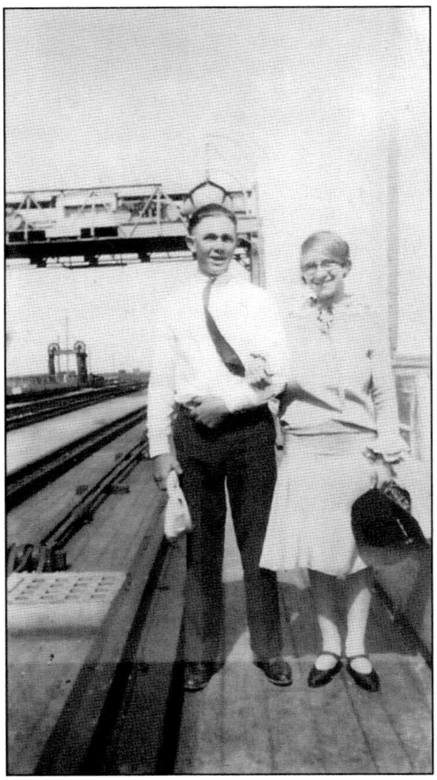

At 7:00 a.m. on September 24, 1903, Train No. 1 once again pulled out of Beaumont, headed for Port Bolivar. It resumed the run started three years earlier. Gulf & Interstate officials honored any ticket from the 1900 run that had not been collected. About 12 of the original passengers showed up still carrying their 1900 tickets. The daily passenger service was operated until 1930. Operations were then reduced to three times per week. At that time, service was "mixed." Passenger cars and cattle-shipping pens, along with flag stops (allowing passengers on the train with the wave of a flag from the side of the track) were included. This combination made for a very irregular train schedule. The 27 miles of rail between Port Bolivar and High Island was abandoned in 1942. Years later, this photograph was taken of Jack and Myra Simpton on a rail barge off Old Frenchtown Road. (Courtesy of the Simpton family.)

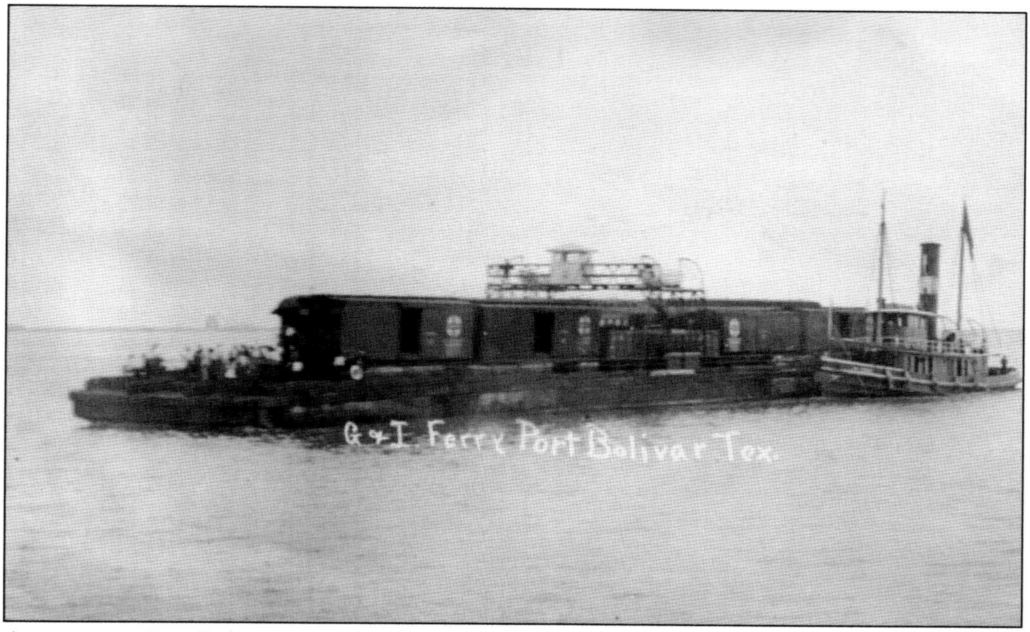

At one time, Port Bolivar was a thriving port. The Gulf & Interstate Railroad was built in 1896 to connect Galveston and Beaumont. Port Bolivar took in cargo ships and loaded freight for transport on the G&I. This photograph of the train barge was taken in 1911. (Courtesy of Ralph Stenzel.)

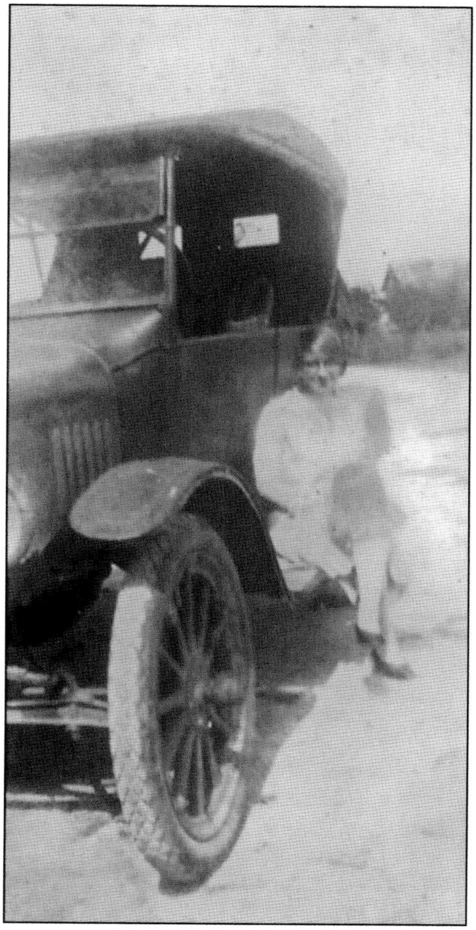

Myra Bouse sits on the running board of the family automobile. In those days, the beach was wide and smooth. Youngsters would frequently drive the length of the peninsula on the beach all the way to the cutoff at High Island. (Courtesy of the Simpton family.)

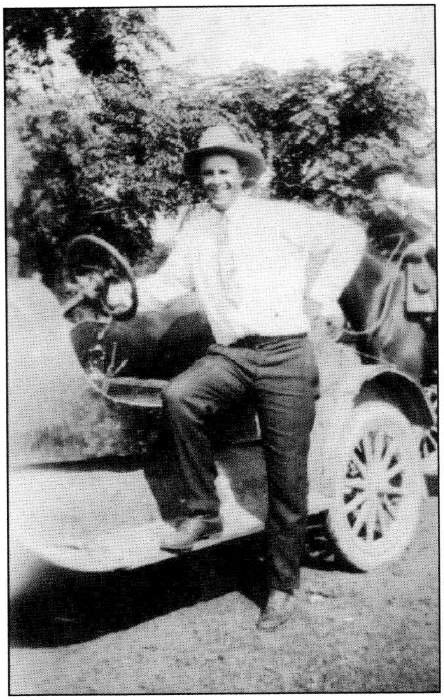

This proud motorist poses with his automobile. Notice the interested horseman behind the vehicle. (Courtesy of the Simpton family.)

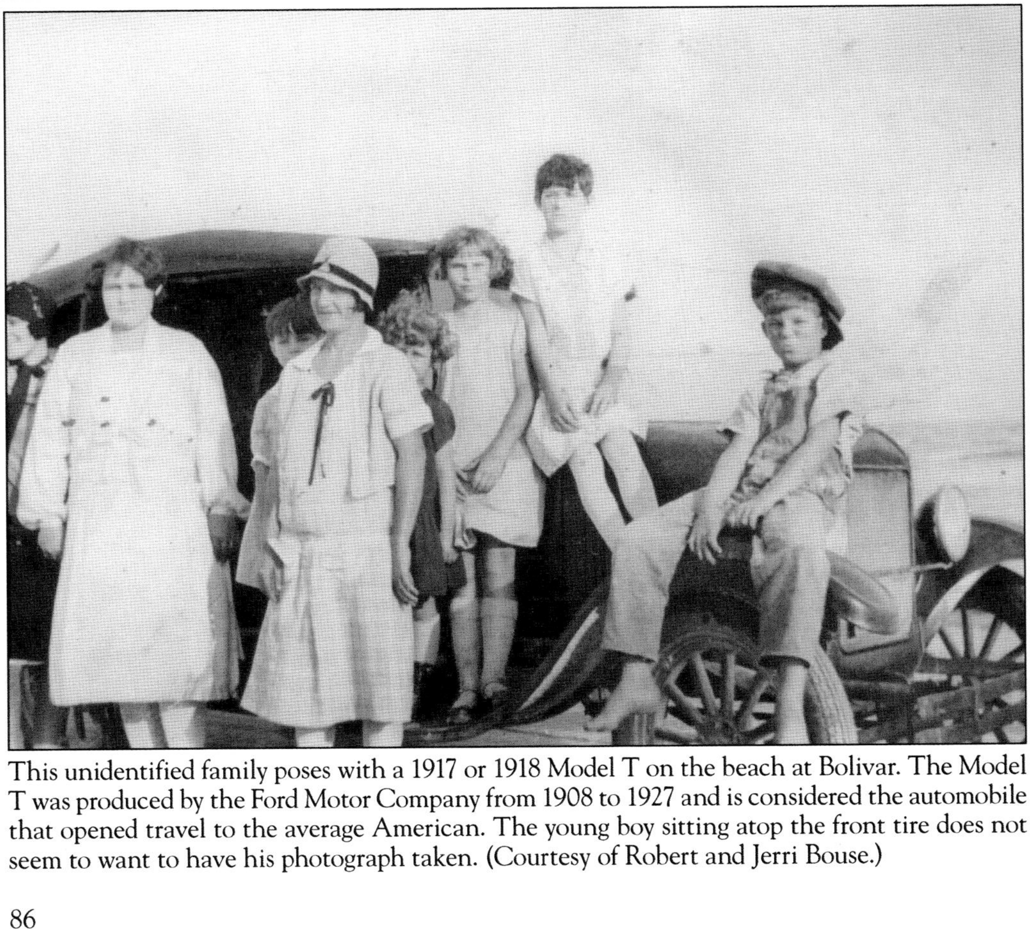

This unidentified family poses with a 1917 or 1918 Model T on the beach at Bolivar. The Model T was produced by the Ford Motor Company from 1908 to 1927 and is considered the automobile that opened travel to the average American. The young boy sitting atop the front tire does not seem to want to have his photograph taken. (Courtesy of Robert and Jerri Bouse.)

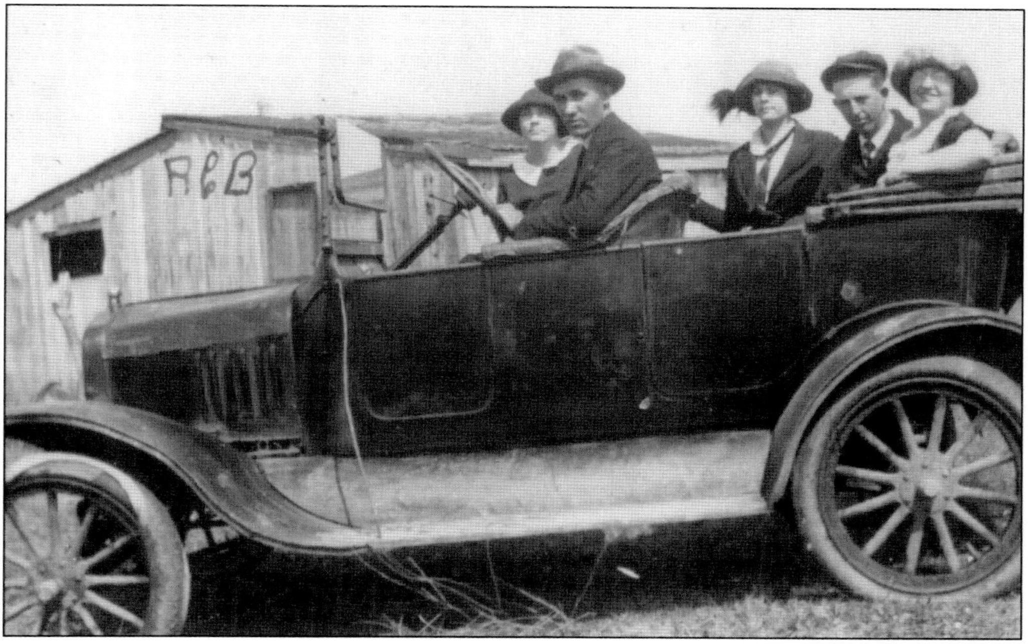

These passengers, dressed up possibly for church, are shown in front of property owned by Raymond Clarence Bouse (note the letters *RCB* painted on the barn). (Courtesy of Robert and Jerri Bouse.)

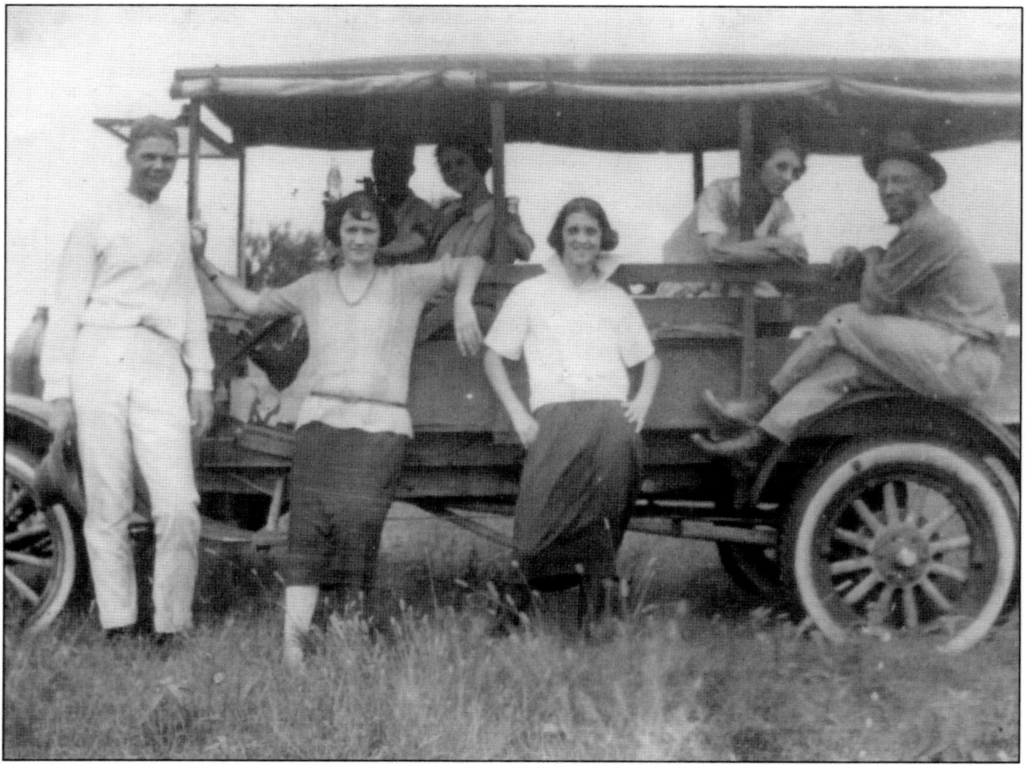

This group of vacationers is pictured with an automobile just perfect for riding on the beach. (Courtesy of Robert and Jerri Bouse.)

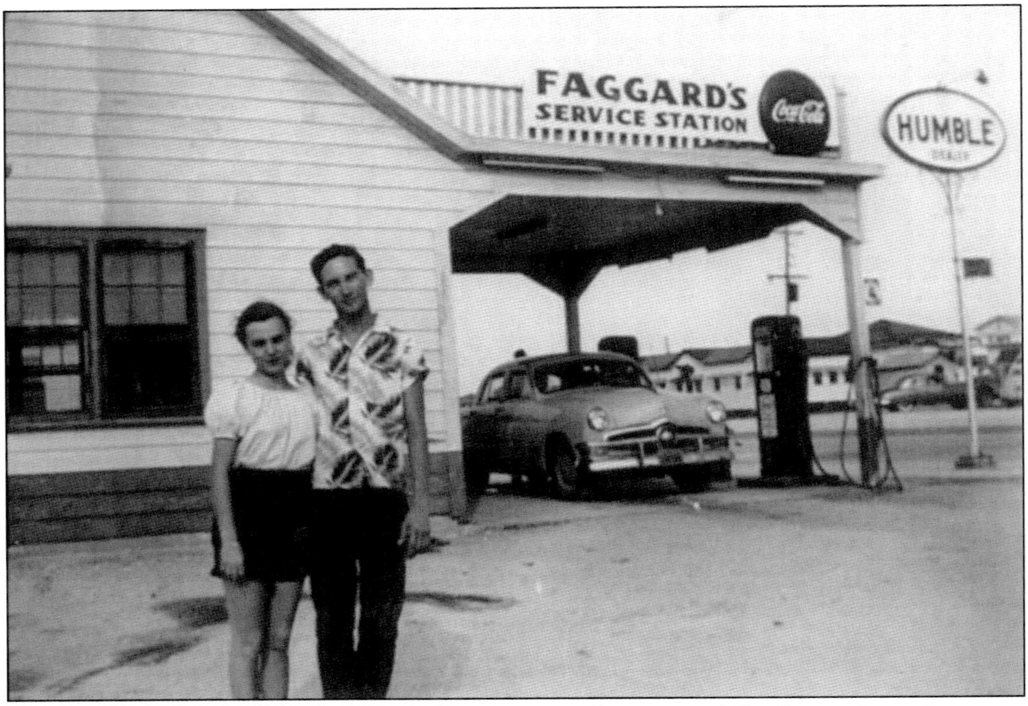

By 1930, more than half the families in America owned an automobile. Gas stations, tire stores, and repair centers began to appear to service the new trend. The Faggard's Gas Station in Gilchrist was one of the first to offer these services on the peninsula. Pictured here are Blaine Brigance and Ann Faggard, daughter of the owner of Faggard's Service Station. (Courtesy of Blaine Brigance.)

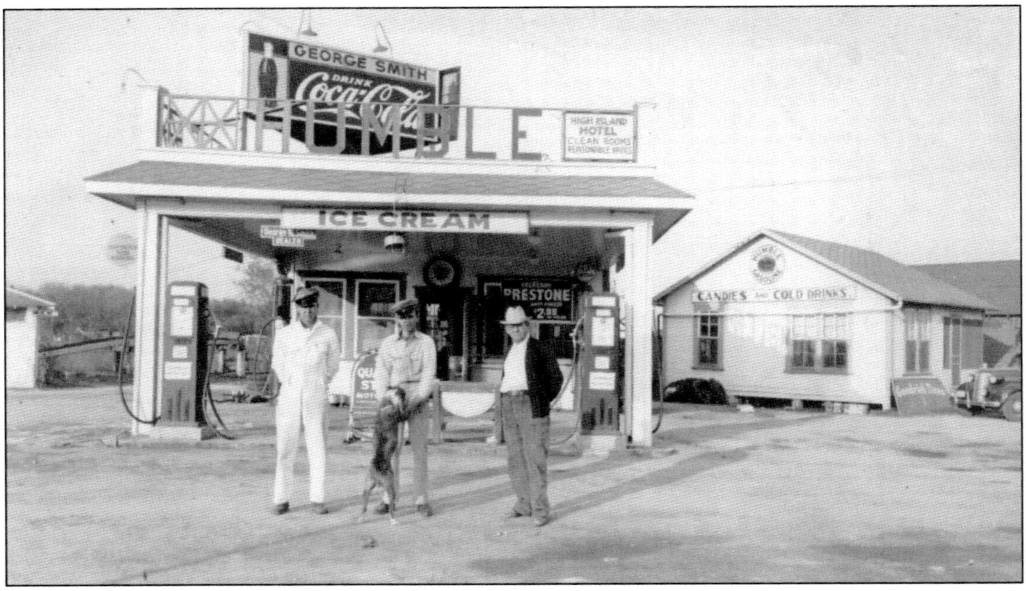

George W. Smith's Humble Station, located in High Island, is pictured here. Notice the attendant uniforms worn by the men on the left and in the middle. These were the days when filling station attendants performed services other than just accepting payment. Tasks usually included pumping fuel, cleaning the windshield, and checking the oil level. (Courtesy of Blaine Briggance.)

In this photograph, Myra Bouse sits at the gas pump at the Bouse Store. (Courtesy of the Simpton family.)

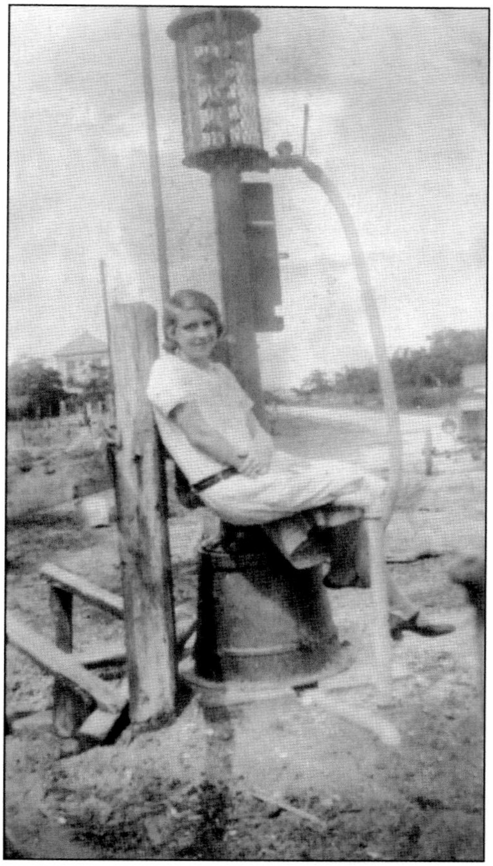

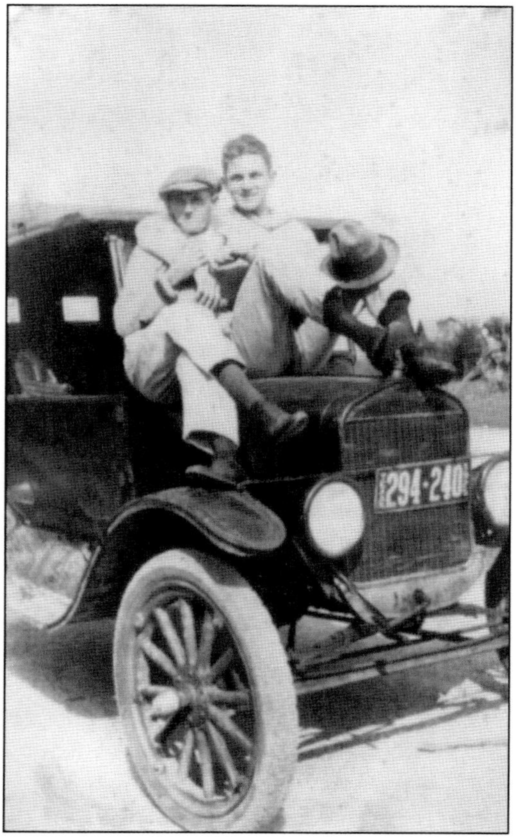

Benny Simpton (left) is pictured enjoying a day on the open road. (Courtesy of Simpton family.)

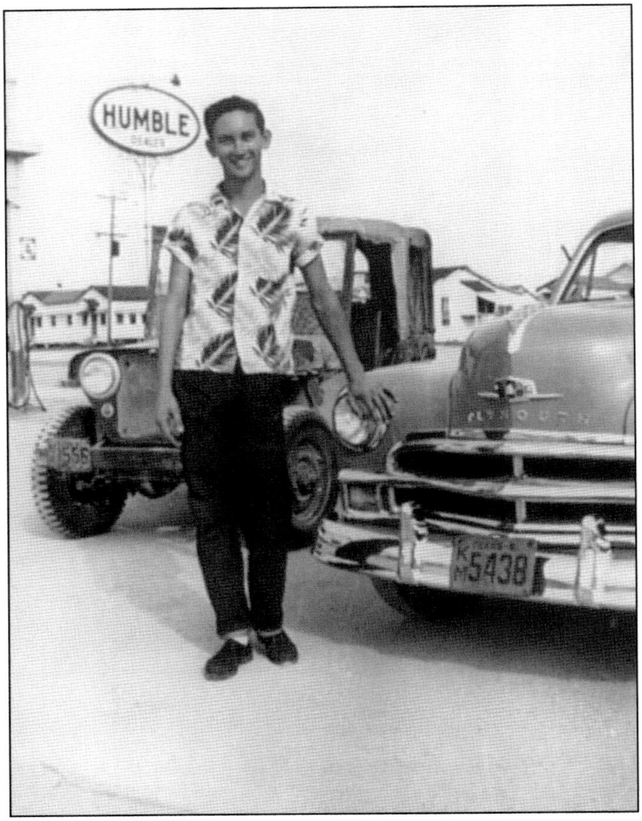

Blaine Brigance poses with a Plymouth around 1950. (Courtesy of Blaine Brigance.)

Five years after Texas was admitted to the union in 1845, coastal business interests began to connect portions of the state's coastline by dredging links between the natural bays, lakes, rivers, and bayous. The original canal ranged in depth from three to six feet. (Courtesy of the Library of Congress.)

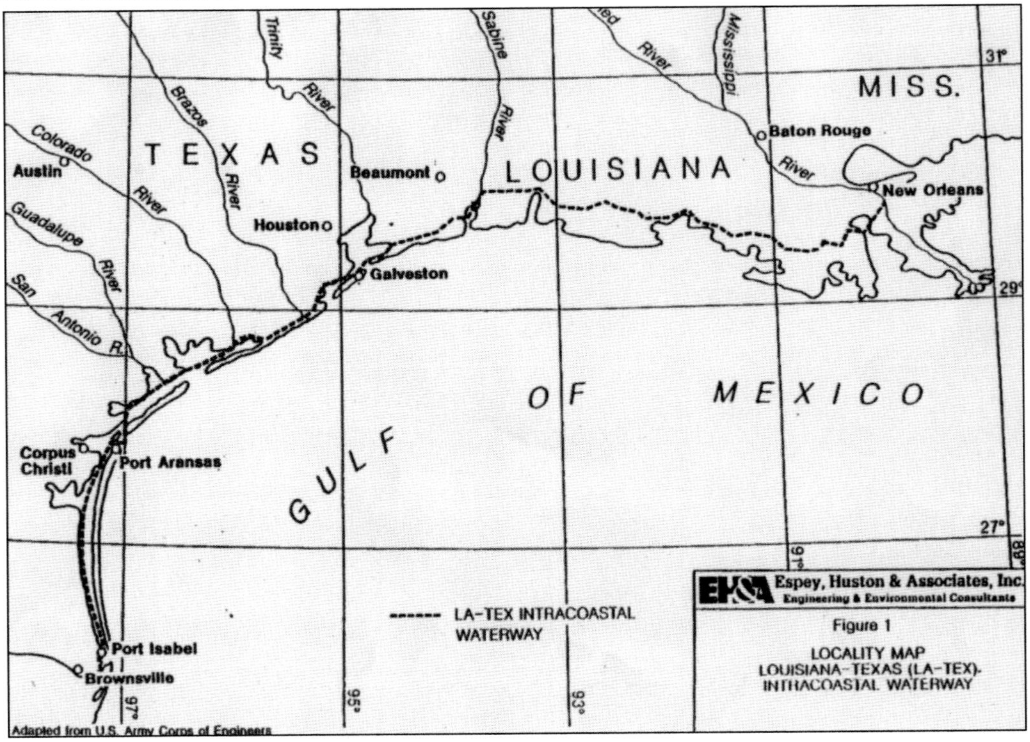

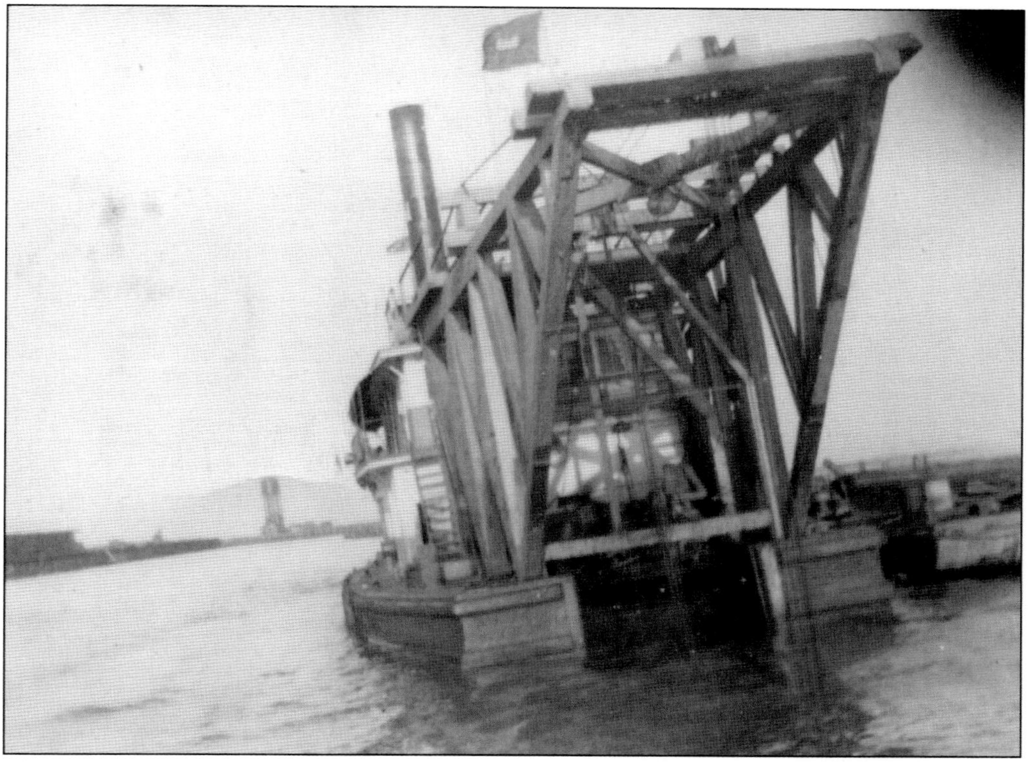

The Rivers and Harbors Act (1873) was the start of the development of the intracoastal waterway. This act appropriated funds for a survey to "connect the inland waters along the margin of the Gulf of Mexico." One of the initial functions of the canal was to provide protected inland transportation of goods and troops during World War II. Pictured here is a dredge used in 1927. (Courtesy of Robert and Jerri Bouse.)

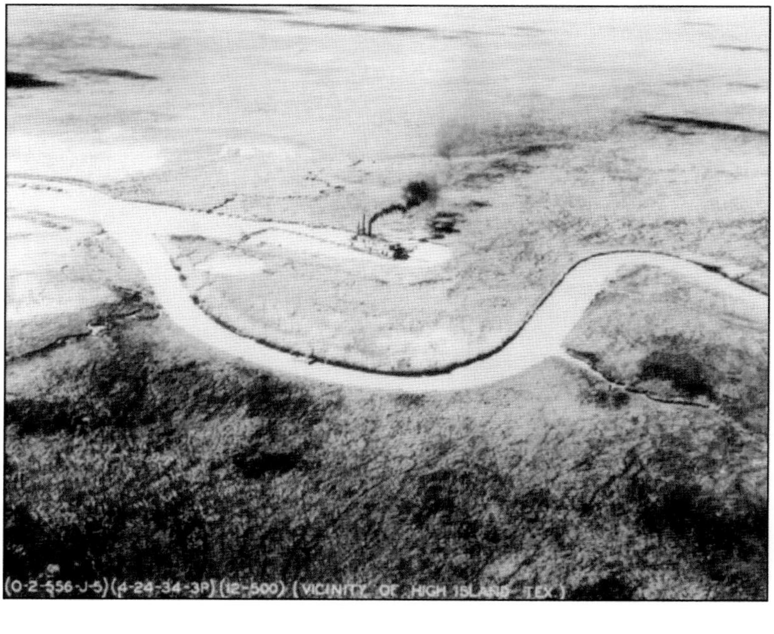

The GIWW has since evolved into a multipurpose waterway used for fishing, skiing, sightseeing, and protected water routes for travelers along the coast. Its commercial uses include the movement of cargo, harvesting of fish and shellfish, and servicing the coastal oil and gas industry. (Courtesy of US Army Corps of Engineers.)

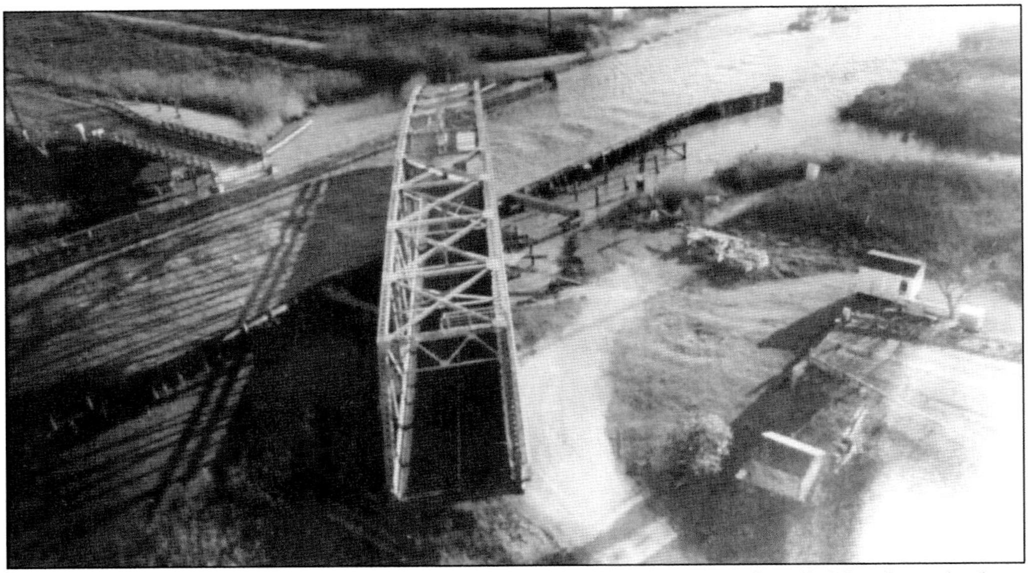

The swinging bridge over the intracoastal canal between Winnie and High Island was built in 1933 in conjunction with planning efforts for the construction of the New Orleans–to–Corpus Christi portion of the Louisiana-Texas (La-Tex) Intracoastal Waterway (now called the Gulf Intracoastal Waterway, GIWW). The swinging bridge was replaced with the current bridge in 1978. It is reported, however, that for several years after the swinging bridge was replaced, students at the High Island school were still using that bridge as an excuse for their tardiness to school. (Courtesy of the Library of Congress.)

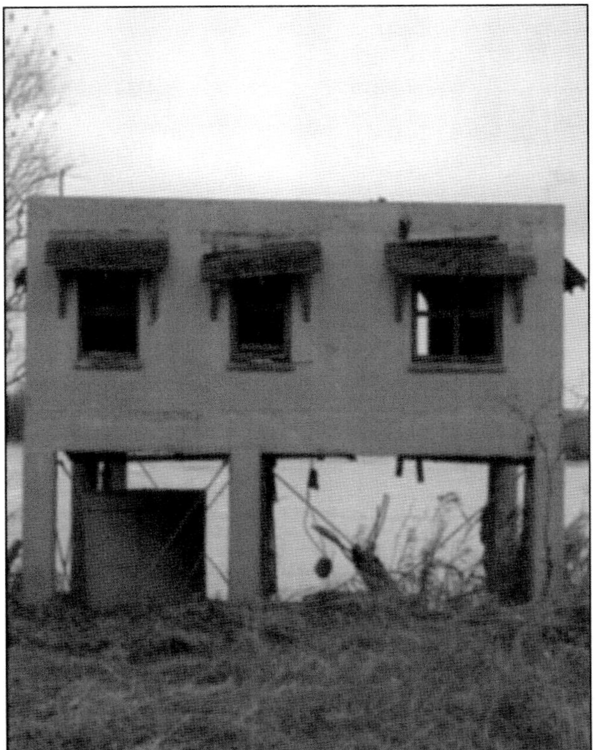

The High Island bridge tender's station and residence was built in 1933 to house engineering personnel who operated the swing bridge at the Gulf & Interstate Railway Company's crossing of Mud Bayou near High Island, Texas. From their perch, resident engineers coordinated the railway bridge's movement to allow for safe passage of commercial, military, and civilian vessels traveling along the waterway east- and westbound from Beaumont and Galveston. The men who worked on the bridges during World War II were plane spotters. They searched the skies with binoculars to make sure no enemy planes sneaked in from across the gulf. Currently, the Gulf Intracoastal Waterway (GIWW) is the nation's third-busiest waterway, with the Texas portion handling over 58 percent of the traffic. (Courtesy of the Library of Congress.)

Six

Teaching and Preaching

Schools and Churches

Regular church attendance is a part of life to many on the peninsula. Churchgoers report that church provides a social as well as a spiritual outlet. The churches also provide important benevolent services on the peninsula by contributing to local food distribution and other charitable causes.

The peninsula offers many religious options. There are about a dozen churches from Port Bolivar to High Island. Before 1915, a minister would come on the train and hold meetings in homes. For many years, there was a single church building in Port Bolivar. One Sunday, the Baptist circuit rider would hold services, the next week, the Methodist, then the Pentecostal. Most of the parishioners attended all services. The same shared experience took place in High Island, with Methodists, Baptists, and Pentecostals sharing a space for many years.

This neighborly tradition has continued through the years when hurricanes have damaged different church buildings. Congregations join together, opening their places of worship to one another in times of need. It is the Bolivar way.

The children on the Bolivar Peninsula can choose to attend school in the Galveston Independent School District that includes Crenshaw Elementary and Middle School and Ball High School on Galveston Island. Another choice is the High Island School in the High Island Independent School District, which offers prekindergarten through the 12th grade. Both options provide small class sizes, excellent teachers, and a small-town school experience for the children.

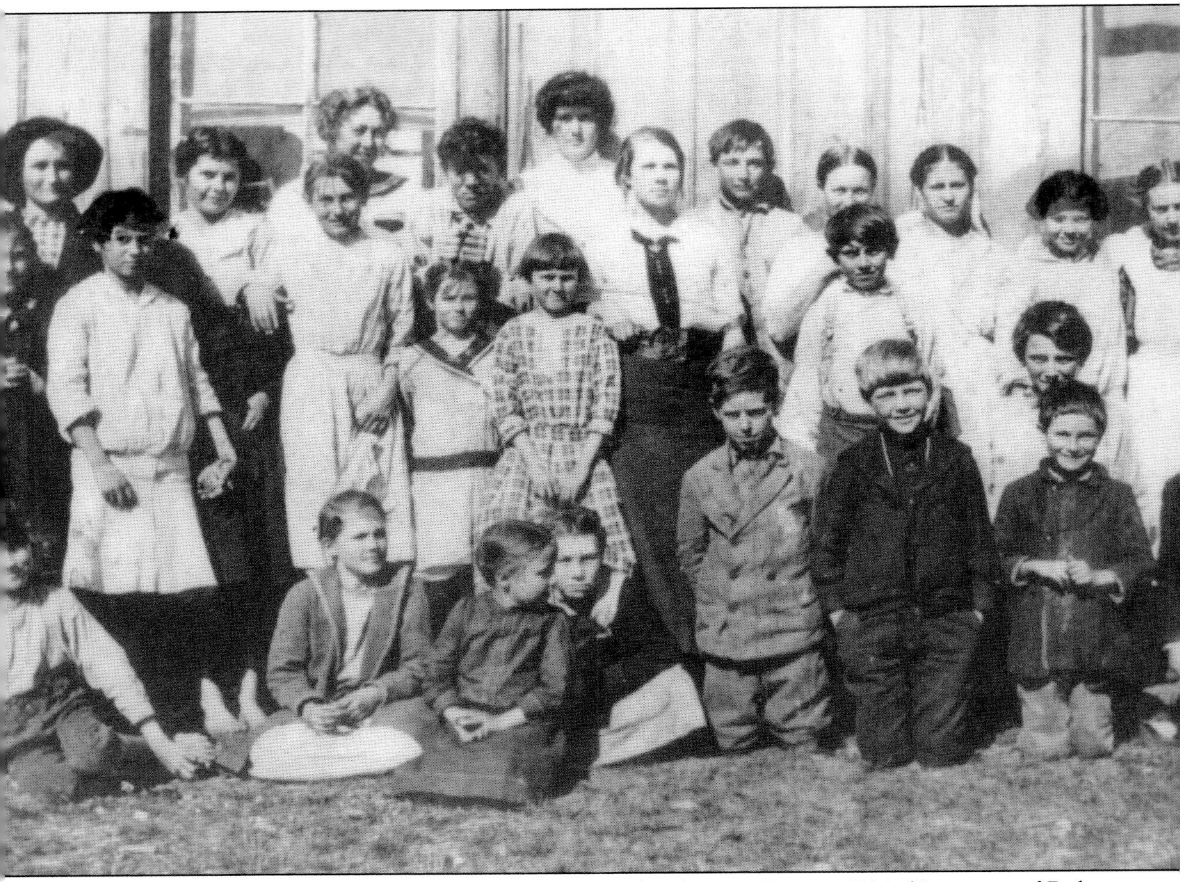

This photograph of the students at the Patton School was taken in 1914. (Courtesy of Robert and Jerri Bouse.)

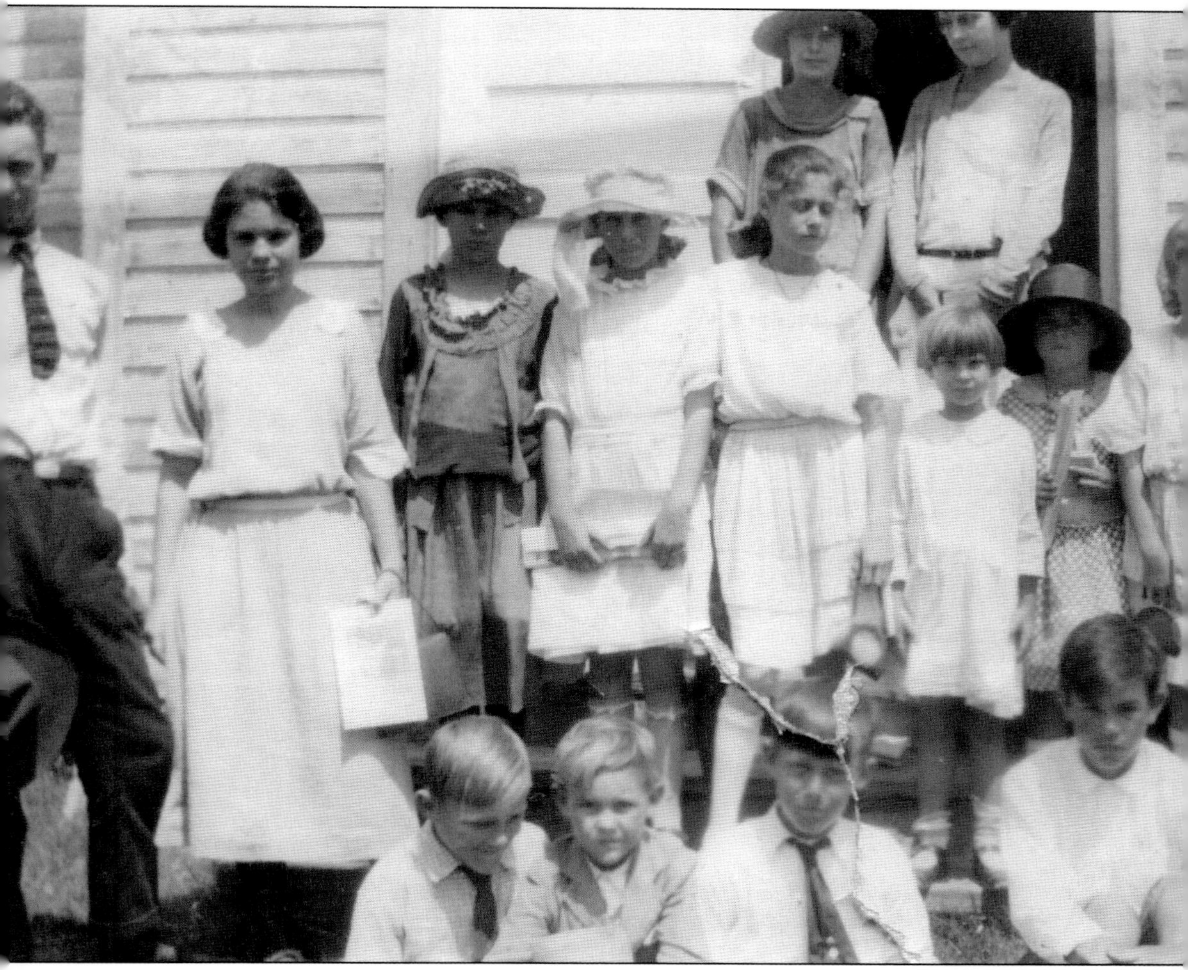

Soon after the 1900 storm, the citizens of Bolivar, who had moved down the peninsula from low-lying areas, started a county school. The Bolivar Common School District, located on Madison Street between Fourteenth and Sixteenth Streets, was operated under a county superintendent. The 1915 storm moved the school to the other side of the highway. In 1917, a two-room frame building was constructed on the site of the Bolivar School. The school was surrounded by barbed wire and had a stile for crossing because cattle roamed free in the area. The wooden school building was moved and became a recreation hall in 1955–1956. (Courtesy of Robert and Jerri Bouse.)

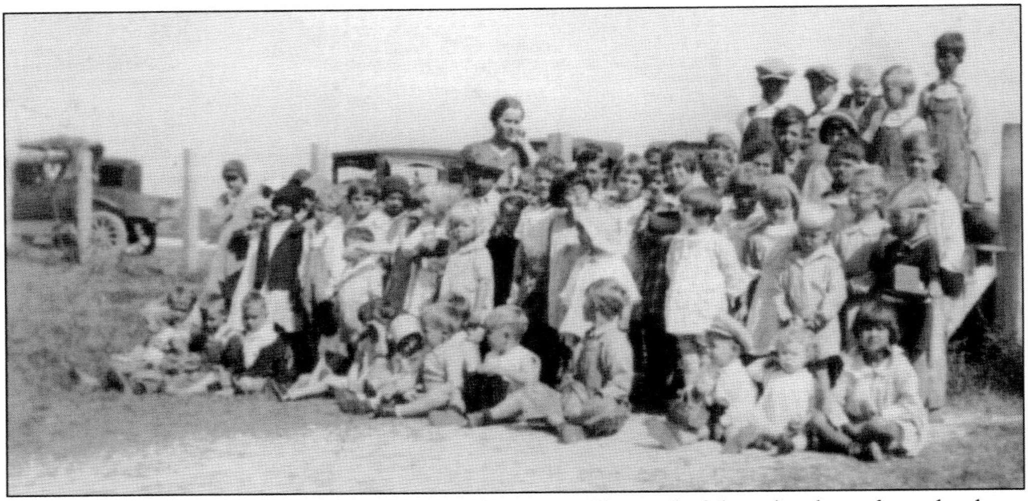

These are students at the Bolivar School in the 1930s. The yard of the school was fenced to keep the cows out. A new brick school building was dedicated on November 18, 1956. Consolidation with the Galveston Independent School District was accomplished on September 1, 1960, and kindergarten was added in 1968–1969. Students attended the new brick school until Crenshaw Elementary and Middle School was opened in 2004. (Courtesy of the Simpton family.)

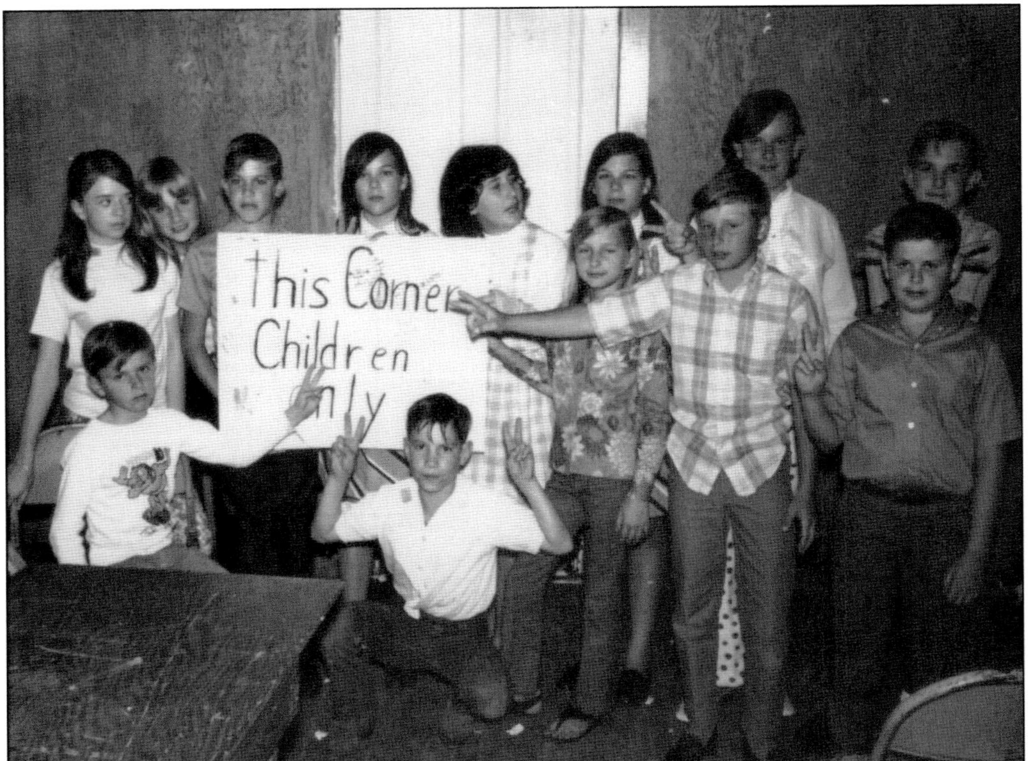

Bolivar School sponsored community dances for the youth of the peninsula. This photograph was taken in 1966 at a dance featuring Don Westmoreland and the Rhythmaires. (Courtesy of Terri Simpton.)

These students are participating in a bicentennial celebration at the Bolivar School in 1976. (Courtesy of Terri Simpton.)

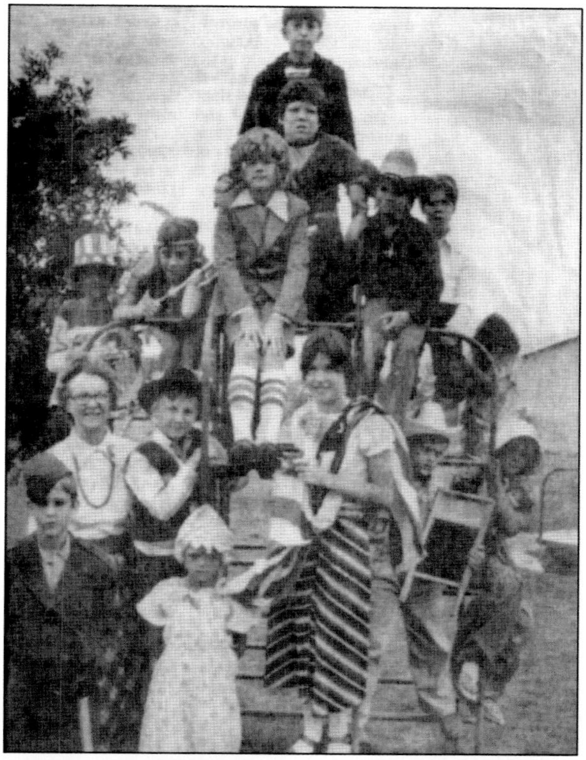

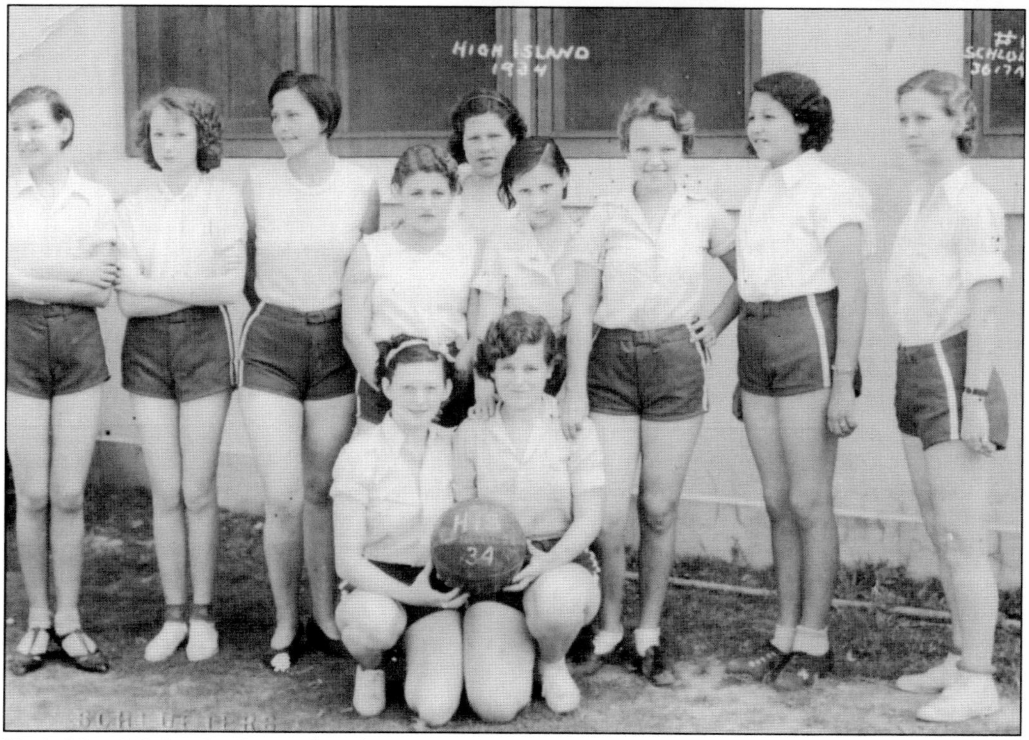

High Island School is located at the east end of the peninsula. The High Island girls' basketball team from 1934 is pictured here. (Courtesy of Elsie Devers.)

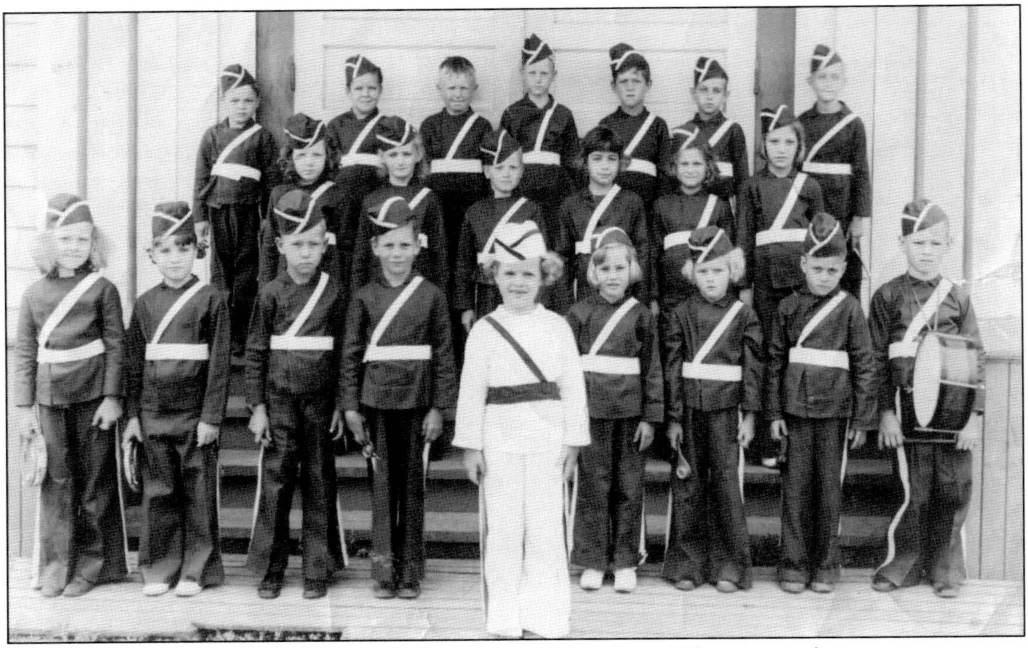

Here is the High Island Drill Team Band of 1941. (Courtesy of Elsie Devers.)

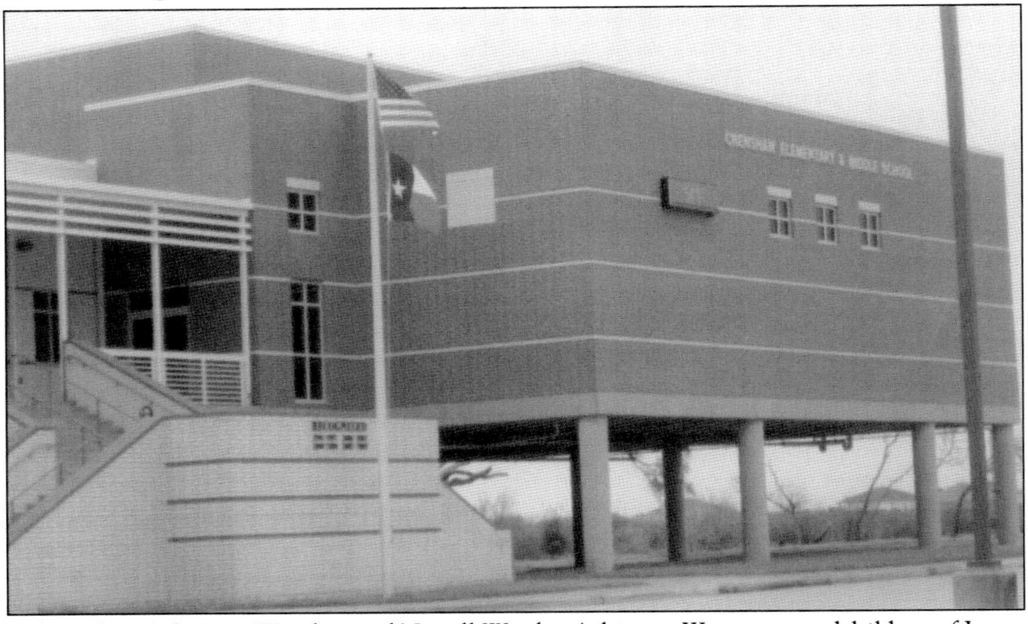

Helen Clare Atkinson Wonders and Newell Wrigley Atkinson III, great-grandchildren of James Anderson Crenshaw Sr. and Henrietta Barker Elliot Crenshaw, were contacted by the president of the Bolivar Elementary School with a request to purchase land for a new school in the early 2000s. The sister and brother chose to donate the land. Wonders, a schoolteacher, and Atkinson, a pecan broker, donated 30 acres for the newly planned campus. They requested that the school be named after their grandmother Helen Crenshaw, who grew up on the property, which her parents bought in 1872. They requested that the library be named after their mother, Gertrude Atkinson, a retired schoolteacher. The ultimate result is a state-of-the-art education facility for the children of the Bolivar Peninsula. (Photograph by the author.)

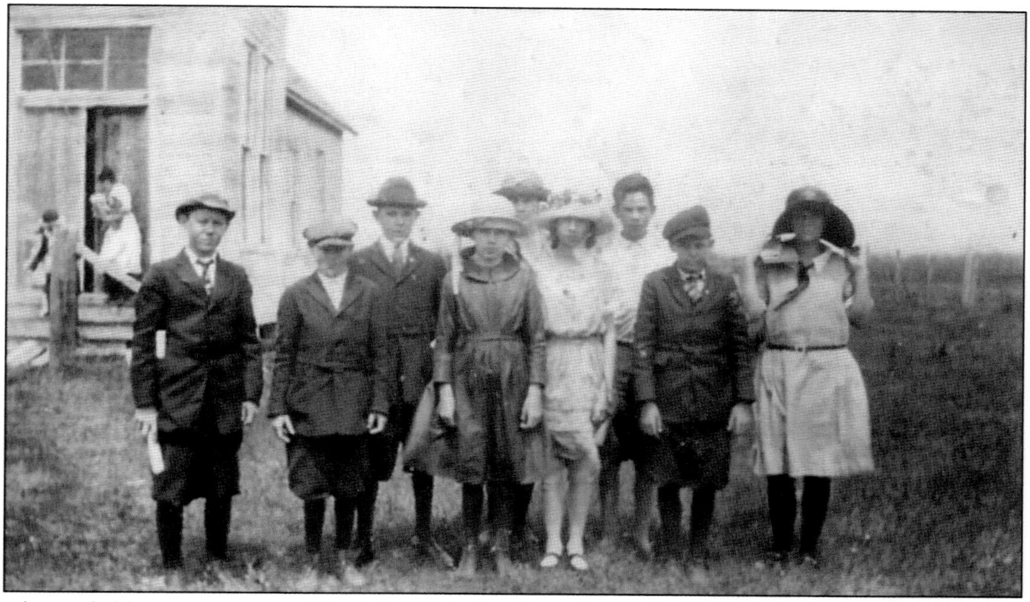

These children are a part of Susie Kahla's Sunday school class at the Port Bolivar Methodist Church. Frank L. Simpton is third from left. (Courtesy of the Simpton family.)

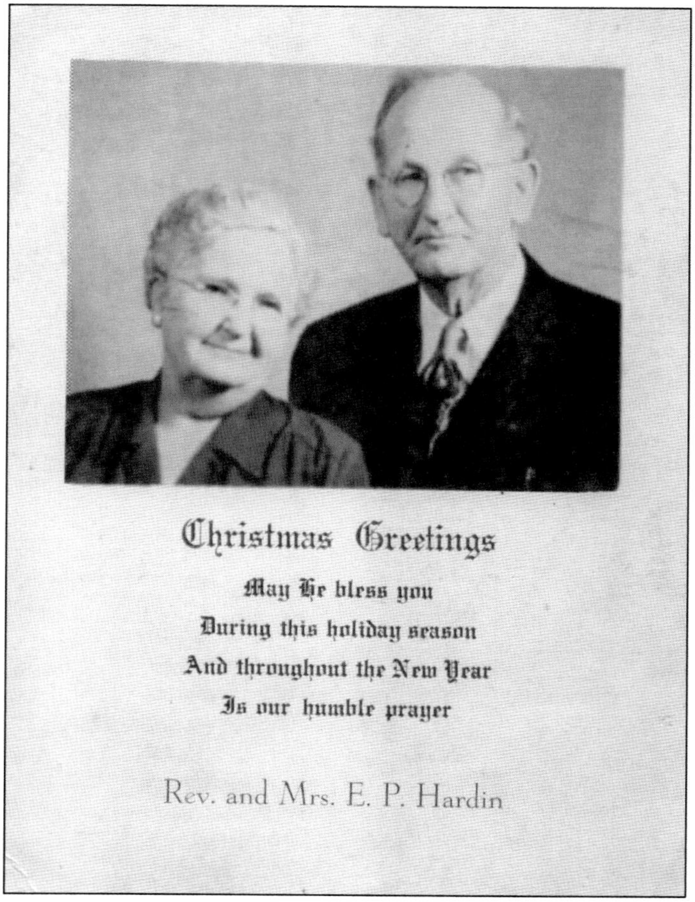

The First Baptist Church of Port Bolivar was started in 1927. Pictured here are the Reverend and Mrs. E.P. Hardin, early ministers at the church, offering Christmas greetings to the congregation. First Baptist Church of Port Bolivar was the mother church for First Baptist of Crystal Beach. (Courtesy of Robert and Jerri Bouse.)

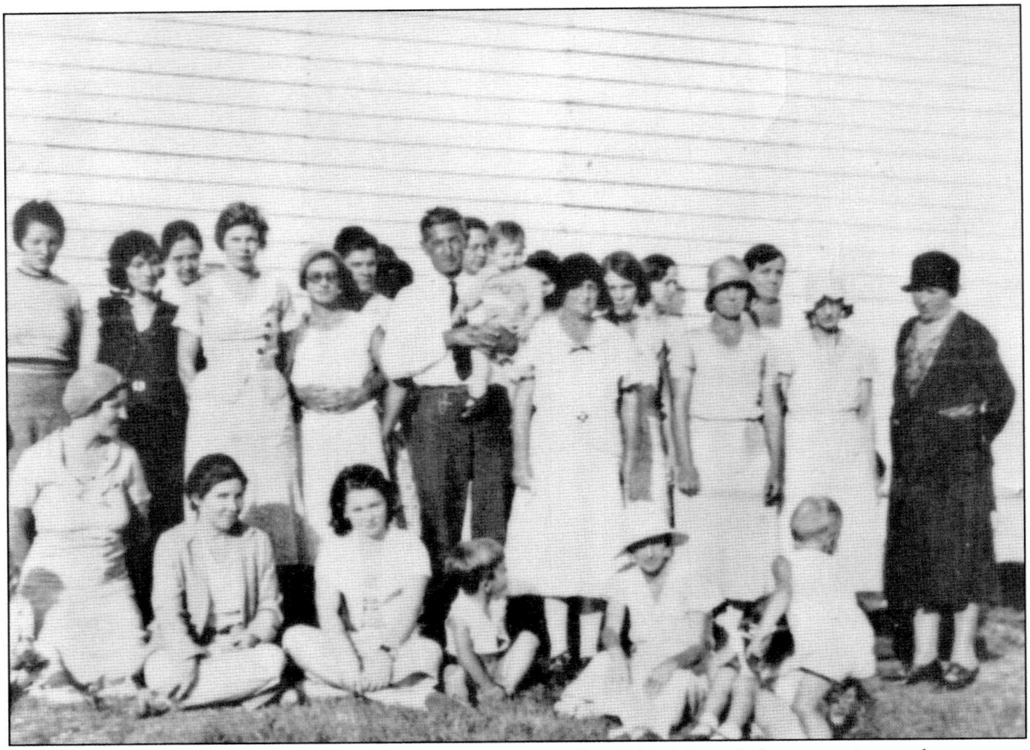

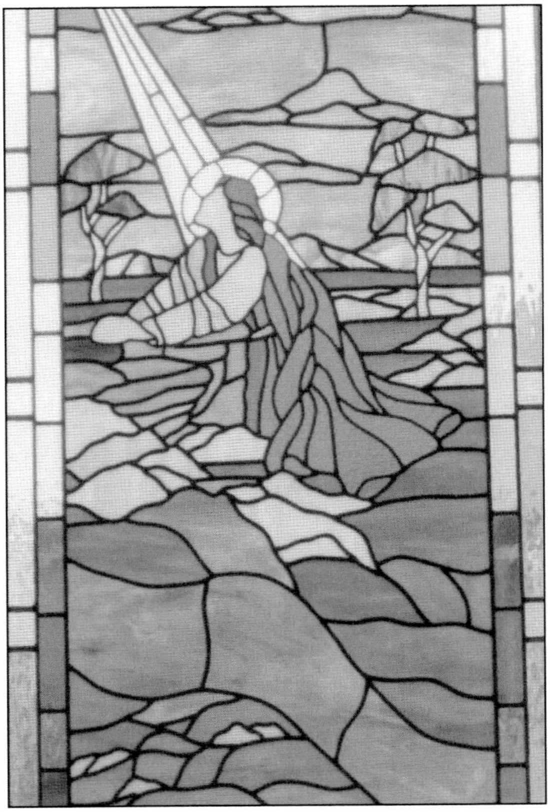

In 1880, Nena Johnson, pictured at the far right in the black ensemble, founded the first Methodist church on the Bolivar Peninsula. She also played piano at the Methodist church. (Courtesy of Robert and Jerri Bouse.)

The stained-glass window of Jesus in the Garden of Gethsemane (from the passage in Luke 22:39–46) was created by artist Harold Guidry for the First United Methodist Church of Port Bolivar and dedicated shortly before Hurricane Ike. The window was undamaged in the storm. (Photograph by the author.)

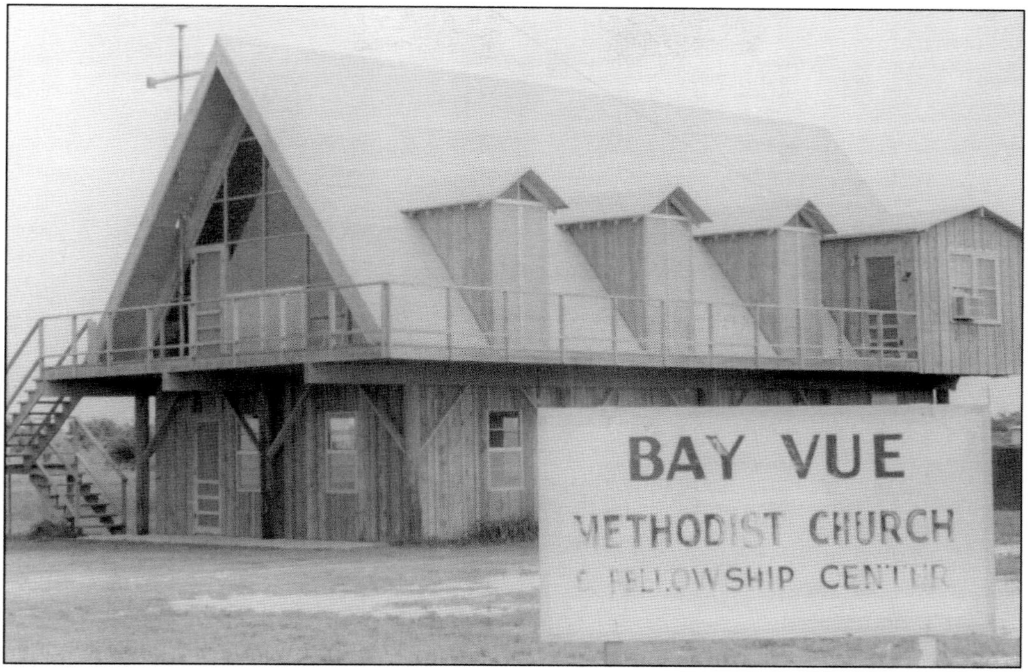

Ground was broken for Bay Vue Methodist Church on the Bolivar Peninsula in early 1963. Bay Vue is a mission of the First United Methodist Church of Port Bolivar. The unique place of worship was made of rough cypress and designed in much the same manner as the summer beach cottages on the peninsula. The sanctuary is at the top of the stairs and designed with a glass front overlooking the Gulf of Mexico. The parsonage was located behind the chapel. (Courtesy of Rev. W.C. Hall.)

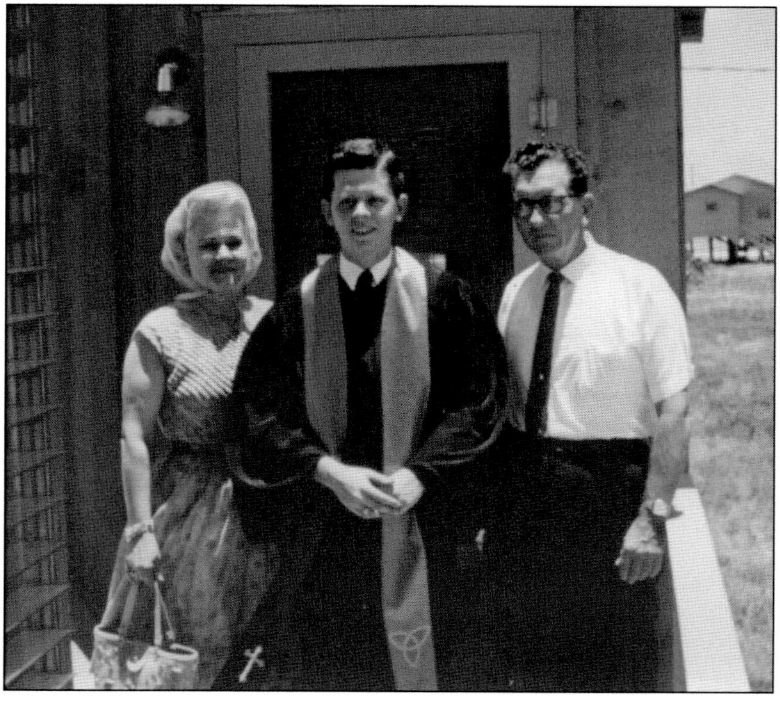

A very young Rev. W.C. Hall is pictured with his parents, W.C. Hall Sr. and Arlene Hall, on the first day of services at Bay Vue Methodist Church. On April 13, 1969, Bay Vue United Methodist Church dedicated its new church and parsonage buildings. (Courtesy of Rev. W.C. Hall.)

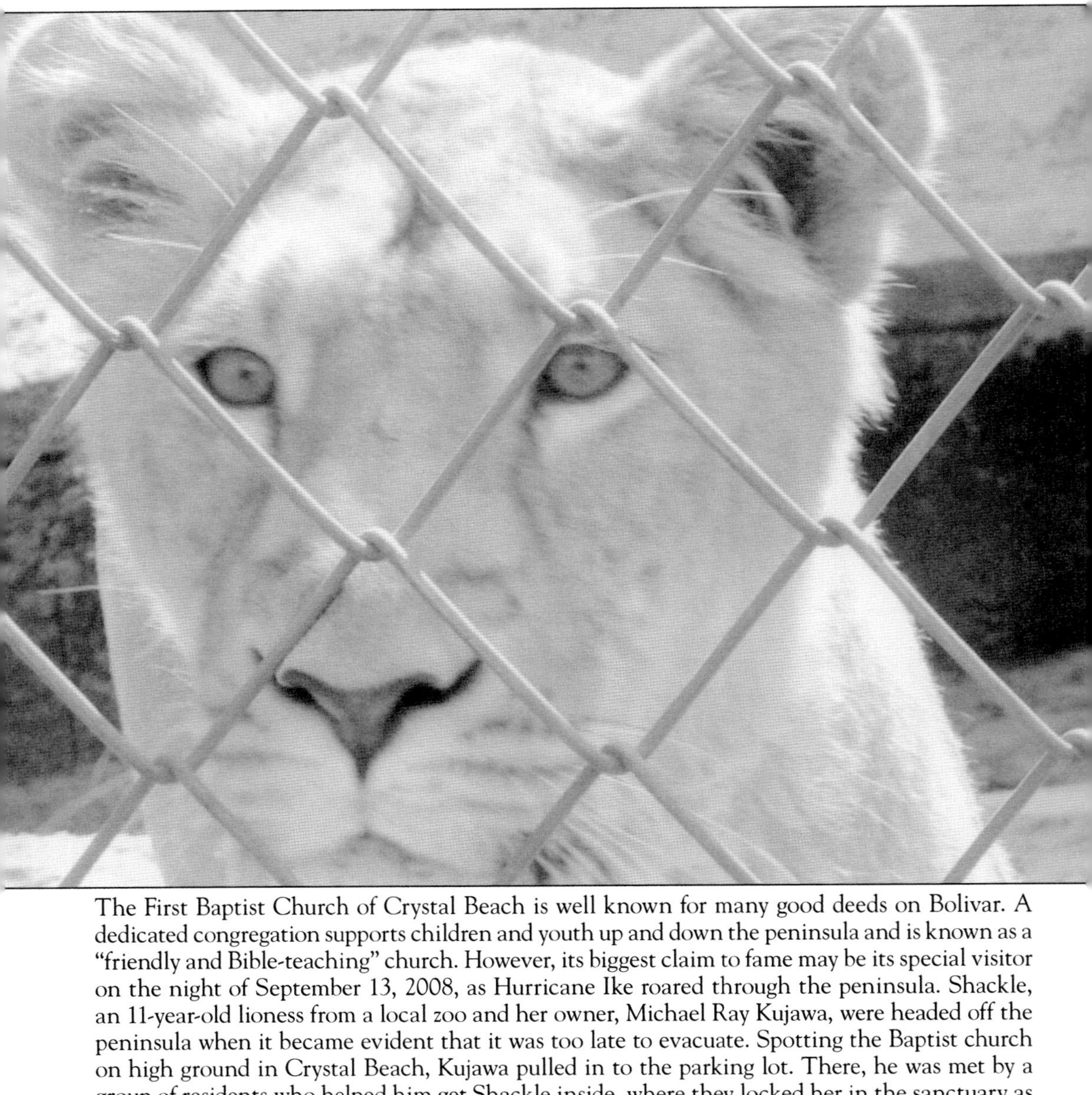

The First Baptist Church of Crystal Beach is well known for many good deeds on Bolivar. A dedicated congregation supports children and youth up and down the peninsula and is known as a "friendly and Bible-teaching" church. However, its biggest claim to fame may be its special visitor on the night of September 13, 2008, as Hurricane Ike roared through the peninsula. Shackle, an 11-year-old lioness from a local zoo and her owner, Michael Ray Kujawa, were headed off the peninsula when it became evident that it was too late to evacuate. Spotting the Baptist church on high ground in Crystal Beach, Kujawa pulled in to the parking lot. There, he was met by a group of residents who helped him get Shackle inside, where they locked her in the sanctuary as the storm raged. "They worked pretty well together, actually," said Kujawa. "When you have to swim, the lion doesn't care about eating nobody." (Photograph by the author.)

Second Going, a resale shop, began as an outreach of Bay Vue Methodist Church around 1970. Donations of household items, clothing, tools, and furniture are sold to finance this ministry. After Hurricane Ike in 2008, the Bolivar Peninsula Community Outreach agreed to repair the building, and the church allowed them to use the name Second Going. Food is provided through the Galveston County Food, in partnership with the Houston Food Bank. Pictured here are, from left to right, Dot Walker, Virginia Hill, and Mildred Starke, who along with many others in the community were instrumental in starting the Second Going Shop. (Courtesy of Rev. W.C. Hall.)

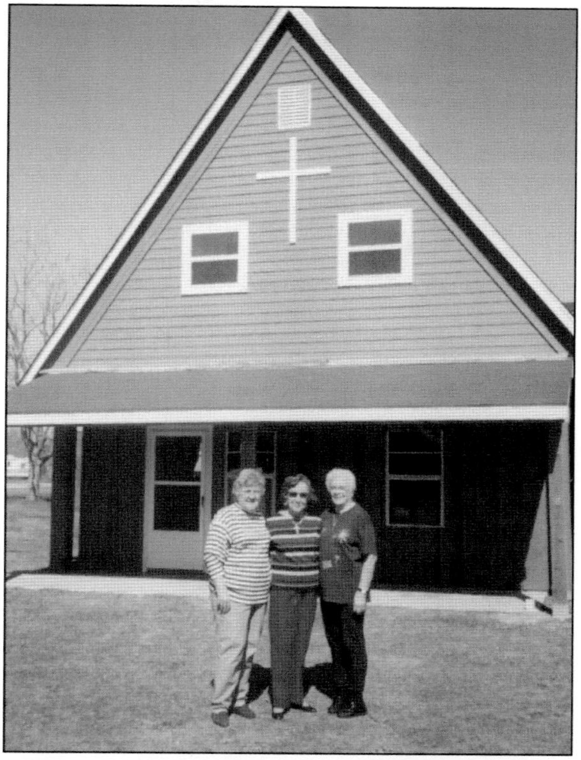

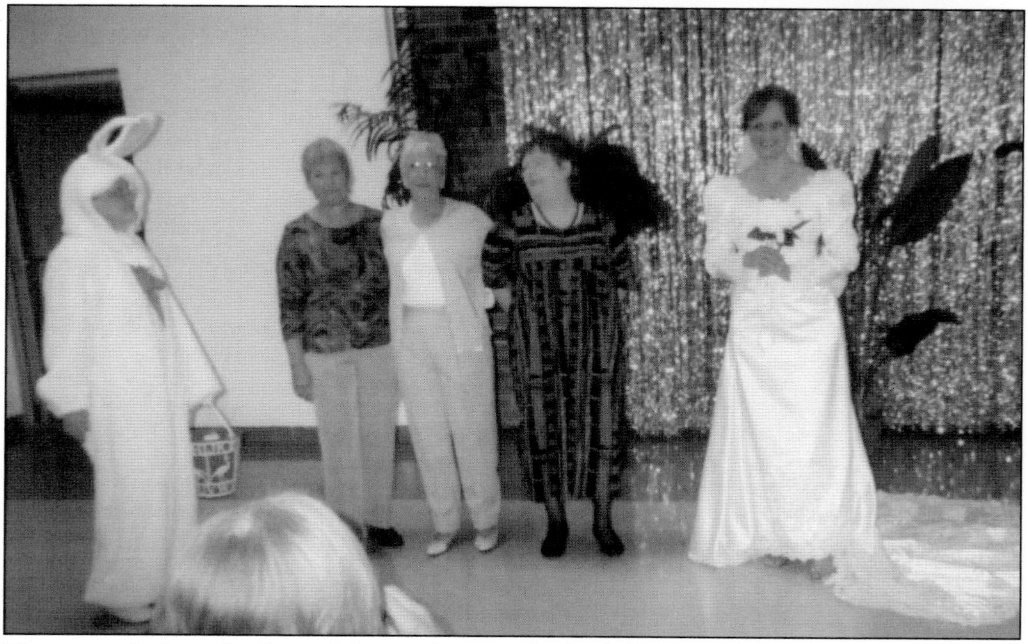

The proceeds from the Second Going shop pay for food that is provided for 180 families each week and is distributed at High Island, Gilchrist, Crystal Beach, and Port Bolivar. Fundraisers like this fashion show help raise money to continue this ministry. Pictured here are, from left to right, Marianna Gage, Grace Moore, Marian Davis, Linda Peak, and Brenda Hughes. (Courtesy of Rev. W.C. Hall.)

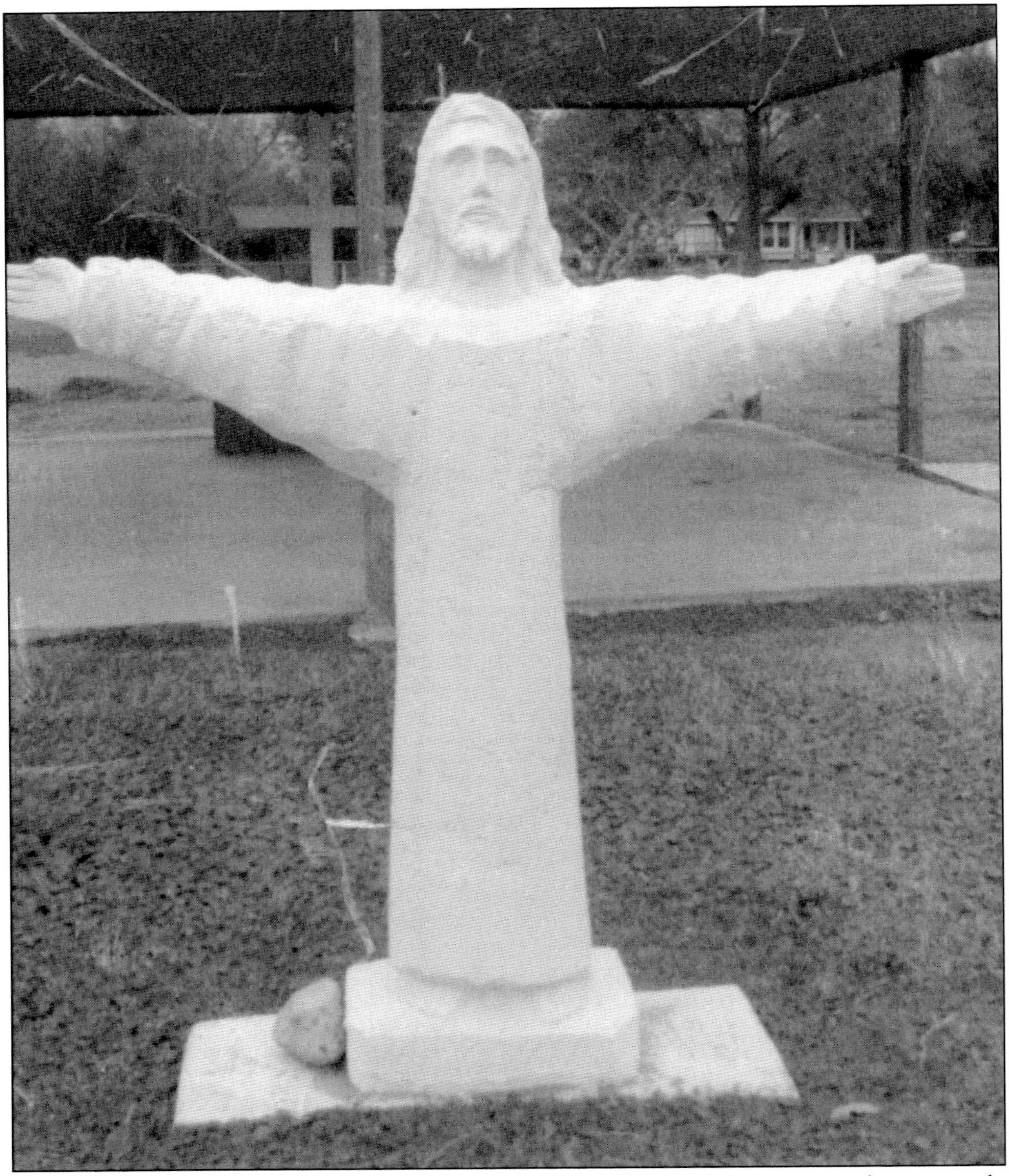

There are several other churches on the peninsula; each one is important to the peninsula and to its congregation. First United Methodist Church of High Island, First Baptist of High Island, the Crystal Beach Community Church, the Bolivar Peninsula Church of Christ, and the Lighthouse Apostolic Fellowship are all vibrant, important contributors to the spiritual life on the peninsula.

Seven

Going Down to Take the Breeze

Life at the Breakers

The Breakers, which stood at Caplen for over a century, was a symbol of fine resort living on the Texas Gulf coast. The Sunday *Beaumont Enterprise* of August 14, 1921, describes the beautiful home as "equipped with gas lights and sewerage and painted white and a soft green within to soften the glare and with rugs and hangings to harmonize while numbers of nest vases filled with yellow wild flowers add that ineffable homey charm."

Lumber for the home came by schooner from Pensacola, Florida, and was floated to shore. Framed with heart pine and put together with cypress pegs, the house was built in 1884 by a ship carpenter for Terence Meche and his wife, Carrie Weaver Meche, as a small farmhouse. Meche lived in the house until his death. Meche's wife and child left well before the 1900 storm.

In 1905, William D. and Ruth McLean Gordon purchased the house and named it the Breakers. They used the home as a vacation destination for many years, making renovations and additions in 1914 and 1930. During the 1915 storm, the house was washed from its blocks and filled with approximately two feet of water. It was placed back on a creosoted piling foundation and reinforced with double floors and brick flues.

Marie Eddins Gordon accepted the care of the Breakers from Ruth McLean Gordon in the 1950s. Many happy family memories were made at that iconic beach house. Ownership of the home was passed to Barbara Gordon McNeill and her family in 1998. At that time, the Breakers was moved back from the gulf because of beach erosion. The home continued to be the setting for many pleasant gatherings of friends and family members, maintaining the tradition of happy times on the Texas Gulf coast.

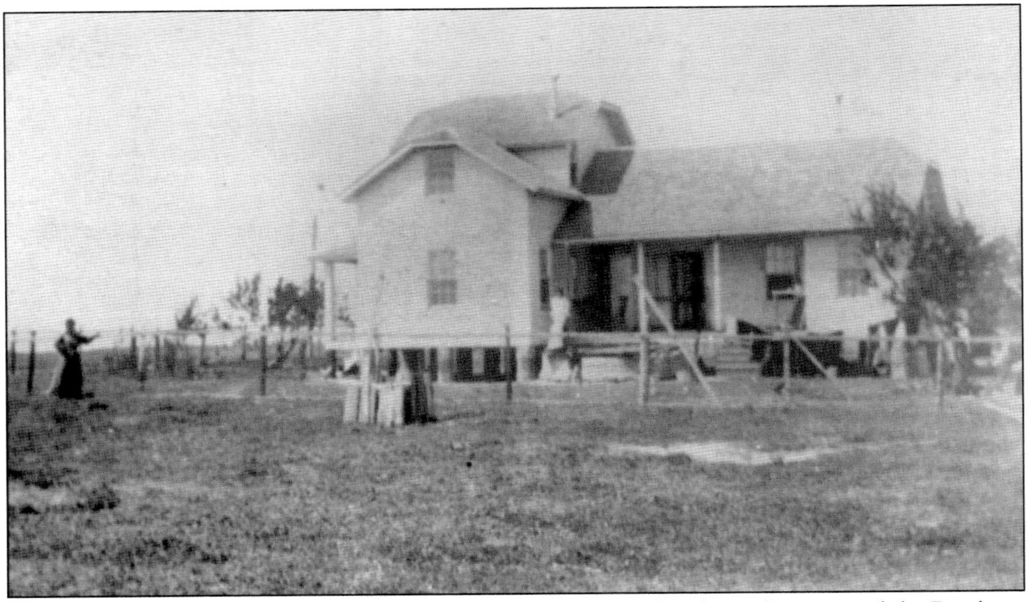

Terrence and Carrie Weaver Meche were the original owners of the home later named the Breakers. The original structure was a small farmhouse, constructed by a shipbuilder in 1884. The home was built using materials shipped from Pensacola, Florida. (Courtesy of Barbara Gordon McNeill.)

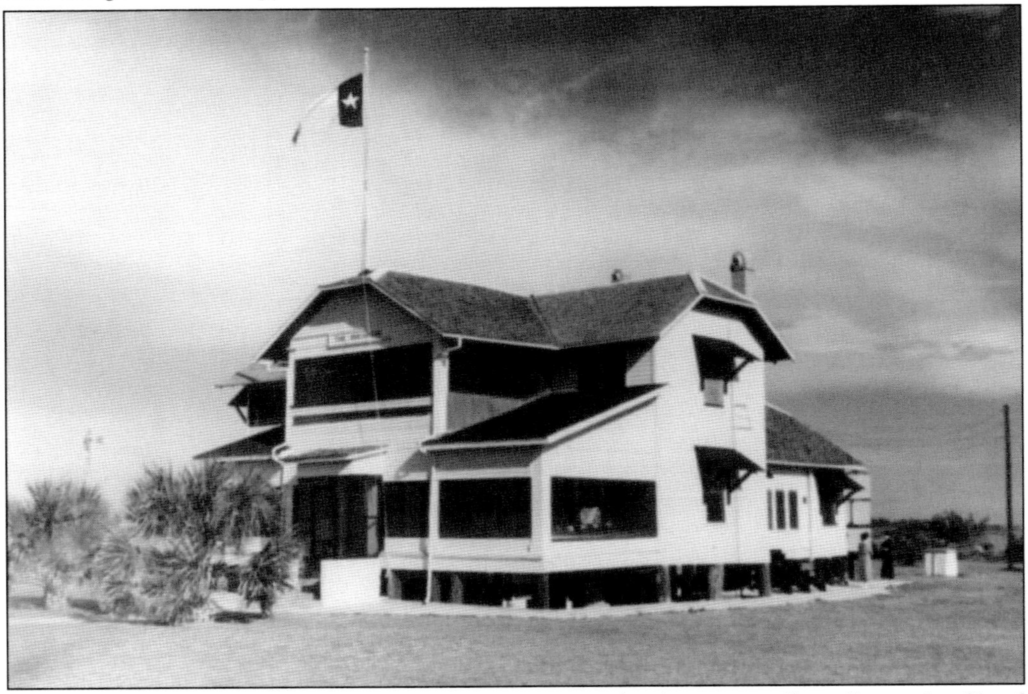

Caplen became a summer colony in 1914, and W.D. Gordon began to sell small parcels of land for vacation homes. The *Beaumont Enterprise* suggested, "Probably nowhere in America is there greater opportunity for the development of beautiful and comfortable summer seashore homes than along the Gulf Coast of Texas, where real communication makes resorts of the sort easy of access, and where a plentitude of building material enables the construction of elaborate buildings of reasonably low cost." (Courtesy of Barbara Gordon McNeill.)

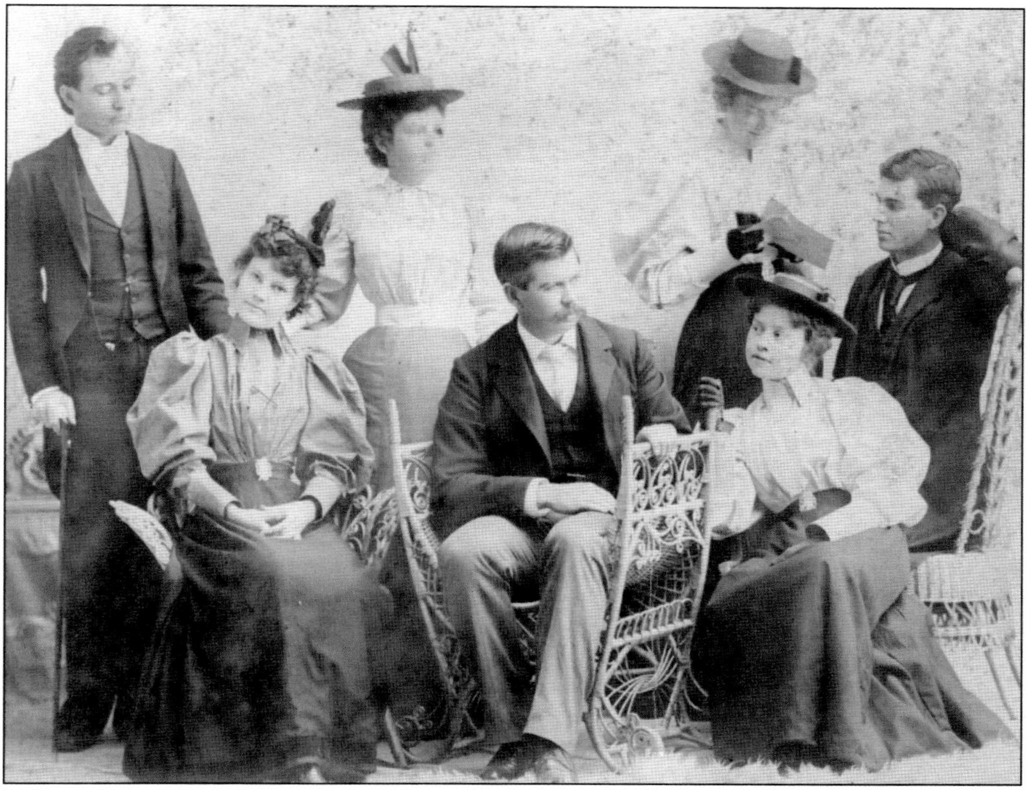

William D. and Ruth McLean Gordon purchased the house in 1905, naming it the Breakers. The Gordons used the house as a vacation home for many years, making renovations and additions in 1914 and in the 1930s. Pictured here around 1896 is their bridal party. (Courtesy of Barbara Gordon McNeill.)

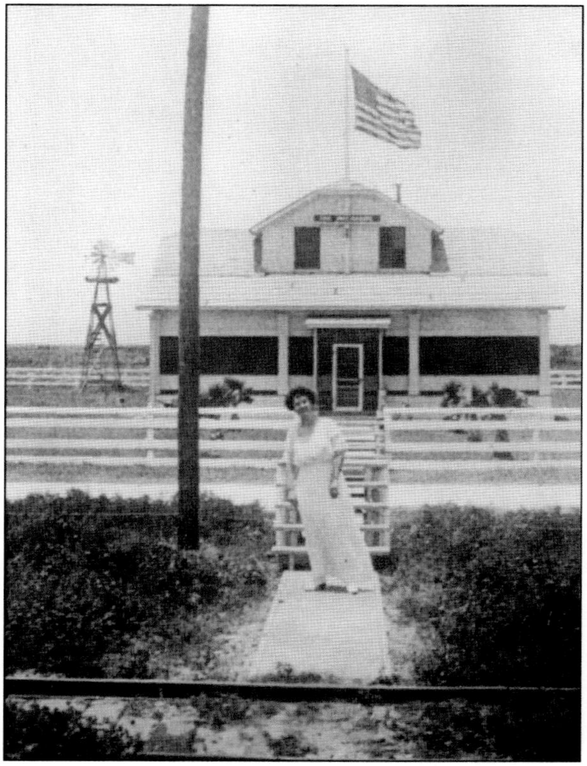

Pictured is Ruth McLean Gordon, sometime before 1915. Note that the train tracks are in the foreground of the photograph. They were moved after the 1915 storm. (Courtesy of Barbara Gordon McNeill.)

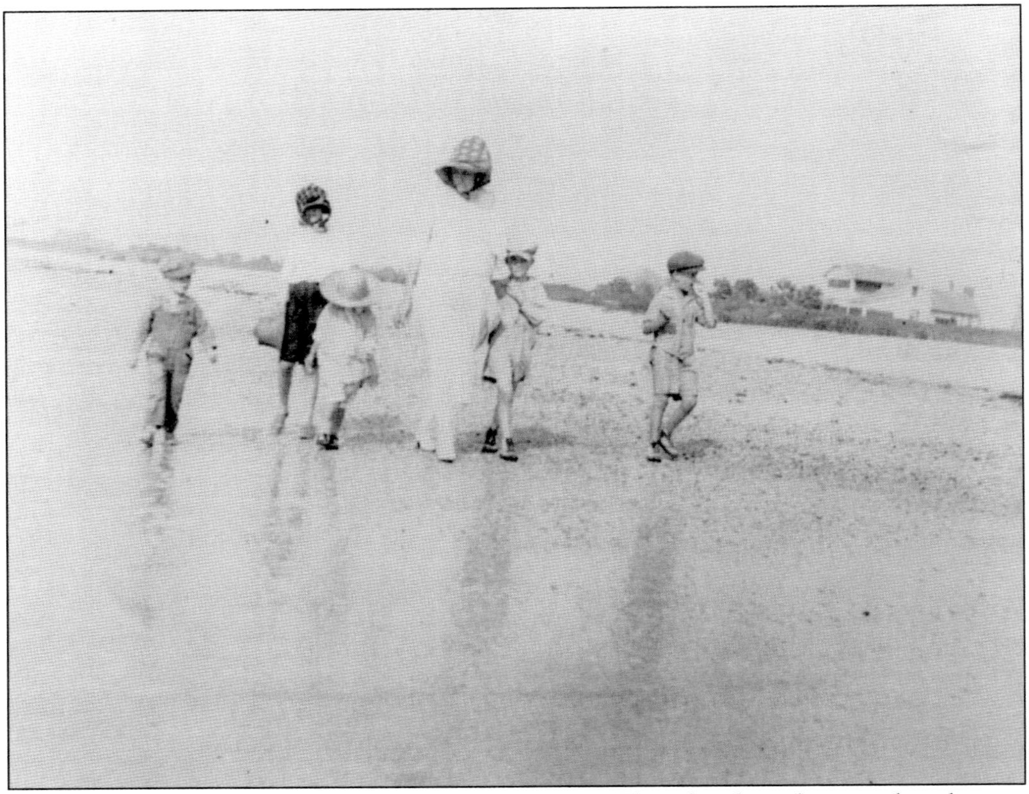

These beachcombers are thought to be the niece of W.D. Gordon and her five children. (Courtesy of Barbara Gordon McNeill.)

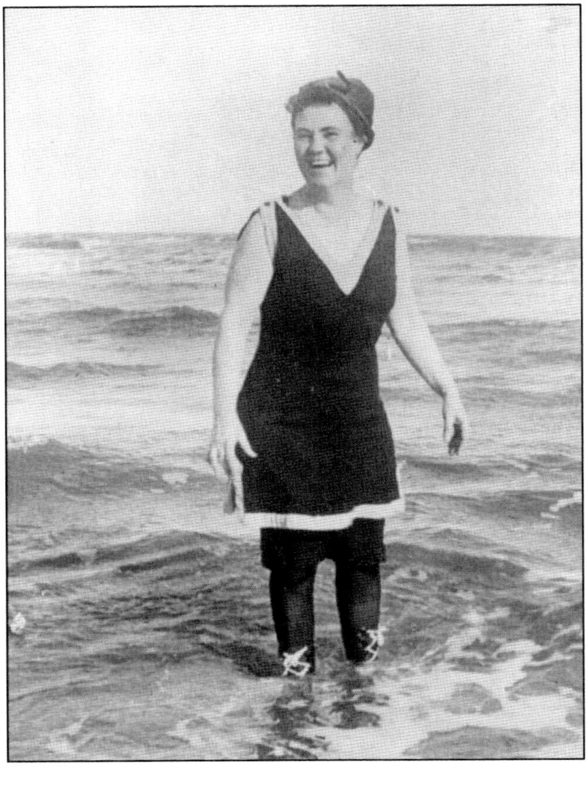

Ruth Gordon is pictured standing in the gulf, wearing a woolen bathing suit. (Courtesy of Barbara Gordon McNeill.)

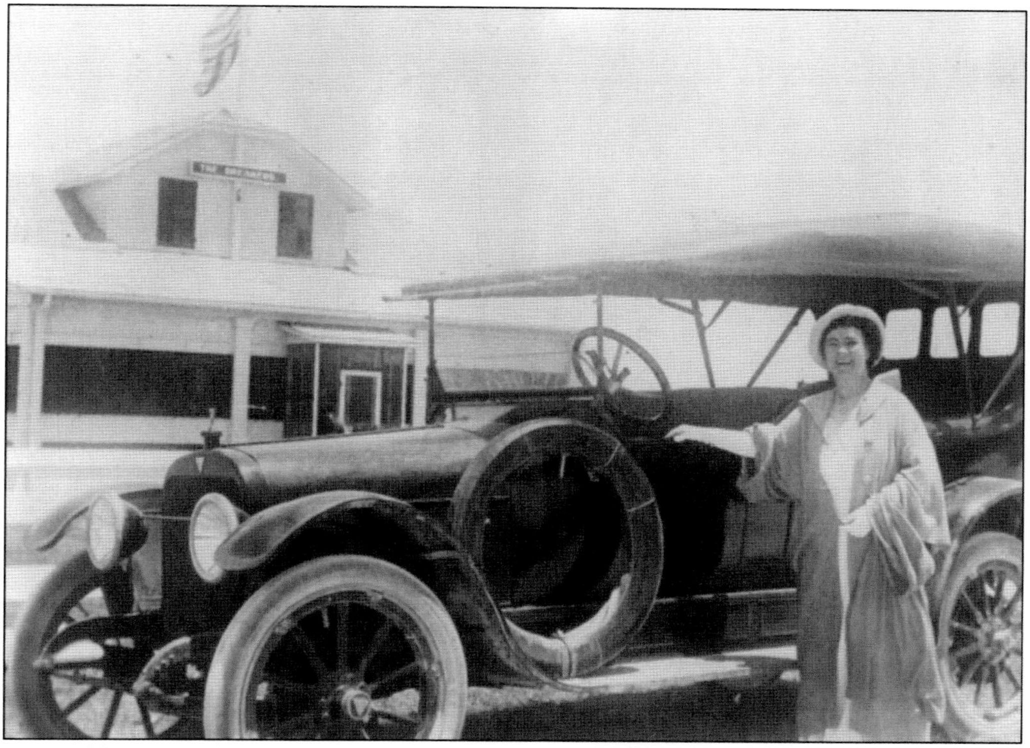

Pictured here is Ruth McLean Gordon. (Courtesy of Barbara Gordon McNeill.)

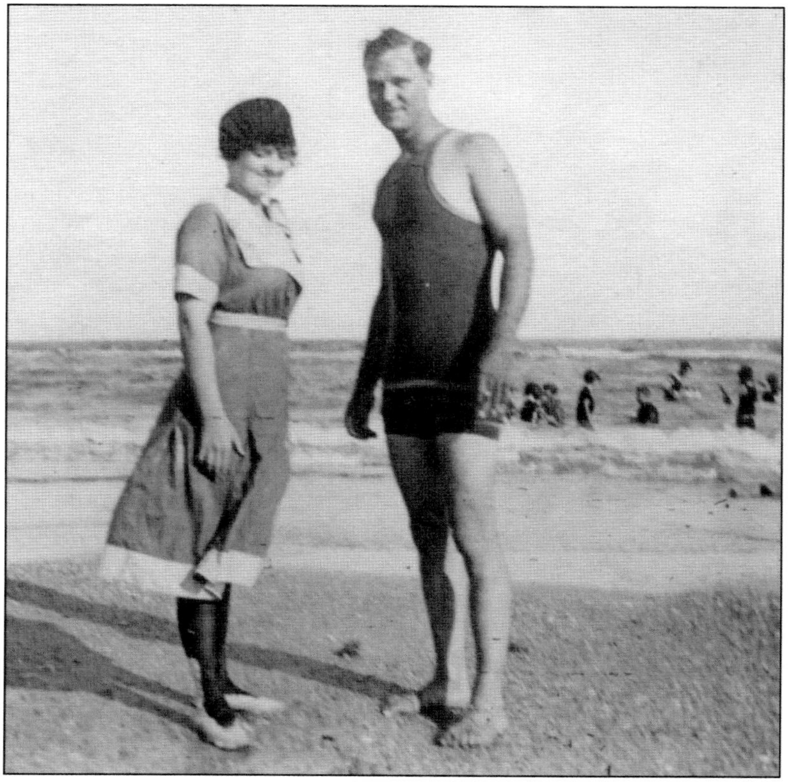

Marrs and Verna McLean are on the beach in front of the Breakers in 1918. (Courtesy of Barbara Gordon McNeill.)

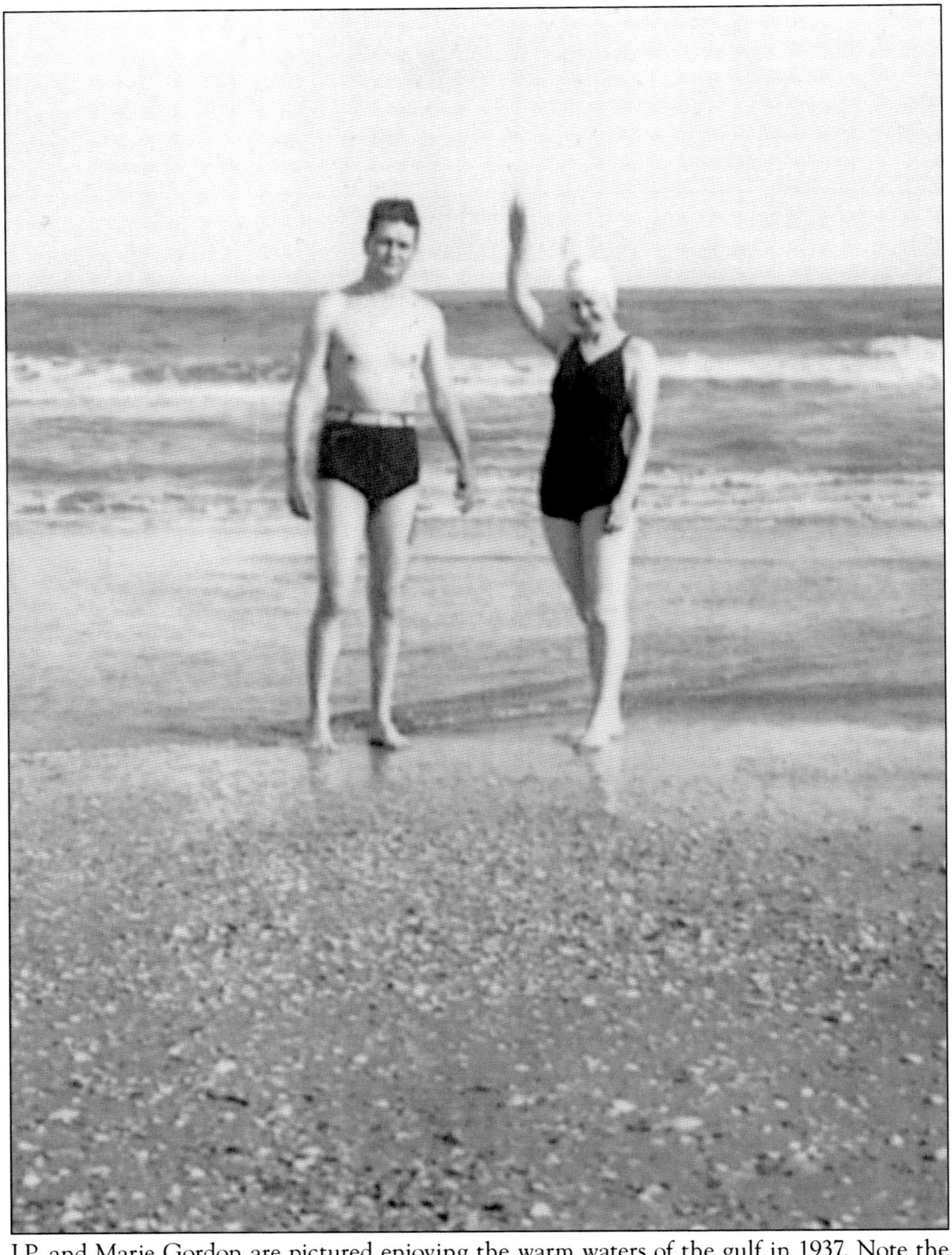

J.P. and Marie Gordon are pictured enjoying the warm waters of the gulf in 1937. Note the plethora of seashells in the forefront of this photograph. The Bolivar Peninsula is famous for its shell-laden currents, carpeting the glimmering sands with angel wings, moon shells, augers, and an occasional sand dollar. (Courtesy of Barbara Gordon McNeill.)

John and Marie Gordon accepted the care of the Breakers from Ruth McLean Gordon in the 1950s, preserving it for future generations of fortunate family members and guests. The relocation and restoration of this beautiful Bolivar beach house saved this iconic piece of Bolivar history for many years. (Courtesy of Barbara Gordon McNeill.)

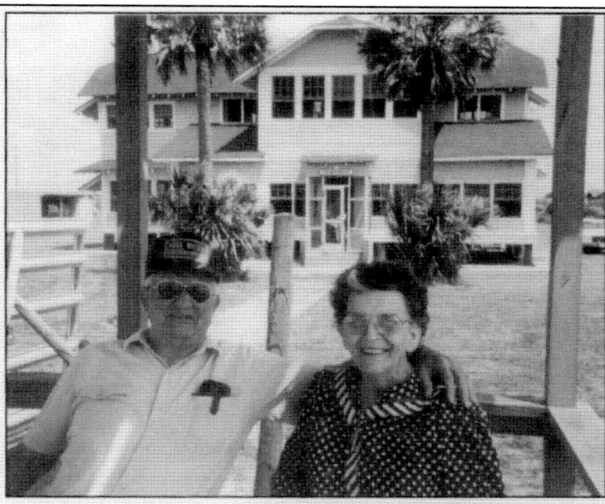

John B. and Marie Gordon
1994

The relocation and restoration of this beach home is lovingly dedicated to my mother, Marie Eddins Gordon, who accepted the care of "The Breakers" from Ruth McLean Gordon in the 1950s and who preserved it for future generations and for the continuation of Bolivar Peninsula history.

Barbara Gordon McNeill

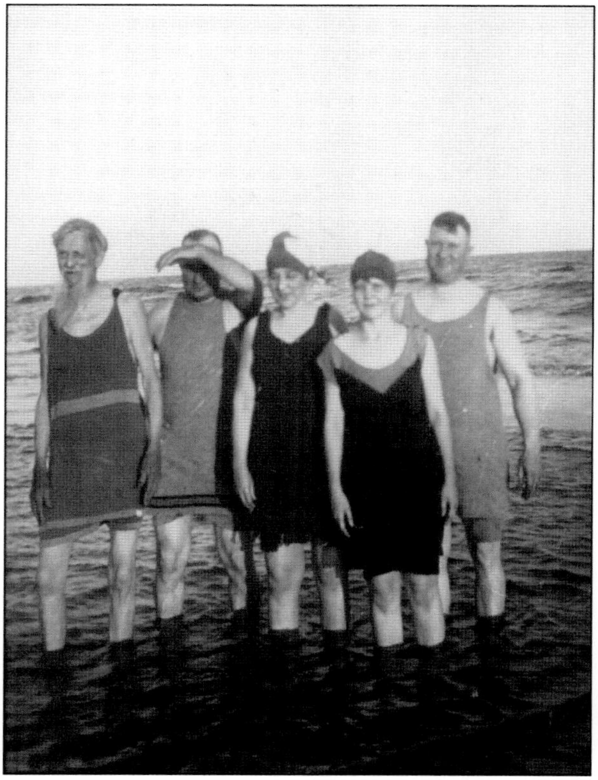

The Gordons found a trunk of old woolen bathing suits such as the ones pictured here when they took ownership of the Breakers in the 1950s. Guests often dressed up in those bathing suits for fun. (Courtesy of Barbara Gordon McNeill.)

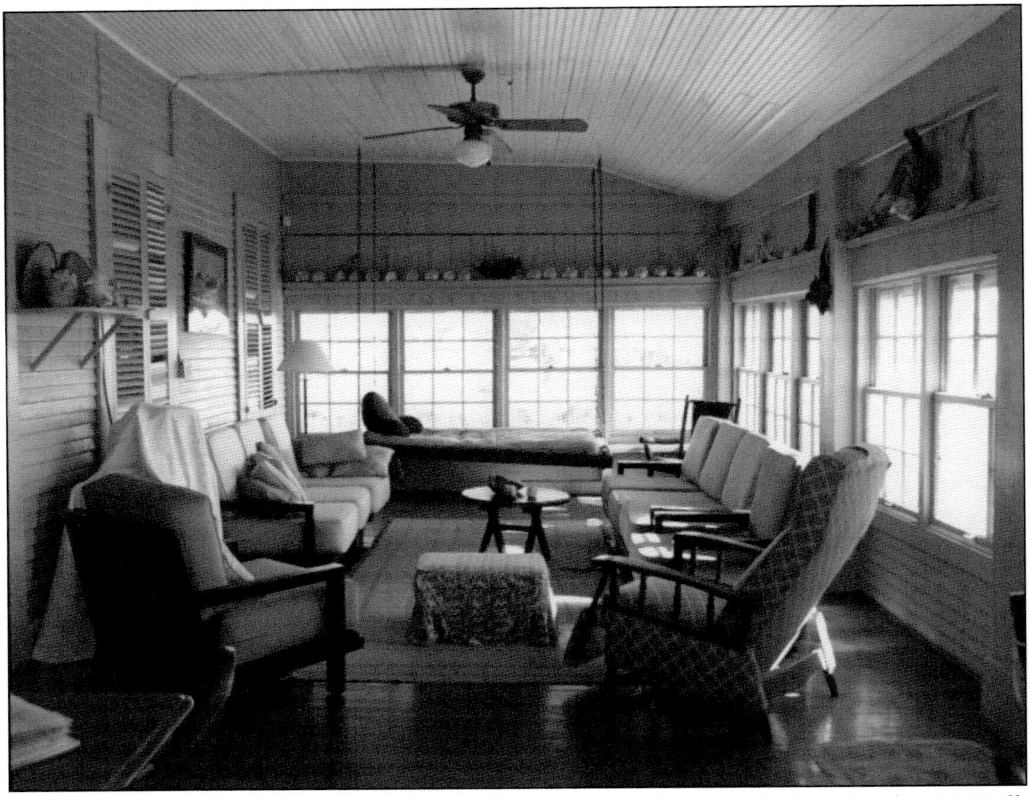

Many happy hours were passed on this gulf-side porch at the Breakers. Barbara Gordon McNeill, grandniece of W.D. and Ruth Gordon and most recent owner of the Breakers said, "Napping was a priority—at least for the adults." Notice the swinging bed at the far end of this porch. That swinging bed (and the matching one at the other end of the porch) were prime, coveted spots on hot summer afternoons. Decor on the porch included "a big old platter filled with seashells (that) sat on the front porch, along with examples from a shark tooth collection." (Courtesy of Barbara Gordon McNeill.)

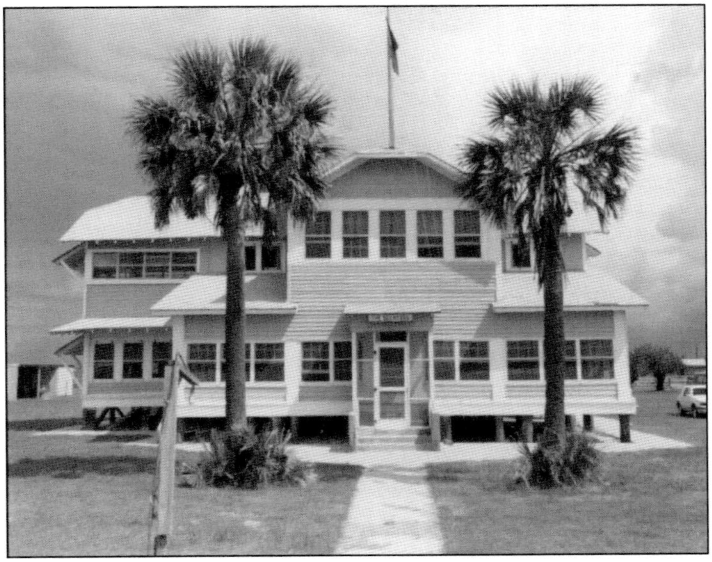

When the owners arrived at the Breakers, the first tasks were to raise the flag and the 87 windows, making for a perfect breeze on a summer day. Family members remember scampering to close those windows when the inevitable thunderstorms struck in the middle of the night. (Courtesy of Barbara Gordon McNeill.)

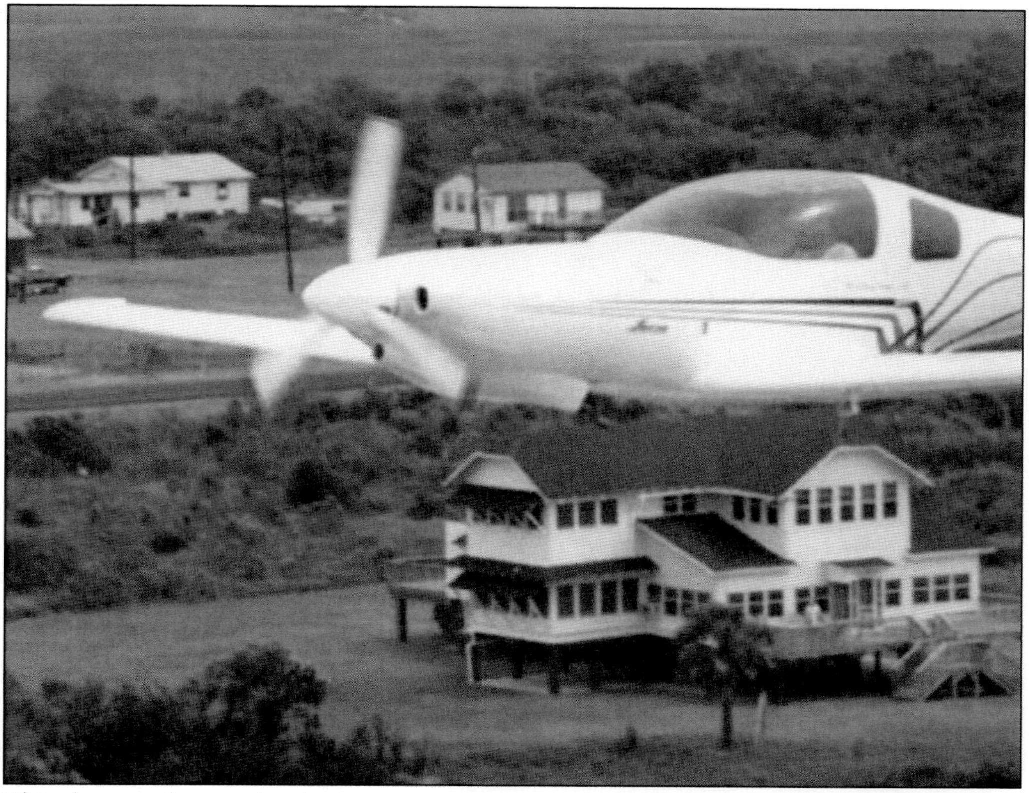

This photograph was taken by a second private plane, passing over the Breakers as owner Barbara Gordon McNeill waves from the porch. (Courtesy of Barbara Gordon McNeill.)

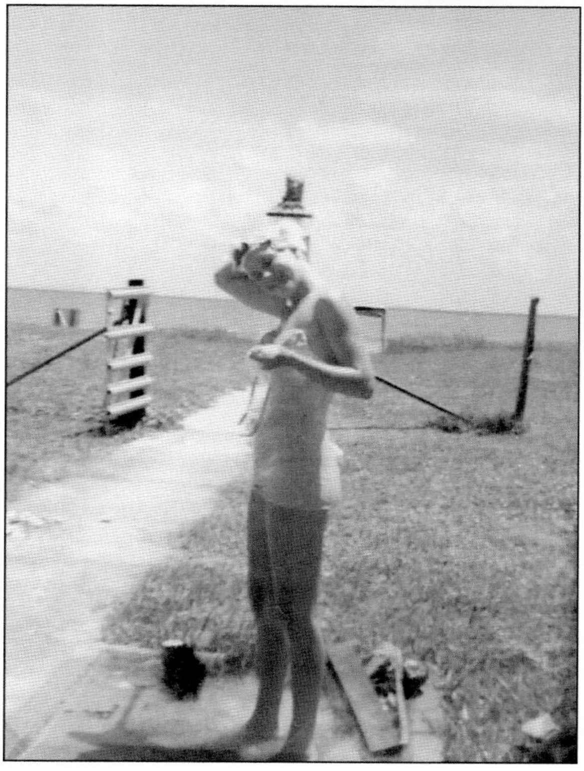

Barbara Gordon is pictured showering off the gulf salt and sand in this outdoor shower. When a cistern still supplied shower water at the Breakers, outdoor bathers would often be surprised with a dousing of cold cistern water tossed over the top of the shower from a kitchen window. Beach cabins all along the Gulf coast still boast outdoor showers—a rite of passage for kids throughout the generations. (Courtesy of Barbara Gordon McNeill.)

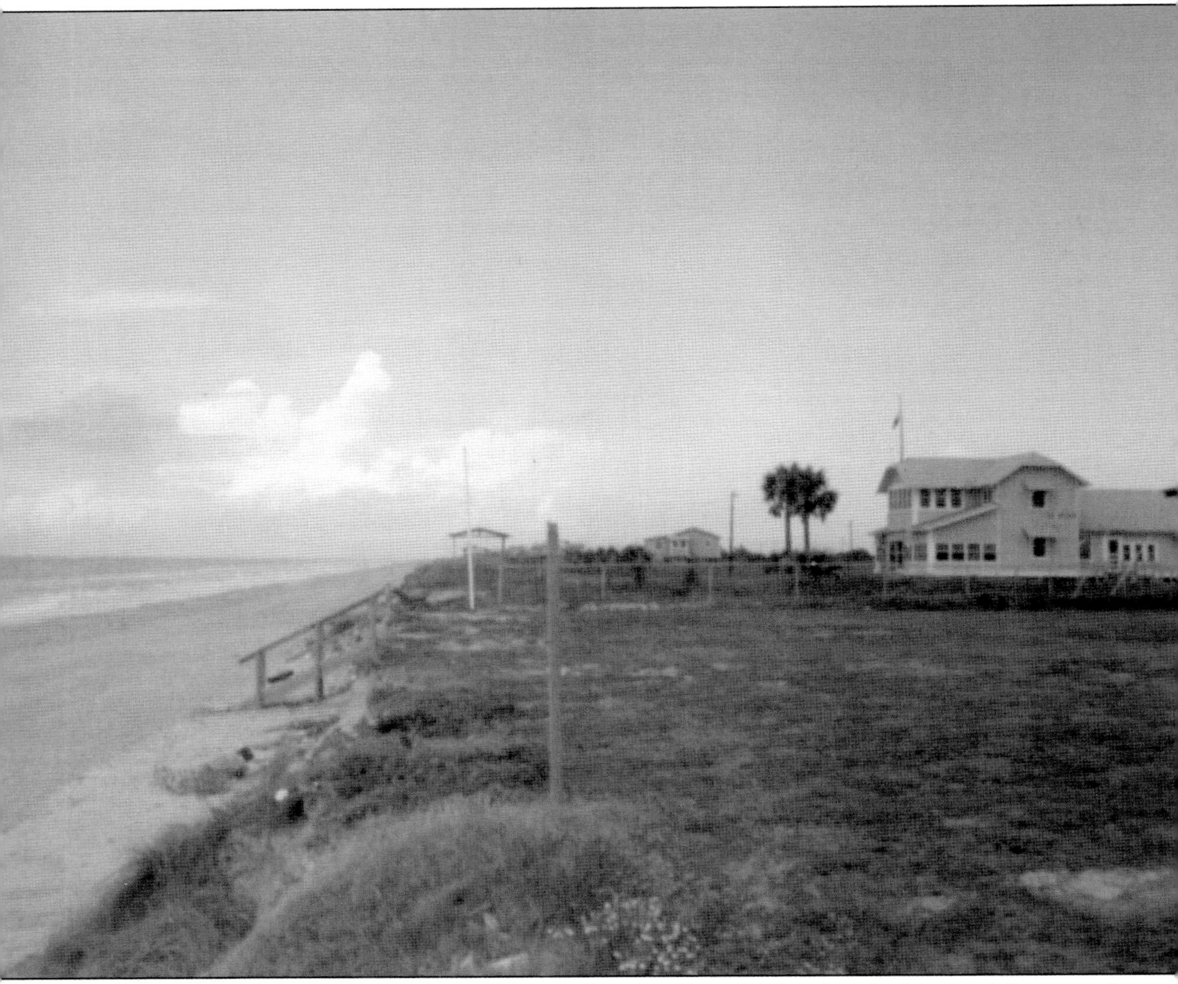

The Breakers was recorded as a Texas Historic Landmark in 1990 and in the National Register of Historic Places in 1998. The Breakers survived countless major storms along the Gulf coast while retaining a high degree of historical and architectural integrity, but it succumbed to Hurricane Ike in 2008. (Courtesy of Barbara Gordon McNeill.)

Eight

This and That

Too Good to Miss

It would require an encyclopedia of multiple volumes and a hundred chapters to do justice to the fascinating history of the Bolivar Peninsula. In this format, of course, that was impossible. This chapter includes interesting people, places, and tales that just did not fit elsewhere but were too good to leave out.

Throughout the years, family-owned stores were important meeting places for community members. This was especially true on the Bolivar Peninsula, where residents were fairly isolated. The stores on the peninsula served as post offices, message boards, and phone booths, as well as places to buy groceries. The Stingaree Restaurant is, perhaps, the peninsula's most famous eating establishment. "You catch 'em, we'll cook 'em" reads the sign that hangs in the lobby. Peninsula residents, along with boaters from the intracoastal and motorists from East Texas, enjoy tasty seafood dinners throughout the year.

Every family who has lived at the beach has a hurricane story to tell. While the hardy residents of Bolivar Peninsula do not like to dwell on the negative, hurricane tales show the ingenuity, resilience, and spirit of the peninsula.

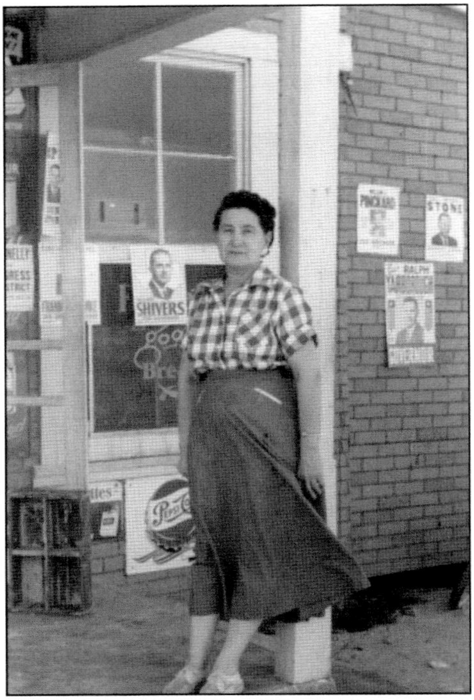

"Where Friends and Fishermen Meet" was the motto of the Faggard's Store. Notice the political posters adhered to the front of the building. These indicate that the year was 1952, when Ralph Yarborough unsuccessfully challenged incumbent R. Allan Shrivers for the governorship of Texas. The original owners of the store, Clyde and Lou Faggard (pictured), came to Bolivar in the late 1920s. Customers would drive down an oyster-shell road to reach the store, which was started in a building made of tar paper and had a dirt floor. The post office was next door. Shan Faggard, grandson of the owners, remembers that he and all of his cousins worked at the store. They earned $5 a day plus a meal. Their grandmother wrote them a check each day and cashed it at the store register in order to keep an accurate record for taxes. Shan remembers that he learned values and a strong work ethic from that experience. (Courtesy of Shan Faggard.)

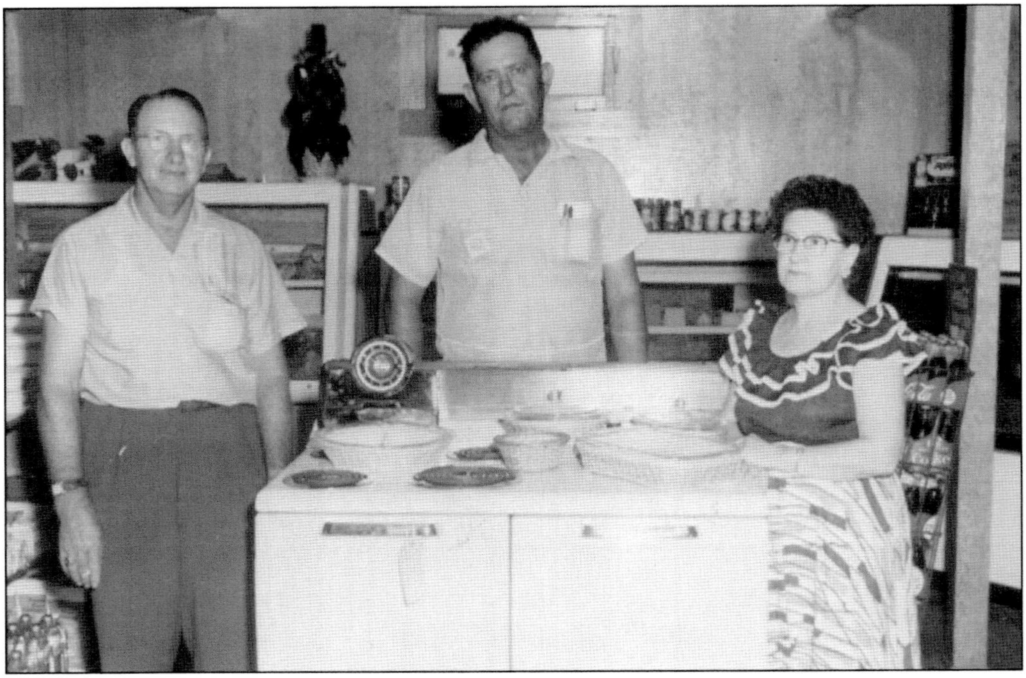

Faggard's Store was a popular meeting place throughout the 1950s. In this photograph, taken around 1954, Pat Lee (center) and Lou "Ma" Faggard (right) show off some of their new wares. The gentleman on the left is unidentified but assumed to be an electrical-appliance salesman. Notice that the stove is electric. In the 1950s, electric appliances revolutionized the kitchen, giving women (who were at that time still generally considered to be the homemakers) more leisure time while still creating a comfortable home for their families. (Courtesy of Shan Faggard.)

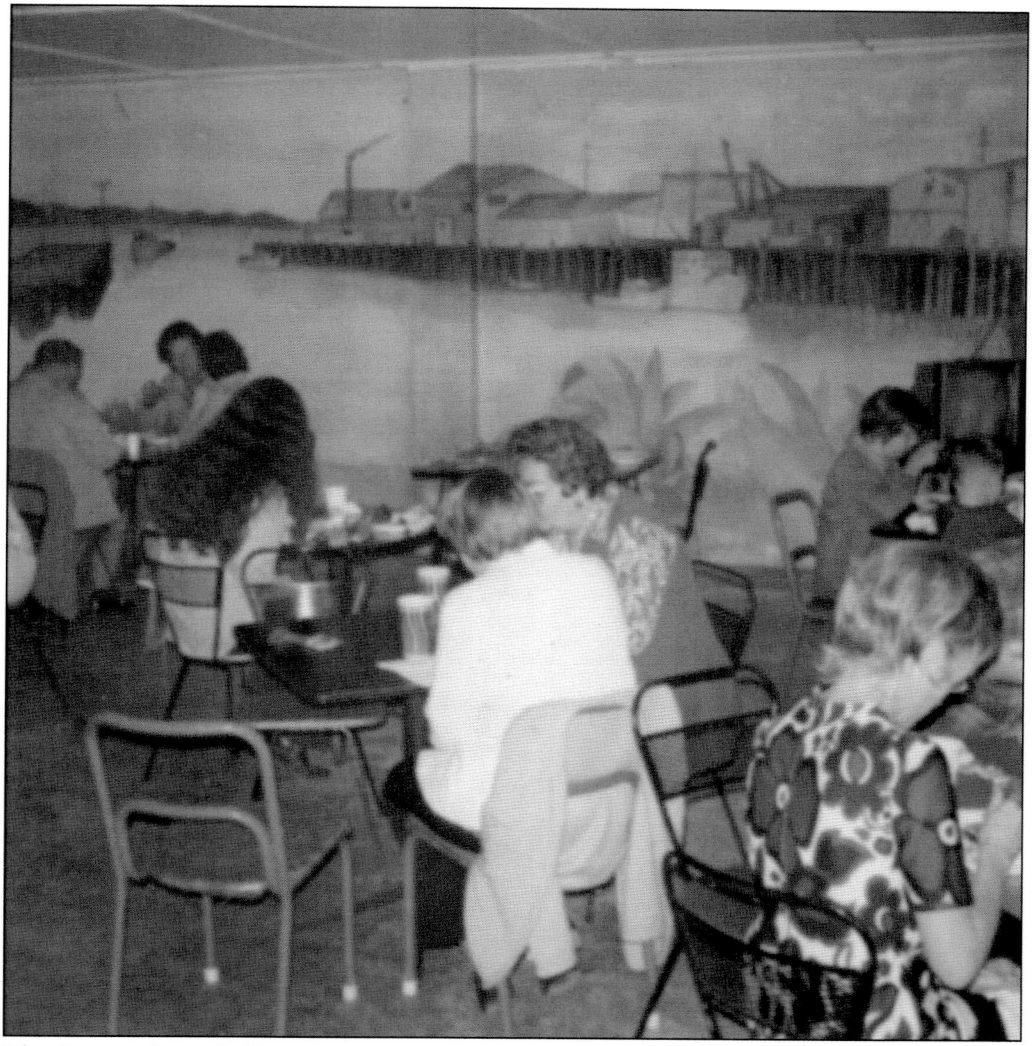

The Corner, formerly King's Corner, was a popular diner in the heart of Gilchrist. Originally built by Kinky Fox in the 1950s, the diner was sold to Charles and Bobbie King in the 1970s, then owned by Mary Ellen Smith in the 1980s and 1990s. The restaurant was actually a restaurant, bakery, service station, and general store. The mural was painted by a drifter in the 1950s. It depicts Rollover Pass, which was located across from the restaurant and dredged in 1955. The restaurant survived Hurricanes Carla and Alicia, but strangely, it burned to the ground shortly after being bought and renamed the Firehouse. The Corner had a ghost. At least, anyone who worked there could not be convinced that there was not one. The story goes that there was a group of drifters staying near the Corner. One of them was found dead, hanged on a piece of construction equipment. The story continues that the death was ruled suicide, though he was found with his feet on the ground and his hat on his head, making for a pretty unhappy ghost. As late as the 1990s, the owner, her business partner, and staff would feel the presence of a ghost at nighttime. The jukebox would mysteriously begin playing, chairs would move, and strange noises would be heard. Even though he seemed to be a very friendly ghost, it was hard to convince the waitresses to come in to open up in the early mornings. (Courtesy of Charles and Bobbie King.)

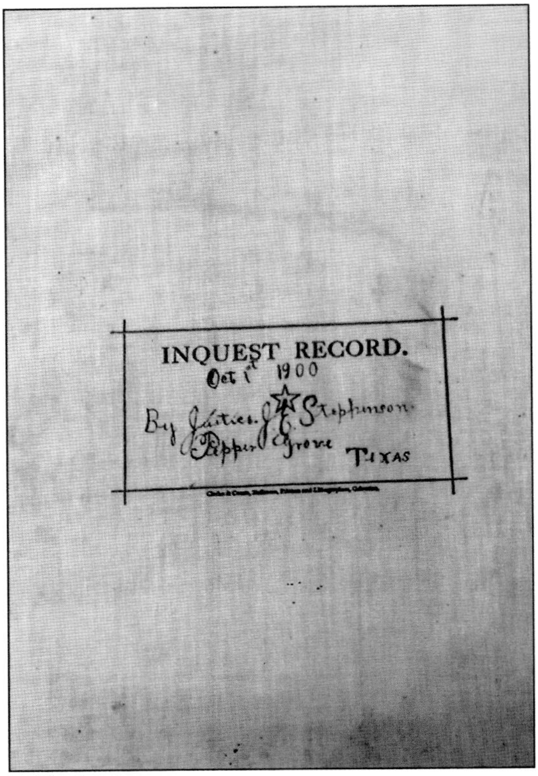

INQUEST RECORD.
Oct 1st 1900
By Justice J. F. Stephenson
Pepper Grove
TEXAS

It is known that 210 people sought shelter at the Bolivar Lighthouse during the 1900 hurricane. All of them survived. Other stories of survival include residents drilling holes in the floors of their homes to accommodate rising water, lashing their homes to trees, and even tying themselves to the tops of trees to survive. Sadly, however, many did not survive. The Inquest Record from the Coroner's Office, dated October 1, 1900, lists the personal items found when victims were recovered. Documented in great detail, many of these artifacts are currently housed at the Galveston County Museum. (Courtesy of Galveston County Museum.)

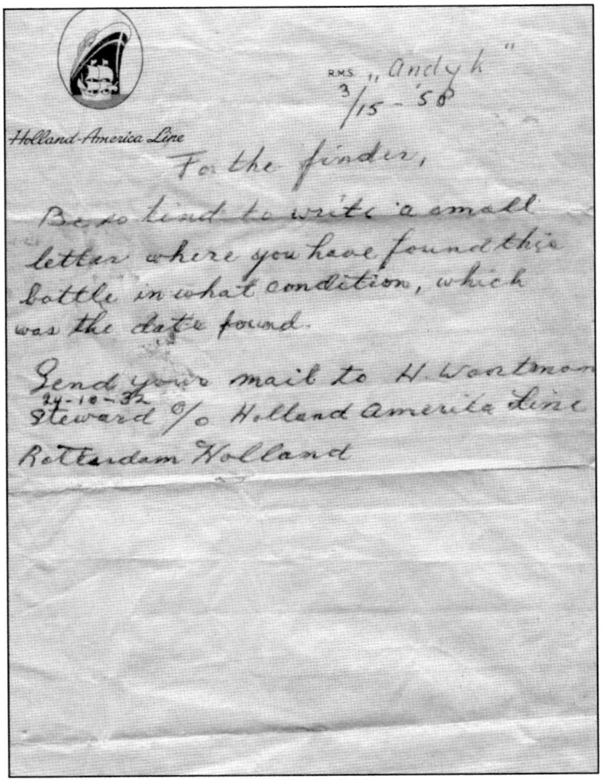

R.M.S. "Andyk"
3/15-58

Holland-America Line

For the finder,

Be so kind to write a small letter where you have found this bottle in what condition, which was the date found.

Send your mail to H. Woortman
24-10-32
Steward c/o Holland America Line
Rotterdam Holland

The romance of the sea was brought to life when a member of the Bouse family found this message in a bottle washed up on the beach. Written on March 15, 1958, the note was thrown overboard from the Holland American Line cruise ship by a resident of Rotterdam, Holland. (Courtesy of Robert and Jerri Bouse.)

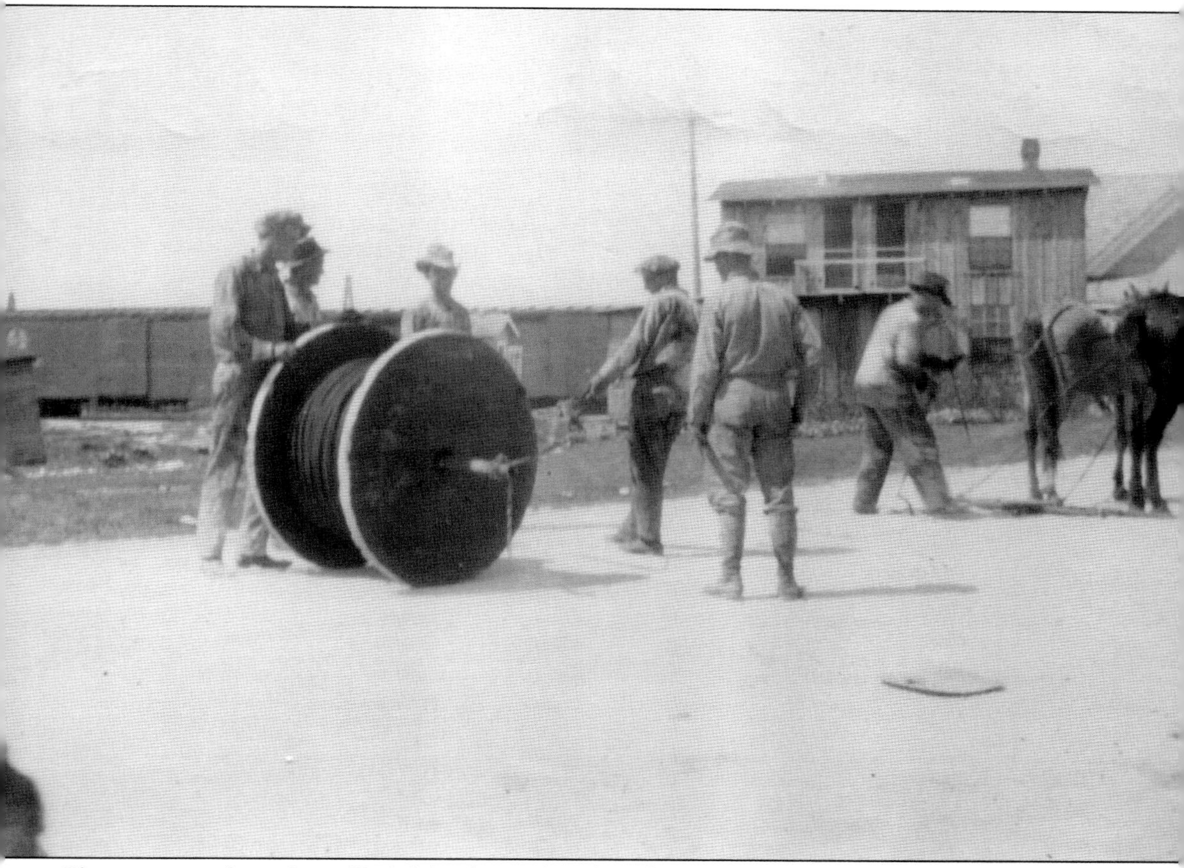

Electricity was brought to High Island in 1931. This photograph depicts the beginning of that process. (Courtesy of Elsie Devers.)

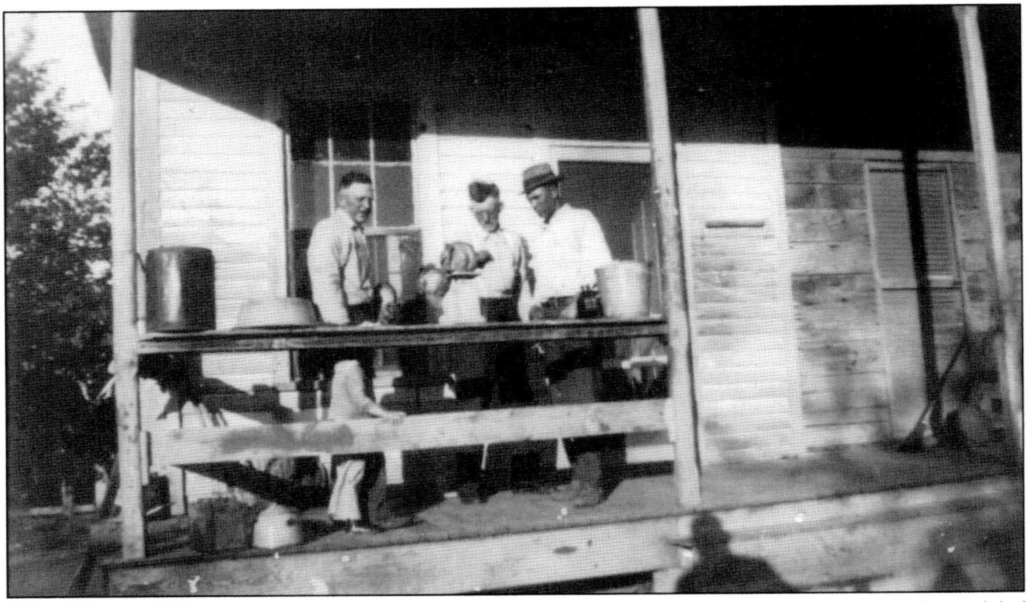

Leslie Fern Simpton and others are pictured weighing a chicken on the porch of the Kahla/Simpton house on Tenth Street and Madison Avenue in Port Bolivar. The Simpton and Kahla families were among the first settlers on the peninsula. (Courtesy of the Simpton family.)

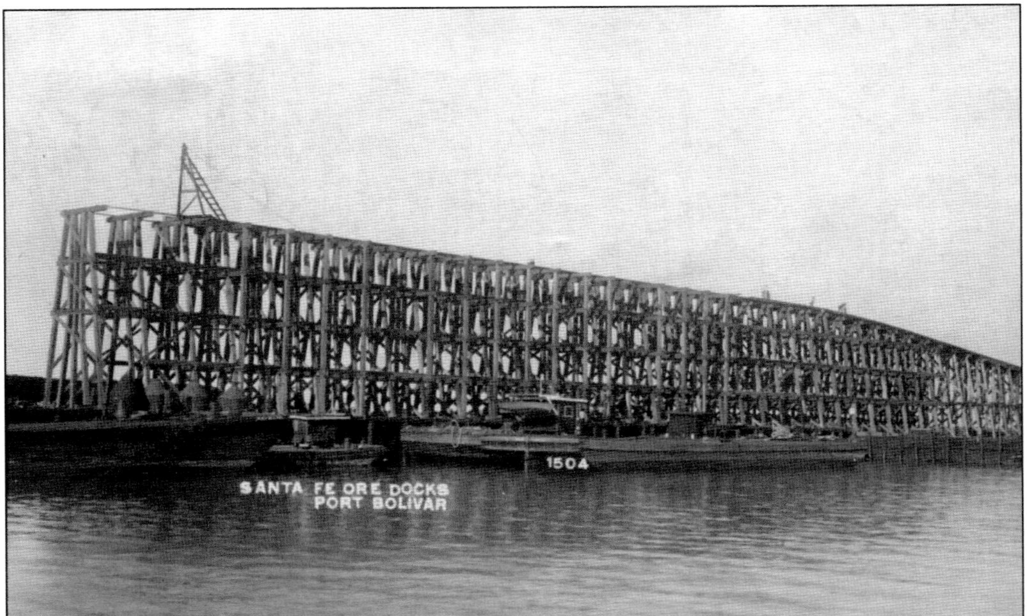

The Port Bolivar Ore Dock was completed in 1912, when iron ore was discovered near Longview, Texas. From the ore dock in Port Bolivar, the ore was transported to Philadelphia, Pennsylvania, for smelting. The docks at Port Bolivar never regained their vigor after being damaged in the hurricane of 1915. After that hurricane, East Texas shipping began to go to new deepwater ports in Port Arthur, Orange, and Beaumont. (Courtesy of Ralph Stenzel.)

Nine

Jane Long
Mother of Texas

Jane Herbert Wilkinson Long was born in 1798 in Maryland. She later moved to Natchez, Mississippi. Known for her beauty, Jane was said to be a "tall, vivacious dark-eyed girl with ringlets of black."

When her husband, Dr. James Long, physician turned filibusterer, went to the Bolivar Peninsula for a second trip in 1820, Jane, their infant daughter Ann, and servant girl Kian accompanied him. Living at Fort Las Casas at Point Bolivar (probably near where the lighthouse now stands), Jane is said to have loved the beautiful wildflowers, wild game, fish, and oysters.

Jane dined (without James) with the pirate Jean Lafitte aboard his favorite ship, the *Pride*. She described the pirate as "an impeccable gentleman who was polished, even graceful . . . six feet, two inches tall, with dark curly hair, swarthy complexion, and eyes as vivid as lightning and as black as ebony."

Long left his wife, daughter, and servant girl at the fort in 1821, promising to return and imploring Jane to wait for him on the peninsula. One by one, the remaining soldiers left the fort, ultimately leaving Jane and the children alone during the bitter winter of 1821–1822. Legend goes that Jane Long used her red petticoat as a flag, running it up the flagpole each morning after firing the cannon, to make the natives think that the fort was still inhabited. Mary James Long, Jane's third daughter, was born at the fort on December 21, 1821.

Jane Long was one of the most politically powerful women in Texas in the early 1800s. To assist Stephen F. Austin, Jane entertained Mexican officials at her Brazoria-area hotel, organizing a ball at the hotel when Austin was released from a Mexican prison. Here, Austin gave his first speech calling for independence from Mexico and setting off the Texas Revolution.

Jane was courted by many of the Texas revolutionaries, including William Travis, Stephen F. Austin, Ben Milam, Sam Houston, and Mirabeau B. Lamar. She never remarried, however, citing her enduring love for Dr. James Long.

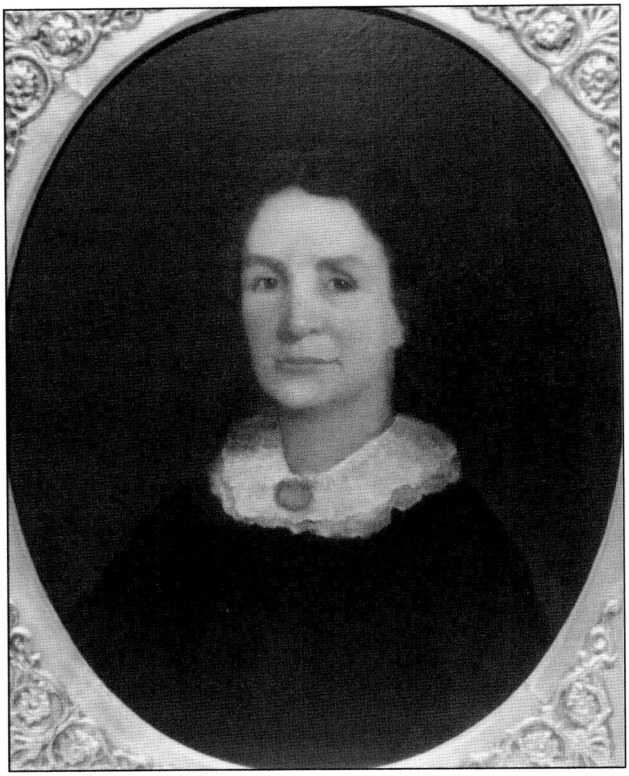

Jane Herbert Wilkinson Long was a Texas pioneer who was married to Dr. James Long. She joined him at Fort Las Casas on the Bolivar Peninsula in 1820. Jane was left alone with her young daughter Ann and servant Kian in the winter of 1821. They faced frigid winter temperatures, a lack of food and supplies, and danger from the native Karankawas. During this frigid winter, Jane gave birth to another daughter, Mary James Long, leading to her honorary designation as the "Mother of Texas." (Courtesy of Fort Bend County Museum.)

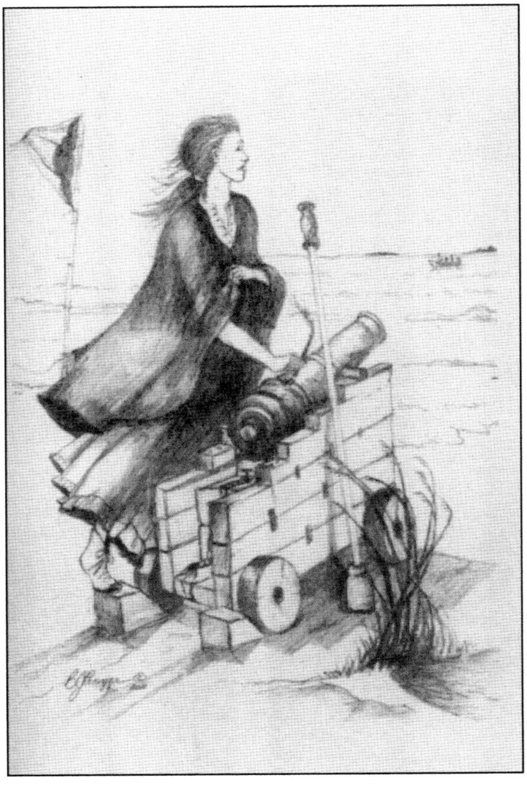

After her husband's death, Jane Long received her own headright of land (usually accorded only to a male head of household), settling in San Felipe de Austin. Jane opened her boardinghouse for rallies and meetings, stored arms and munitions, and gathered information from Mexican officers during the Texas War for Independence. She is remembered as a Texas patriot and a pioneer of the Texas frontier. (Original art by Barbara Pringer.)

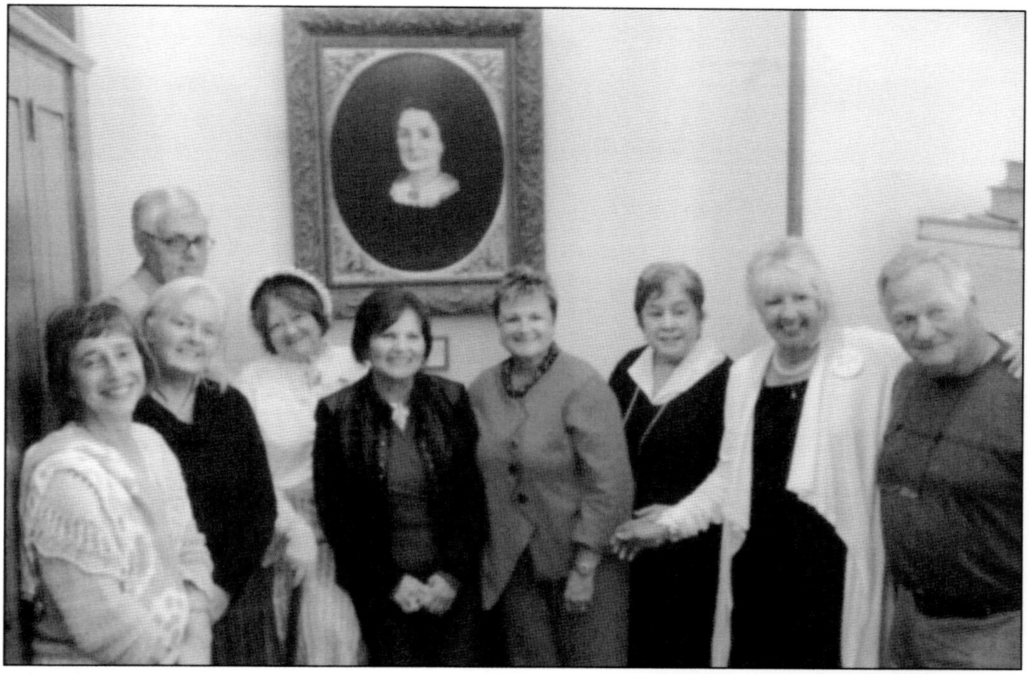

After discovering that there was no recognition of Jane Long at the capitol in Austin, Margo Johnson, Bolivar Peninsula Cultural Foundation director, wrote a letter to Galveston County commissioner Stephen H. Holmes, saying, "We need your help in our quest for recognition of Jane Long, the Mother of Texas. Hurricane Ike dealt a devastating blow to Bolivar Peninsula. Yet the vibrant people of our community are following Jane Long's example of survival." Eventually, the Jane Long Society and the Bolivar Peninsula Cultural Foundation were given permission to present a portrait of Jane Long, copied from an original painting belonging to the Fort Bend County Museum, to the library. The portrait of Jane Long now hangs in the prestigious legislative reference library at the Texas State Capitol. Pictured are a contingent of Bolivar residents who traveled to Austin to view the portrait in its new home. From left to right are Betty Wind, Melanie Wallace, Mack Wallace, Helen Mooty, Margo Johnson, Eve Bradford, Brenda Beust-Smith, Linda Elissalde, and Marcel Elissalde. (Courtesy of McHenry Wallace.)

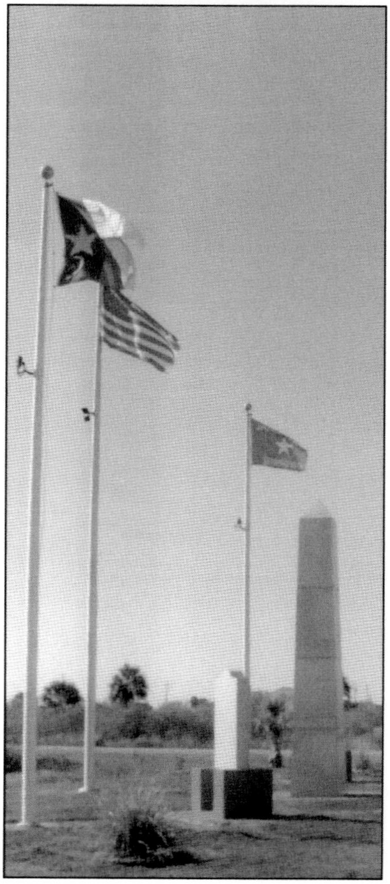

The Jane Long Memorial was dedicated on October 13, 2012. The memorial consists of a monument, historical markers for Bolivar Point and Jane Herbert Wilkinson Long, and three flagpoles flying the US flag, the Texas flag, and the Jane Long flag. The pavilion-like area is located at the entrance to Fort Travis directly off Highway 87 (now the Jane Long Memorial Highway) and includes benches and personalized pavers. (Photograph by the author.)

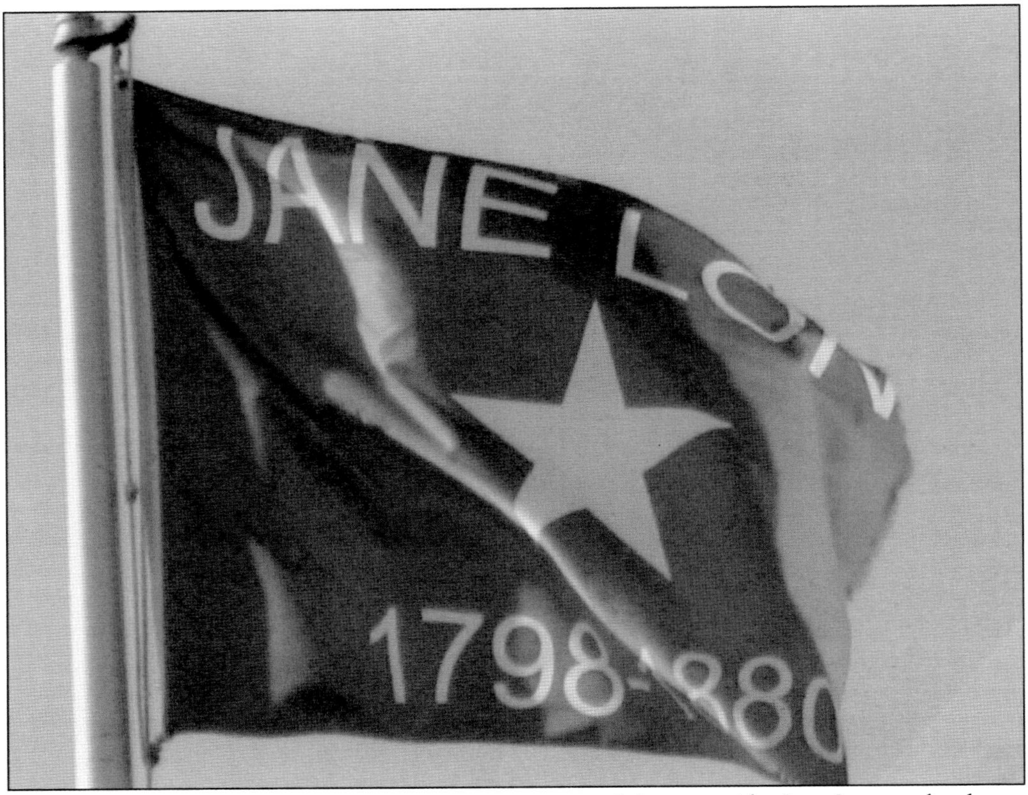

Many consider Jane Long to be the first female advisor in Texas. She is known to have served as confidante and archivist for Ben Milam, Sam Houston, and Mirabeau B. Lamar. Dr. James Long carried a solid red flag bearing a white five-pointed star in the center that was made by his wife, Jane, during his invasions in 1819–1821. This was the first Lone Star image used in a Texas flag. The Jane Long flag, flown at the memorial on the Bolivar Peninsula, is fashioned after this flag. (Photograph by the author.)

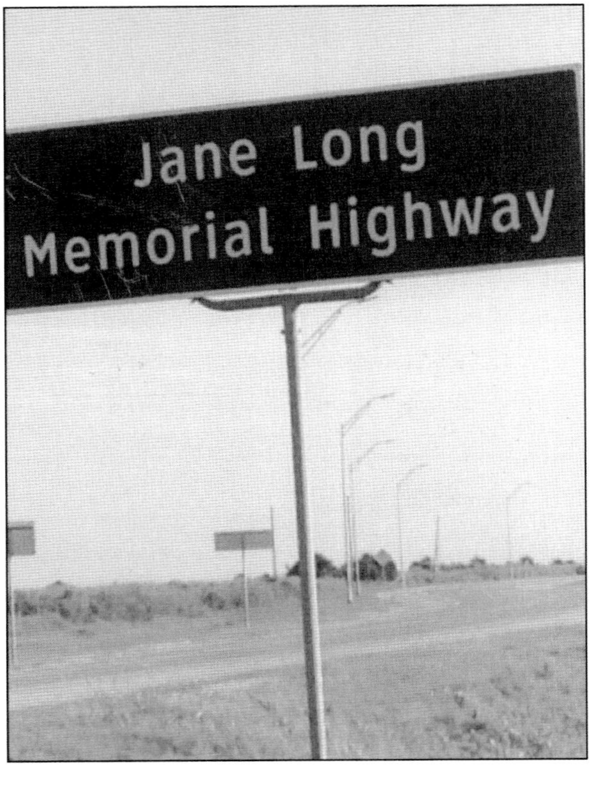

On December 18, 2012, Highway 87 was officially renamed the Jane Long Memorial Highway. (Photograph by the author.)

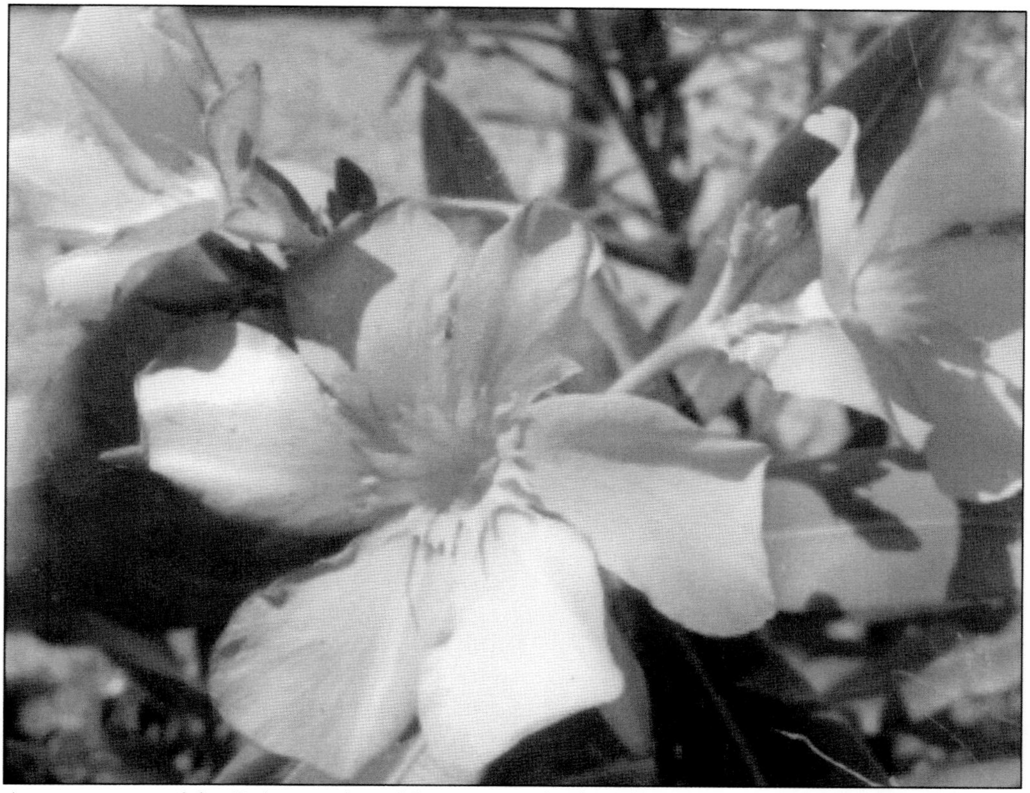

A joint project of the Galveston-based International Oleander Society and the Jane Long Society of the Bolivar Peninsula Cultural Foundation introduced the Jane Long oleander at the 2013 Jane Long Festival. The beautiful pink bloom was hybridized by Robert Newding of the Oleander Society. It is unique in that it has a white stripe down the center and many of the flowers have six petals. Most oleanders have only five. (Courtesy of the Bolivar Peninsula Cultural Foundation.)

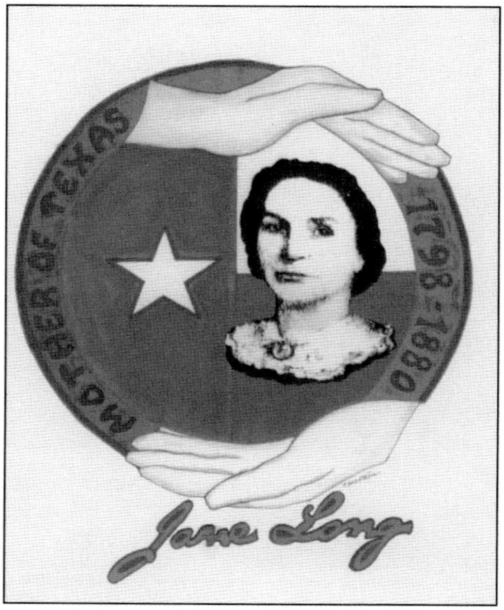

The spirit of Jane Long, Mother of Texas, survives and thrives on the Bolivar Peninsula. The Jane Long Festival was conceived as a response to the devastation of Hurricane Ike in 2008. During the difficult months following the hurricane, a group of hardy residents came up with the idea of "a little skit and some hot dogs" to celebrate the spirit of the Bolivar residents. The festival opened to rave reviews and is now a staple on the Texas Festival circuit. Held on the second Saturday of October each year, the Jane Long Festival celebrates history, art, and music in an entertaining tribute to the courage of Jane Long. Admission to the festival, held at the most beautiful festival site in Texas, Fort Travis, is free. (Original art by Patricia Hagstrom.)

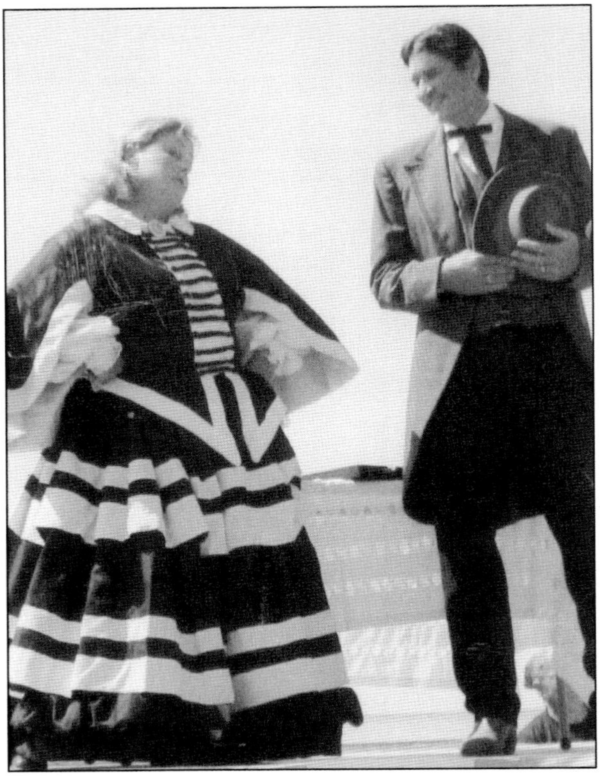

Penned by Linda C. Elissalde, *Pirates and Petticoats* is performed to rave reviews at each Jane Long Festival. The entertaining play tells the story of Jane Long during her years on the Bolivar Peninsula. Music, dance, and humor bring the story of Jane Long to life every October. Here, Melanie Wallace plays the part of Jane Long, and Sid Bouse portrays Gen. James Long. (Photograph by the author.)

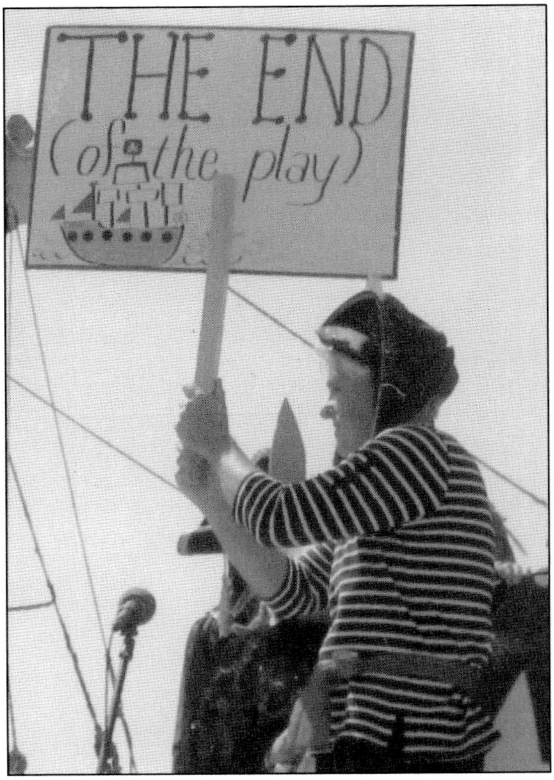

Signman Mack Wallace entertains the audience with descriptions of the action onstage at the annual performance of *Pirates and Petticoats*. His final sign announces the end of the play, but the "Beginning of the Rebirth of the Bolivar Peninsula." (Photograph by the author.)

About the Organization

The Bolivar Peninsula Cultural Foundation, formed in 2006, has been active in bringing recognition to the long history and strong resilient spirit of the Bolivar Peninsula. The mission of the foundation to "preserve and honor the art, history, and music of a vital community" has been specifically accomplished through the story of Jane Long, the Mother of Texas.

As a part of the Bolivar Peninsula Cultural Foundation, the Jane Long Society was formed to address projects specific to maintaining the memory of Jane Long. To that end, when it was discovered that there was no recognition of Jane Long at the capitol in Austin, members of the society commissioned an artist to copy the only known portrait of her, which was located at the Fort Bend County Museum. In April 2011, the portrait was hung in the library at the capitol in Austin, Texas. The plaque reads, "Jane Long Mother of Texas Donated by the Bolivar Peninsula Cultural Foundation and the Jane Long Society."

BPCF raised money for the construction of a monument at the entrance to Fort Travis that honors Jane Long. The foundation provides flags for the monument and keeps informational brochures stocked for the many visitors who stop to learn more about the peninsula and Jane Long.

The foundation successfully lobbied for the renaming of Highway 87 from the ferry landing to High Island. That portion of highway is now officially named the Jane Long Memorial Highway. The International Oleander Society has propagated a new oleander, named in honor of Jane Long.

Each October since 2010, the foundation has hosted the annual Jane Long Festival at Fort Travis. The festival, held on the second Saturday of October, is a celebration of the spirit of Jane Long, the spirit of survival that she displayed during her time on the peninsula, and the spirit that lives on with the hardy residents of the peninsula today. Through the generous help of the Galveston County Parks and Cultural Services Department, Battery Kimble has been opened to fascinated visitors during the festival each year.

The annual Jane Long Lecture Series, which has recently been extended to take place throughout the year, along with scheduled art exhibits, continue to enrich the lives of residents, as well as increase knowledge and understanding of the art, history, and music of this history-rich peninsula. Through the Bolivar Peninsula Cultural Foundation, the legacy of Jane Long, the Mother of Texas, continues to survive and thrive.